The Way to the Labyrinth

Portrait by Mac Avoy

The Way to the Labyrinth

MEMORIES OF EAST AND WEST

Alain Daniélou

TRANSLATED BY MARIE-CLAIRE COURNAND

A NEW DIRECTIONS BOOK

PHOTOGRAPH CREDITS

Sophie Bassouls, photograph 18. Raymond Burnier, photographs 7, 9, 10, and 12. Jacques Cloarec, frontispiece and photographs 14, 15, 16, 17, 19, and 20. From the Alain Daniélou Collection, photographs 1, 2, 3, 4, 5, 6, and 8. Alain Daniélou, photograph 11. Dominique Nabokov, photograph 13.

First published in France as *Le chemin du labyrinthe: Souvenirs d'Orient et d'Occident* in 1981. First published clothbound and as New Directions Paperbook 634 in 1987. Published simultaneously in Canada by Penguin Books Canada Limited.

Manufactured in the United States of America
Book design by Sylvia Frezzolini

Library of Congress Cataloging-in-Publication Data
Daniélou, Alain. The way to the labyrinth. (A New Directions Book)
Translation of: Le chemin du labyrinthe. Bibliography: p.
1. Daniélou, Alain— 2. Musicologists—France—
Biography. 3. Orientalists—France—Biography. I. Title.
ML423.D16A3 1987   780'.92'4 [B]   86-28660
ISBN 0-8112-1014-6   ISBN 0-8112-1015-4 (pbk.)

New Directions Books are published for James Laughlin
by New Directions Publishing Corporation,
80 Eighth Avenue, New York 10011

TABLE OF CONTENTS

Illustrations

Illustrations are to be found facing page 5 and in an eight-page
section between pages 214 and 215.

Here is Alain Daniélou, author of *Hindu Polytheism*, brother of Père Jean Daniélou, and son of Madame Daniélou, who nearly founded an order and was quite possibly a saint. Only by looking very closely at this curiously "asiatized" face does one begin to notice a family resemblance. He writes about Hindu religion in a scholarly and highly objective way, without the slightest trace of fervor. A family is a wondrous thing! Years ago I wrote *The Frontenac Mystery*. Who will write the mystery of the Daniélous?

François Mauriac
July 14, 1960

"The rightness of the path you have chosen will be measured by your happiness."

—ARISTOTLE

PROLOGUE

Time is only an illusion, a chain of separate moments in man's journey through the everlasting present. As we travel along the spiral of life, there are moments when we come very close to other points of time, past or present, only to move away. Is our destiny foreseen, foreseeable? We only have a vague sense of it; but when we reverse the march of time and follow the unfolding course of our lives from old age back to childhood, a great many things begin to make sense and suddenly fit together. Chance is no longer a factor, nothing happens by accident. Childhood is the consequence of maturity, the culmination of the future. It is not a question of predetermination, simply a reality of the world. Every moment of our life exists simultaneously in the wondrous and divine substratum of eternity.

Each of us lives several different lives. We can describe a man in many different ways, all of them contradictory; but we should never try to combine these portraits, incomplete as they may appear. Our spiritual destiny—the role each of us must play in the great comedy of the world—is independent of our emotional, sensual, even our intellectual lives. Moralists are always led astray by their desire to connect these different aspects of man's nature. We often find ourselves struggling against our fate, when it frightens us or seems too heavy a burden to bear. But there are times when we must be totally open and surrender to those mysterious inner forces that inspire our most irrational acts, sometimes in defiance of human law; for it is in those very actions that we most truly fulfill not only ourselves but the humble role we have each been assigned in a world whose ultimate design we cannot know.

Our destiny—the part we are called upon to play in the world of men and in the history of our species—justifies the unique gifts we have been blessed with and the strange, otherwise inexplicable paths we have followed, which have led to what we are and to what we have achieved. As we reach different points on the spiral of life, and when the time is right for us to fulfill a specific part of ourselves and of our destiny, certain patterns of thought, of being, seem to repeat themselves—astrology can sometimes explain this. Each night we rediscover the independent world of dreams, each day our normal sphere of activity; but they are totally unrelated. The same is true of all the different aspects of our lives. I have never tried to become anything or anyone in particular. I have always given myself completely to the present moment, thrown myself into the widest range of activities. Yet it seems clear to me now that fate was waiting for me at every turn, that it used me and led me to play a certain role without my ever having desired or chosen it. The fact that I had so many interests, such a total lack of ambition, that I had no ties of any kind and never sought a career or a conventional place in society, created the very conditions that made it possible for me to become a link between two civilizations. Considering the kind of man I was, it was the perfect role for me. Was it mere chance, or foresight on the part of the gods who always do with us exactly as they please? Hindus believe that our freedom to be what we are—our right to live and think without social constraint—is the basis of all human progress, individual or collective.

It is not out of vanity that I shall mention in these memoirs the successes, the praise and encouragement that greeted my various experiments in different fields in which I could have made a career. As I consider my past life, it seems as though my gifts were only a series of temptations, like those of certain kinds of yogis who gradually discover their own hidden powers but can never use them if they mean to reach their goal.

My versatility also allowed me to adapt to a totally new world and come to know its real meaning through a number of peripheral activities, where a more direct approach would only have met with obstacles and defeat. The same was true when I returned to the West. The gods offered me endless possibilities, but all the while they were deceiving me so that in the end I would accomplish my destiny—a destiny for which I have never felt myself responsible.

As time passes, death takes away those who have experienced with us the same events, learned the same things, and shared the same emotions. Places we have loved are gone forever. All those people, those adventures, those passions and hatreds live only in our memory, outside of which they might never have existed; they simply return to the magma of non-being and nothingness. That long-gone house in Valognes where Tate died, only I have seen it, with its great stone staircase, its lattice windows, its five centuries of family history. Should I let it slide back into oblivion, or at least allow it some kind of grave or memorial, some bit of that concrete matter ghosts so fiercely cling to in their struggle to remain alive?

One does not write memoirs for others, or even for oneself, but to revive the memory of people and things, for without us they would never have existed or lived but remained in limbo forever. One also writes for those whose memory has been perverted or betrayed, whom posterity has turned into empty puppets stripped of human reality and passion. All of these I shall mention so that they will have been born, will have lived, will live again. For a short while I shall lift the veil of time and give them, and myself, the illusion of having lived.

I do not intend to verify the facts and dates of which my memory is unsure. I wish only to sketch a few portraits so that long-gone shadows may cling to them and reclaim their humble place in the illusory and blessed world of the living.

I have never taken notes; apart from a few letters, I have kept no documents. The shadows of the past that I shall reawaken will appear of their own free will, bounded only by my memory, where they have long lain asleep.

1. Charles Daniélou,
a young Breton poet

2. Madeleine Clamorgan,
founder of a religious
order, was also my mother

3. Catherine,
Jean, Alain,
and François
in 1913

CHAPTER ONE

The Discovery of the Divine

THE RETREAT IN THE FOREST

I was a sickly child. All the "doctors," those kindly and learned men who play the role of soothsayers in times of illness, had predicted that I would not live long. I was never sent to any of those noisy places called schools; for a boy without a future, this was considered a useless ordeal. I never knew other children besides my brothers and sisters.

My father had bought a property in Britanny, the land of his ancestors; it stood above the old village of Locronan. In the foreground, you could see the square tower of the ancient church and its slate roofs covered with golden moss. In the distance were the sea and the three crests of the Menez Hom. My father had built a large, very uncomfortable stone house, where we had to spend all our summers. He had a passion for trees and used to plant new ones every year. Then he would savagely cut down their branches, because they always ended up blocking the view. He loved fog and would go on long solitary walks with his dog. He usually came to Locronan when his family was absent.

In one of the farthest corners of the property was a thick wood with trees planted too close together. It was like an abandoned tree nursery, grown wild and as impenetrable as a jungle. I had cleared several narrow paths through the woods and spent long hours nestled among the friendly trees. Here, alone, I could sense a mystery far greater than that of the ordinary human world. I created small sanctuaries and adorned them with sacred objects, symbols of the forest gods. These

objects were of all kinds—anything I happened to have:
crosses, holy images of the Virgin or Saint Ronan, small
rounded pebbles. It did not matter what they really stood for;
they were fetishes through which I could communicate with
the higher mysteries.

One day my hiding places were finally discovered. What
could this child be doing among the trees? They found my
altars, my idols, my offerings of flowers. The temple was
violated. I was in despair, but the grown-ups, who never
understand anything about children, were filled with pride. I
was a saint, a Tarcisius reborn. They found the crosses and the
images of the Virgin, paying no attention to the pebbles. Now
they had to consecrate this small doomed saint. In those days
my mother had close ties with Pope Pius X, through whose
support she had founded a new religious order for women
who wished to pursue a teaching career. Pope Pius X granted
me a golden cross personally blessed by himself, and authorized the celebration of my first communion, although I was
only four years old. It was a very grand affair. Even my
godmother, the Baronne Pierard, with her luxurious gowns,
her jewels, and a long white lock curling beneath her ear, came
to Britanny for the great event; also Madame Lefer de La
Motte, a defrocked Mother Superior from a Spanish order
who, at the time, was the spiritual guide of many artists and
intellectuals in Paris. All this left me sad and indifferent. Although I was the hero of the day, I have no recollection
whatsoever of the ceremony. I already sensed that the religion
of men had nothing to do with the divine reality of the world. I
never went back to my profaned, desecrated retreat. Years
later, in order to pay for some of those trifles that mean so
much to an adolescent, I sold the golden cross.

THE PRIORY OF RESSON

All that remained of the ancient Abbey of the Templars was
the church. It has been subdivided: the chancel was left intact
and still served as a chapel, but the nave had been fitted up
with two rows of cells, separated by a central corridor. A small
parish house was built later, to the left of the chancel. I spent

two winters in this house with a maiden lady who gave me lessons and a servant woman who made delicious soups and would warm up my nightshirt in front of the fireplace before tucking me in under an enormous red eiderdown. In the morning she would light a great fire and heat up the leftover soup, which I feasted upon while watching the star-shaped frost crystals melt on the window panes. Near the house was a high, alfalfa-covered field which sounded mysteriously hollow when I ran across it; huge ruined chambers were probably lying underneath. A small brook, called Le Resson, ran swiftly through the meadow; a bed of watercress lay within a wire fence. During the coldest part of the winter, an ice bridge formed over the brook, and the water sang gaily through its underground tunnel. Beyond the brook there was an old farmhouse, where lived a very fat woman. She had dropsy and liked to call the illness her "position". "Because of my position," she would say, "I can't pick up wood, etc." I was very fond of her and often helped her with her chores. The following year she was gone. No one ever told me she was dead; I only understood it later. I spent two long seasons at Resson, the winters of 1917 and 1918.

It was wartime. On the road along the garden, military trucks would roll by, filled with soldiers. They were covered with earth-colored mud and their faces were gray. One day we had to ride our bicycles to a military hospital twelve miles away, beyond the upper village, well-known for its excellent cheese. The lady who gave me lessons needed to have a tooth pulled out. She must have suffered agonies in the icy wind which threatened to knock us down. But I knew nothing about it. People never explain anything to children.

The old chapel held a strange fascination for me. I hated for anyone else to go inside. I would stay there for hours on end, my mind completely blank. The red-shaded oil lamp threw dancing shadows on the wall. I was not afraid, though I felt an unknown presence beside me. I would perform all kinds of strange rites which seemed guided by some mysterious force. I invented a complete ritual—was it really invented by me?— and as I lay flat on my stomach with my arms stretched out in the aisle, I would make a vow. I did not know what it was;

when spirits exercise their will upon one's mind, they never express themselves through words. I vaguely sensed that I had been chosen for a special destiny and must pledge myself to it with no questions asked. That was my first real initiation. I was ten years old.

CHAPTER TWO

The Years of Childhood

PORTRAIT OF A FAMILY

My mother was very proud of her family which, according to her, descended from ancient nobility. Clamorgan was presumed to be a Viking name, "son of the sea clan."* As children we did not take our mother's aristocratic pretensions very seriously. We thought she had made most of it up. We were greatly surprised to inherit a set of ancient parchments, some dating back to the thirteenth century, which seemed to prove that we were in fact related to the Dukes of Clamorgan and Shakespeare's Glamor.

When I was a child, the ancient home of the Clamorgans had long since become the Municipal Hall of Valognes; all that remained in the family was an old house with Gothic windows and large, worn, centuries-old staircases. It belonged to a maiden aunt of my mother's whom we called Tate. As a very small child I visited her several times in Valognes and also stayed in a house at Saint-Vaast-la-Hougue, where the garden stretched all the way down to the sea. At low tide you could see a vast expanse of rocks and seaweed, which were filled with thousands of little holes teeming with crabs, shrimp, and all kinds of small fishes. At Saint-Vaast I learned many of the colorful canticles that are sung by the sailors of Normandy:

*A cousin, the Count of Clamorgan, has just recently died. Not long ago Jean Canu, the parish priest of Valognes, published a thousand-year genealogy (1056–1980) of a Norman family, the Clamorgans; it ends with my mother and her four brothers, who all died heirless.

Si l'ancre vient à chasser
Gardez-nous de nous froisser
Chassez loin douce Marie
De tribord et de bâbord
Les troubles et la crierie
En nous tenant bien d'accord
. . . .

Tendez la main belle lune
Aux besoins de vos dévôts.

When the anchor drags,
Sweet Mary guard us from
   discord,
Drive away our petty quarrels
From starboard and from
   portside
Drive them far into the sea
And help us keep in harmony.
. . . .

Hold out your hand, beautiful
   moon,
To those who worship you.

Tate died. It was I who accompanied my mother at the time of her death. I was not allowed to see her. For several days I heard her ravings until, all of a sudden, a chilling hush fell over the house. Mother told me that she had spent hours wiping away the many layers of paint and enamel on the old woman's face. I have no memory of the funeral. My mother spent several days putting Tate's various papers in order, especially her father's letters. Apparently she had been his closest confidante, and the letters moved my mother profoundly.

After my mother died, my sister Catherine gave me two family heirlooms in her memory: a beautifully carved Renaissance chest and a smaller one of the same period, containing several flasks of Venetian glass which some ancestor had once used to carry wines and liqueurs on his hunting jaunts.

In addition to these two chests my mother had also brought home a Louis XV settee; her brother Pierre had died on it after an attack of hemoptysis, and you could still see the blood. Apart from the few articles of furniture inherited by my sister, we never saw anything else of Tate's legacy. I have always felt that my mother was unwilling to let her children inherit anything from "her" family.

General Clamorgan, my grandfather, had died of cholera in Indochina, in 1912 or thereabouts. It was rumored in army circles that in his youth he had been an aide-de-camp and a favorite of Maréchal Lyautey. He was a very handsome man with a passion for gambling and duels. In order to solve his financial difficulties he married a rich heiress from Britanny, Lucie Cuzon du Rest, whose fortune he then proceeded to squander on horses, hunting, gambling. She was forced to sell her château in Saint-Maur-des-Fossés and eventually settled in Paris. She lived in a charming little apartment on the Ile Saint-Louis, which was cluttered with priceless Oriental objects, gifts of the King of Annam and other Indochinese dignitaries. The general's married life does not appear to have been very happy. My grandmother's interminable sea voyages and long sojourns in Cochin-China were, I believe, great trials to both of them.

In my childhood I often paid visits to my grandmother, who seemed very fond of me. She would tell me stories about "pirates" who carried off European women and tortured them by hanging them by their toes until the proper ransom was paid; when finally caught, these incorrigible desperadoes were tightly bound to ladders to keep them from running away.

Not far from my grandmother, in a dingy garret which he used as a studio, lived one of her two surviving sons, Pierre, a sensitive and musically gifted painter. His lungs had been ravaged by poison gas in the First World War. I used to pay him visits from time to time. A position had been found for him at the Jacquemart-André Museum, where he was curator, but his poor health made it very difficult for him to do any kind of work.

Paul, the other son, had chosen the priesthood and for many years was parish priest in a working-class section of Paris before finally being named canon at Saint-Pierre de Chaillot. He was a hard, ascetic man and had a great deal to do with the inflexibility of my mother's attitude; he was one of her closest confidants. He was hateful toward me, falsely accusing me of sins I had not committed and calling me a liar when I tried to defend myself. He had cunningly guessed my inclinations and was convinced that such tendencies were never innate but the result of experience and as contagious as a disease. "You are all the same," he would sneeringly tell me, at a time when I had no knowledge of this species except myself and was still inno-cent, in terms of actual practice, of the behavior of which I was accused.

At one time my mother hoped very much to solve Pierre's difficulties by marrying him off to one of her disciples, a rich heiress both sweet-tempered and musically gifted; but she was afraid to put too much pressure on her ward. I heard Paul lecturing her: "He is your brother. Your duty towards him must come first." The young girl finally became rebellious and married a well-known music critic.

My uncle's behavior did not surprise me. I already knew that people who equate good morals with sexual frustration are usually dangerous and unprincipled in other areas.

Chastity, when not used as a screen, is a form of masochism: it is normal that it should lead to sadistic behavior and a distorted sense of values. Hindus are never allowed to make vows of chastity unless they have experienced sex. It is impossible to renounce something that one does not know. A poor man who renounces wealth is not virtuous.

One of Uncle Paul's many functions was serving as Grand Exorcist of the Diocese of Paris. He was therefore involved in all kinds of diabolical hocus-pocus and sprinkled holy water over hysterical young girls who were considered "possessed." My uncle, so much admired for his piety and his life of privation and sacrifice, terrified me with his calm cruelty. He was the perfect type of the Inquisitor—cold-blooded, domineering, imperturbable, and supremely self-confident. I was sure that in another day and age he would have sent me to the stake for good of my soul and for the greater glory of God. In my later life I had occasion to meet other sadistic types; they behaved exactly like my uncle, but at least the glory of God played no part in their strange rituals.

There were two other brothers in my mother's family. The eldest, whose name was Jean, died of typhoid fever when he was twenty; Michel, the youngest in the family, went off to war in 1914 at sixteen and was killed almost immediately.

One of the general's brothers, Uncle André, was still alive. He was an Inspector of Finance—a tall, elegant gentleman with gray hair. I had met him in Valognes and we were very fond of each other. Uncle André, having no son of his own, would have been happy to take an active role in my life. My mother prevented it. She did not want her children to have anything to do with "her" family.

The truth was that my mother thought of her children as bastards; because she was an uncompromising woman, she must surely have faced that problem at some point in her life. She always refused to introduce us into "her" world, nor could she bear to see us mingle with her husband's political friends, whom she considered vulgar and corrupt. Once, at her home in Britanny, she left the table because my father, without warning, had invited "a divorced woman" along with some other friends. My mother had spent time in Indochina with her father but never spoke of it. Her family always remained a closed, secret world. We knew that we had cousins, but we never met them.

My Mother, a Saint

At a time when few women pursued serious studies, my mother had won first place in the *agrégation*, the highest competitive examination for teachers in France. She was gifted with superior intelligence, vast culture, and a remarkable gift for organization. There was no trace in her of that masculine element so frequently seen in high-powered women. She possessed great charm and knew how to use it. She was passionate, perhaps even sensual, and extremely domineering; her greatest goal in life was to mould people's characters. Her role model was not Saint Teresa of Avila but Madame de Maintenon.

Although her father was a general and politically ultraconservative, she had been a passionate supporter of Captain Dreyfus in her youth and married a young man from Britanny, a mediocre poet who later became well-known in the political world, occupied various ministries, and was a strong left-winger and anticlericalist.

It was an odd match, greatly beneficial to my mother; for my father, however, it presented a number of serious drawbacks.

My mother attached great importance to her clothes and dressed with pretentious sobriety. She bore a slight resemblance to the character played by Silvana Mangano in *Death in Venice*: charming, dignified, irreproachable. Her old dresses, which were kept in the dress room where I was locked up for bad behavior as a small boy, were all very elegant. I particularly remember a lace-trimmed sky-blue satin dress whose material I later used to make a theatrical costume. Women's clothes, even then, never caused me the slightest titillation. I had no conception whatever of female sensuality and never imagined that women and feminine artifice could play any kind of sexual role. I was no Oedipus. Four children were born after me, and yet not until my adolescence did I have any notion of a sexual, or even an emotional relationship between my parents; in the family context, that side of their life remained completely hidden. As a result, I never thought of my father as a rival. It never occurred to me that the two pillows in which I loved to nestle in my mother's enormous bed were meant for two people; but I have enjoyed having two pillows in my bed ever since.

Although I never really spent much time near my mother, I was deeply, even excessively attached to her, and this feeling was very much put to the test.

Like all people who take pleasure in dominating and manipulating others, she bestowed her favors with shrewd partiality. I was bitterly jealous of her flagrant, almost indecent preference for one of my brothers, François-Jehan, who was five years younger than myself. She showed this in many small ways. We never did very much for our own birthdays, but celebrated those of the saints whose names we bore. There was no Saint Alain in the church calendar and so I never had my "saint's day"; what was worse, my birthday happened to fall on the day of Saint François. My mother would shower presents upon my younger brother and always forgot me. Each year I would await the bitter day, expecting the inevitable.

The main feature of my mother's character was her passion for "God." This enigmatic being took precedence over all her human sympathies. Her actions were ruled by his desires and commands, which she never seemed to doubt in any way, and, like a woman with a lover, she relegated her husband and children to second place. Why had she married? I have never been able to find the answer. Her relationship with her husband was highly correct but never betrayed the slightest sign of tenderness. She had six children, but probably bore them more out of duty than desire. Her love for God came before anything else; she seemed at any rate convinced that all her undertakings and notable successes were his will and for his glory.

I was deeply disturbed by the presence of this invisible interloper. My jealousy may have been excessive, but my mother's faith always struck me as a monstrous aberration—at any rate, a betrayal. Christians, like staunch Marxists and Fascists, sometimes come to betray their heretical friends, children, or brothers. I felt that in another time my mother, with a bleeding heart and a magnificent display of sorrow, would have delivered me into the hands of the Inquisitor.

I once heard her say—quoting Saint Augustine's mother I think—"I would sooner see my son dead than committing a mortal sin." My mother spoke these pernicious words with great seriousness, showing an incredible lack of psychological insight. God clearly appeared to be a kind of stepfather and lover, whose whims my mother was prepared to humor even by the sacrifice of her own son. She had read *The Lives of the Saints* so many times that the over-theatrical and melodramatic quality of such a statement did not disturb her. If this God had ordered her to cut my throat, like Isaac's, would she have done it? Or was she lying in order to exercise better control over her sons? However one wished to look at it, she seemed definitely dangerous. She had given herself body and soul to this strange character who, in fact, appeared to be nothing more than a sexophobe; the ultimate sin was touching one's sex, which happened to be very agreeable. My mother's main obsession was to preserve her children's "purity" for as long as possible. All she had to do, then, was create a protective environment, shielding them from reality of any kind. This negative attitude allowed my mother, a very busy woman, to feel that she was performing her duty. Yet with the possible exception of my brother Jean, whom she was able to dominate, she was singularly unsuccessful in bringing up her children to face life. The cause of this failure was probably the very pretext by which she justified her ruling passion. An ideal is an effective tool in politics and all other forms of action. Whether it bears the name of Christ, the pope, the fatherland, the proletariat, Marxism, civilization, or even humanity in general, people ruled by ambition invariably hide behind a myth. This is how the masses are swayed: they are always more naïvely idealistic than their leaders.

Between a mother and her children, however, there is no room for myth. No interference, no rival allegiance can be tolerated. A child's trust is absolute. There can be no gap, no restriction in a mother's devotion; she must always be ready to defend her brood, whether they are morons, perverts, or criminals, and offer them protection when they need it. It was not until many years later, among Italy's lower class (the bourgeoisie there being as patriarchal and hypocritical as it is everywhere else), that I discovered the last bastion of mothers in the Western world: solid, hardworking women who run their tribe, feed it, manage, and protect it. Whether it is a shack or a simple room, the home is a fortress, always a refuge for those who have suffered the vicissitudes of life, always welcoming to the prodigal child. Like a tigress, the *mamma* defends her cubs against society, the State, the Church, and the law. Once the coquettishness of youth is past, she becomes woman, mother, the pillar of society. She never goes to the hairdresser, she never wears makeup; she is the chieftain, and needs no artifice. How pathetic beside her are those feminists who try so hard to emulate the empty role of men.

The failure of my relationship with my mother was mainly the result of a conflict between "God" and those principles which she ascribed to him. One moment she was a mother, the next a priestess. Her passion for this god-lover always took precedence over her maternal feelings. This was made clear to me by a number of small, seemingly trivial incidents that left me deeply scarred.

Because I had tuberculosis as a child, I suffered violent pulmonary attacks, bronchitis, and pleurisy. Every time this happened I was expected to die. When I was about ten years old I had a particularly severe attack. After subjecting me to the tortures of cupping-glasses and poultices, the good Dr. Tolmer felt it his duty to tell my mother that all hope was gone. Mother came to my room with tears in her eyes and tenderly embraced her poor dying child for much longer than usual. Then she went to the convent chapel, which abutted the house. After a while she returned to my room, calm, tender,

with a faint smile on her face. I suddenly had the feeling that
this exemplary mother had offered God the sacrifice of her
most cherished possession, her own son. I was filled with such
anger that, to everyone's amazement, I promptly recovered.
But something had changed. The saint's sublime sacrifice had
been frustrated by this damnable child. It was natural for her
to feel resentful. I watched carefully for signs of ill-humor.
Perhaps I had only imagined it all. I never spoke to anyone of
this, but thought about it for a long time.

We were staying in Auvergne, in an old Renaissance château, and I was about fourteen, taking therapeutic baths in a
zinc tub warmed by the sun—a remedy suggested by some
naturopathic charlatan. In my bed late at night, by the light of
an electric lamp, I would surreptitiously read forbidden books
from the château library. My sister Catherine and I used to
play a secret game which consisted in inventing words we
considered vulgar and gross. The game was very silly and,
though it carried a faint scent of the forbidden fruit, of no
consequence whatever. Catherine, suddenly contrite, ran and
told everything to Mother, who took the matter very seriously. She summoned me into the garden and gave me a long
lecture. She told me how grieved and hurt she was by such
unspeakable behavior, which offended God and endangered
the salvation and the soul of her children, laying a great deal of
stress on the pernicious influence of the guilty Alain on his
poor, innocent sister. I was extremely upset by this interview.
My mother had really played the part to the utmost, with all
the elements of melancholy, gentle sweetness, broken trust.
But a few days later, my brother Jean, who was being educated
by the Jesuits, came home. I happened to hear my mother
telling him the story. She was laughing: "The children were
saying silly words. I had to put an end to it." I was devastated.
My mother had lied to me, made light of my feelings; Catherine, my only friend, had betrayed me. Jean was just a stranger,
living in an unknown world. I was being laughed at in his
presence.
I found myself alone, friendless, with no one to turn to. The
maternal sanctum, that supreme refuge which I kept trying so

hard to build, had once again fallen to the ground. My mother, her morality, and her God were perfidious and false, and nothing but a sham. From that day onward, I ceased to think of my mother's religion as a tenable code of ethics, or her God as a possible reality. All my life I have kept a vivid memory of that insignificant event. It was very useful to me, however, for never again did I feel the slightest twinge in matters of religion or morality.

At sixteen, I was forbidden to read Balzac's *Le Lys dans la vallée*, an "obscene" novel that dwelt too eloquently, it seemed, on a lady's breasts. I studied for several months at the Collège Sainte-Croix in preparation for my *baccalauréat*—the final examination that ends French secondary education—and there met the son of one of my mother's protégées, a boy named Maillart, who later became a well-known painter. He had lent me La Fontaine's *Contes*, which I found very tedious. When my mother discovered the book, there was a terrible scene. In a flood of tears she dragged me to my confessor, a fat Jesuit whose name was Père Jalabert. Without the slightest twinge of remorse, I swore that I had not read the book and, not long afterward, heard my confessor telling my mother: "Have no fear: he has not read it!" The obligatory rites of confession and communion became an endless display of lies and sacrilege. But this did not trouble me: my ties to the Church were severed. Maillart, always my champion against the other boys' cruelties, turned his back on me.

I was twenty-one, and passionately fond of singing and dancing. I had been turned out of my parents' house and lived in a tiny studio on the Boulevard Gouvion-Saint-Cyr; my mother had agreed to pay the rent. I had a few friends, a few affairs.

One day, my mother summoned me: "I have discussed your case with your uncle Paul," she told me. "The life you have chosen to lead has made it impossible for me to help you any longer. I haven't got the moral right." Here, once again, was that unbridgeable gulf between divine myth and motherhood, Olympus and earth. Morality was nothing more than a social prejudice ascribed by men to a mythical god who knew no-

thing about the realities of the world. The break was defini-
tive, quiet and undramatic.

There were never any violent clashes between us, no scenes.
My mother felt it her duty to act according to an abstract,
theoretical, and pre-established plan that probably conflicted
with feelings she overcame in the name of virtue. What appeared as a total lack of compassion was really a sacrifice. She
always showed me a great deal of affection even when, in
compliance with her inflexible principles, she denied me material support and left me without any means of subsistence. She
was willing to let her prodigal child die of hunger, according to
an ideal of heroic virtue that the Christian world likes to call
"saintliness"; perhaps, with that unconscious hypocrisy so evident in her subsequent dealings with my youngest sister, she
kept hoping that I would find "other means."

I continued to go home to Neuilly for an occasional lunch
with my family. I took on various little jobs, dancing and
giving massages. For the first time, my father secretly gave me
money, and so did my grandmother. Others came to my aid,
out of friendship, but also in outrage against my family's
attitude. Those were difficult years: I worked relentlessly,
lived on sandwiches and *cafés-crèmes* and accumulated many
debts.

But I was free. Later on, when I went back to the house on
short visits, my mother always gave me an affectionate welcome and acted as if nothing had happened.

There has been talk of beatifying my mother; it might happen someday. She carried the principles of her faith to heroic,
almost inhuman extremes, often acting against her own nature. My mother was undoubtedly a saintly woman; what she
was for me is another story. Her world of beliefs and ideas was
very different from the one that I later found for myself.

And yet, at the end of her life, she did not hesitate to say:
"Alain is the most intelligent of my children. He knows what
he wants. He is more like me than any of the others." She was
proud, after all, of that one child who had been able to resist
her. In this sense, by freeing me from her world, the one in
which I was born, she really did me a great favor.

Not long ago, after I had made some comments about my

childhood in an interview, I received a number of outraged letters from "decent" ladies. Their children, they said, were "decent" and not a dishonor to their family or a cause of despair and untold suffering to their mother, as I had been. Whose fault? I am what I am. I never asked to be born. I have conducted my life as best I could without wishing harm to anyone—a viewpoint obviously not shared by those cold-hearted mothers of the Christian bourgeoisie who so often turn into ferocious dragons.

A great many years later the famous novelist Yves Navarre, who also belonged to a "good family" of Neuilly, the elegant Parisian suburb, asked to meet me. He told me: "I was the black sheep of my family. But they always used to say to cheer themselves, 'There are black sheep in the best of families—look at Alain Daniélou.'"

Not everyone, it appears, admired my mother. . . . One day, at a reception given by the publisher Pierre Bérès in his apartment on the Avenue Foch, a very elegant woman came up to me and said: "So you are Alain Daniélou! Well! I want to tell you that your mother was a horrible woman." I was really quite astonished. Later I found out that this woman had at one time wanted to divorce her husband, a particularly odious man. My mother had advised her to make some kind of arrangement, even take a lover if necessary, but to avoid at all cost the scandal of divorce. It had been a terrible shock to the woman.

Although in my youth I was forced to defend myself against my mother, there was never any open hostility between us. She showed me great tenderness at times and I felt deep affection for her. Her last letters are full of gentleness. My mother was a prisoner of the Church and its totalitarian ideology, and I believe that at the bottom of her heart she was really glad that I had escaped her influence. As I slowly became submerged in another mode of thought, another religion, another conception of life and death, my hostile attitude gradually melted away; it disappeared completely once the last vestiges of my Christian heritage were gone. If my mother had ever needed me, I feel that I could have protected her and rocked her in my arms, giving no more thought to her ideas than to a child's babble. When I discovered how strong I had grown, how deeply secure, it was already too late; she was gone. She died on October 13, 1956. I was living in Pondicherry, India. I have never visited her grave.

In a beautiful poem published at the time of her death, she expresses that all-exclusive rival love of which I was so painfully aware in my childhood:

O Jésus qui êtes la Voie, la Vérité,
  la Vie . . .
Donnez-nous de vous aimer
D'un amour de complaisance
Qui nous fasse vous préférer à
  tout,
Qui ôte leur saveur aux créatures
Et nous libère de nos attachements
  secrets.
Donnez-nous de vous aimer
D'un amour délicat et tendre
Qui nous fasse pressentir vos goûts
Aller au-devant de toutes vos préfé-
  rences
Percevoir vos moindres appels
Y accorder toute notre vie.

O Jesus who are the Way, the
  Truth, the Life . . .
Grant that we may love you
With love of such docility
That we may prefer you to all
  others,
Make them of nothing worth
  beside you
And free us from our hidden
  bonds.
Grant that we may love you
With such soft and tender love
That we may sense your
  wishes,
Anticipate your pleasure,
Hear your slightest call
And yield our life to you.

A TENDER, ABSENT FATHER

My father's family came from Locronan, where his ancestors had practiced law for several generations. It had once been a city of weavers who made sails for the Navy; but the industry was killed by steam travel, and Locronan turned back into a village. The family then moved to Douarnenez.

My grandfather, Eugène-Lucien-Napoléon Daniélou, born in 1834, was Mayor of Douarnenez from 1871 to 1896 and one of the city's most important tradesmen. He dealt in wine, imported and exported various kinds of produce, and owned several ships. He became extremely rich and gave Douarnenez an iron bridge linking it to Tréboul. My family always spoke of him as a shipowner: it sounded much more respectable.

In my early childhood I met my paternal grandmother several times, but found it very difficult to communicate with her: she only spoke Breton. My mother treated her quite haughtily. My grandfather was a fervent atheist and thought Christianity was nothing but nonsense. He refused to get married in church or to baptize his children; but when he died, the entire population of the city, including its strict Catholic constituency, followed the civil funeral procession. The people of Douarnenez, mostly poor sailors and fishermen, had benefited greatly from his kindness, generosity and staunch support, and remembered him as a kind of saint. When his son Charles ran as deputy for Douarnenez in 1914, at the age of twenty-five, he was elected by a strong majority; he needed only to remind the people that Eugène was his father.

Between the father's death and the son's election, very strange things had happened. The family fortune, which was considerable, had mysteriously disappeared. The eldest son had vanished, leaving no trace; no one ever found out what happened to him. One of his sisters, Marie, had entered a convent. André, the youngest son, went to Paris with empty pockets and no skills, seeking help from his brother Charles. There was also a married sister, Madame Delbart de Bay, whom I never met. I have never tried to find out what really happened. I heard vague talk of wildly dissipated lives which the three sons were presumed to have led, with women and fancy carriages; but all this sounded rather farfetched.

André lived with us when I was a small child. He was a wonderfully kind-hearted young man. I was tremendously fond of him and played with him constantly. I remember the beginning of a little poem that he wrote in my honor:

Sur le boulevard Victor Hugo
Vint à passer une grande auto.
Le sot Alain qui n'voit pas clair
Sous la voiture roule par terre.

One fine day a motorcar
Came speeding down the
  boulevard.
Poor Alain, whose sight's not
  keen
Rolled beneath the great
  machine.

La bonne Jeanne qui est très fine	Out came Jeanne, a kindly soul
Mais qui est aussi une coquine	Though sometimes just a bit too droll,
A la rescousse se précipite . . .	And ran to him to save his life . . .

I was with him in Quimper when he gaily went off to war, with red trousers and a flower sticking out of his gun. He was killed almost immediately, in 1914. I can still see my mother in her room at Neuilly, tearfully reading my father the official telegram that announced his death.

Marie had entered the Holy Order of the Oratorians, later dissolved by the Vatican. She left the order at the same time as her Mother Superior, Madame Lefer de la Motte, and lived under her protection. She was a worthy soul, somewhat nondescript, and I used to see her from time to time. She still had a strong Breton accent.

My father, having apparently dissipated the family fortune with the help of his brothers, had come as a young man to live in Paris. He wrote poetry, belonged to Sully Prud'homme's literary circle, admired Heredia. He then began to frequent a group of artists and writers who had formed around Madame Lefer de La Motte and the Baronne Pierard, a very rich woman in whose house she lived. Madame Lefer, as people called her, then persuaded my father to get baptized; he was unconvinced, but agreed nonetheless. It was in this milieu that he met my mother. He embarked on a career in journalism, grew quite successful, and from there entered politics. He became Aristide Briand's most trusted aide and shared his ideals of pacifism. Briand used to call him his "little mariner" and made him Undersecretary of State each time he was called to the Ministry of Foreign Affairs. At the *Parlement*, my father became president of the Radical Left, a moderate center party and a key group in the formation of any cabinet. In Britanny, he was deputy for Douarnenez and later for Châteaulin (1910); in 1912, he became Mayor of Locronan and remained so until his death. He spoke Breton fluently, which was essential at the time. He was considered a "Red", an anticlericalist, perhaps even a Freemason. In those days, the people of Britanny were either fanatical Catholics or fierce anticlericals;

they despised each other and disagreed about everything, sometimes to the point of imbecility. Thus, according to their convictions, they set their watches by the church (solar time) or by the town hall (official time), which made it very difficult to keep appointments. My mother, of course, observed church time, and my father town hall time.

My father probably loved his children very dearly, but soon gave up having anything to do with our upbringing, our household or our lives. He was a stranger whom we occasionally saw at the dinner table.

My parents sometimes had rather violent scenes, always behind closed doors; all we could hear was the sound of muffled voices. Naturally, we were all convinced that our mother was being victimized by this useless man who called himself our father. It never occurred to any of us that he might have good reason to be irritated.

As I grew more independent, I discovered to my surprise that my father, whom I knew very little and had hardly ever spoken to, was really very kind. He made no unpleasant comments when some scandalous gossip was written about me by reporters who had taken advantage of my naïveté; he only said that I should be more careful next time, that journalists could be dangerous. He never reproached me for my way of life or my ambitions, and sometimes even tried to help me in secret. In time I came to realize that my father understood me quite well; our relationship nonetheless remained distant and indefinite.

I was sure that he had mistresses and imagined romantic *rendez-vous* on the days when his hands were manicured and he wore a slight perfume. His role in politics was important but fairly low-key. I never met any of his political friends. After Munich, he dissociated himself from Daladier and Laval, whom he considered dangerous; he had been a minister in Daladier's first Cabinet, in 1933. Later, he virtually retired from politics. By then, I was already living in India and only saw him again briefly after the war. He died in 1954. I was living in Madras at the time.

He had published a book of poetry and various studies on the politics of his time, which are quite interesting. My father

was at his best as a private negotiator—what French Parlia-
mentarians used to call an *homme de couloirs;* he was a loyal and
valuable collaborator of Briand's, strongly committed to the
cause of European peace which they were pursuing along with
Stresemann. He was very proud of his role as rapporteur of
the 1920 Treaty of Trianon, which confirmed the independence of Hungary but granted Rumania and Czechoslovakia
most of the Transylvanian territories, traditionally ruled by
Hungarians. It was, in fact, one of those very bad treaties that
lead inevitably to future conflicts.

BROTHERS AND SISTERS

From the moment they were born, Mother had definite plans
for the future of each of her children. The first-born belonged
to God, who always had first rights, so Jean was sent to a
Jesuit school in Jersey.

I never knew my eldest brother very well, and saw him only
during the few weeks of summer vacation that we spent in
Locronan each year. Jean had special privileges. Because he
was destined for God, he was allowed private conferences
with my mother; they probably discussed the spiritual life,
Church affairs, and problems of the children's education.
Along with my uncle Paul, Jean was one of the watchdogs of
our virtuous family prison.

While preparing for his *agrégation,* Jean suddenly found himself thrown among artists and intellectuals of the Paris avant-
garde. He became a close friend of Jean Cocteau's and translated his libretto for Stravinsky's *Oedipus Rex* into Latin. Our
father hired him as a private secretary in one of his ministries.
Jean took great pleasure in keeping industrial and various
other prefects waiting while he translated Greek poetry in a
sumptuous office.

With the help of his friend Robert Garric, Jean—possibly
influenced by François Mauriac and the "elegant Christianity"
that was fashionable among Parisian intellectuals of the
time—decided to create a third order for Christian youths
called Les Compagnons de Saint-Paul. In 1925 or thereabouts,
the Compagnons settled in a large building, now called La

Pergola, on the Boulevard Saint-Germain, and turned it into a kind of YMCA. People used to call them "Les Saintpaulins."

Jean was faced with a serious moral dilemma when the chaplain of the association took a fancy to me and made all too obvious attempts to seduce me. I must have been about seventeen or eighteen at the time. He would drag me into his room and kiss and caress me. We spent endless hours lying on his bed talking, but he never dared go any further. I was too shy and inexperienced to respond to his advances; besides, I did not find this plumpish and overly well-groomed Italian priest particularly attractive. Soon afterward he was sent back to Rome.

I think the Compagnons de Saint-Paul and their young charges were confronted with many problems of this kind as well as financial and administrative difficulties. They had obviously chosen the wrong patron saint, and the association was soon liquidated.

My mother was very concerned about Jean's various activities and his connections with a "corrupt" literary and artistic world. She believed that the principal writers of the day were agents of the devil, and the moment my back was turned, she tossed my first editions of Proust and Gide into the furnace. In order to set Jean back on the right path, she devised a clever scheme, though perhaps not quite consciously. For no apparent reason, one of her young novices began to make regular appearances at our house and also spent a summer with us in Locronan. She was an astonishingly beautiful and romantic-looking young girl, and a sentimental friendship of a clearly very intense nature soon developed between her and Jean. They would spend long hours in Jean's room, supposedly translating Francis Thompson's poem *The Hound of Heaven*, on which she was writing her thesis; it was I who suggested "Le Limier du Ciel" as a translation for the title. They often went on long walks together. Once the sentimental situation was clearly established, my mother effected her *coup de théâtre* in the best operatic style. The girl was dedicated to a religious life and was supposed to take her vows; her vocation was about to be destroyed. Now she must submit to the will of God. God and my mother, as usual, were in perfect agreement. The girl disappeared, and Jean, with a "broken heart," entered the Jesuit seminary as planned.

Jean was always perfectly kind to me. He was rarely at home during my childhood and our paths seldom crossed when we were young. I later learned from mutual friends that throughout his life he had felt great guilt for the way my family had treated me and left me without means of support. When he heard of the death of my friend Raymond—whom I shall speak of later—he confided to Pierre Gaxotte that he was very sorry, thinking that I must be suffering greatly from the loss. These words of sympathy, spoken in the corridors of the Académie Française, earned him the respect of Gaxotte, who normally had little love for clergymen. By then I had become a specialist in Oriental philosophy and Hinduism, and several attempts were made to arrange a confrontation between the theologian and the Hinduist; but Jean always refused. On a few occasions, however, and always among intimates, we allowed ourselves to be led into polite discussion. One time in particular, while we were having lunch at my sister's house, the subject of religion was raised by René Maheu, who was then director of Unesco. I found these verbal jousts, where I clearly had the upper hand, rather amusing. Jean's remarkable intelligence could not function beyond a certain point which he dared not pass; it was easy then to deal him the fatal blow. The moment we began to speak of basic principles, his power of reasoning was totally blocked by the obstacle of his faith, and he would resort to arguments that were more or less absurd. Although he was far less stupid than my uncle Paul, their reactions to certain arguments were very similar. When my uncle was challenged with prehistoric evidence completely destroying the Biblical myth according to which the world was created a few thousand years before Moses, he would simply answer: "God is omnipotent. Why shouldn't he have created a world with dead bodies?" There was no possible answer to such an idiotic argument.

Jean's promotion to the rank of cardinal was certainly a great liberation for him. He was free at last of the Jesuitical yoke which I believe had caused him much suffering. His celebrity and election to the Académie Française, his social life, and his links with the Vatican—whose role is more political than religious—added a new dimension to his life and brought him deep joy and satisfaction. He always remained somewhat nervous and agitated, but in the end he finally began to blossom. His last years were unquestionably the happiest in his life.

At the time of his scandalous death, Jean had become one of the most eminent members of the Church; people were already speaking of him as a possible candidate for the papacy. The outcry that followed seemed like a posthumous vengeance, the kind gods sometimes grant those they love best. People often speak of the ironies of fate, and one can hardly help sensing a real intention behind the circumstances of this death, the sort of joke fortune loves to play on powerful men. He suffered a heart attack right outside the door of a woman of doubtful virtue, in a neighborhood of ill-repute. If he had died a few minutes earlier or later, or had been visiting a wealthy lady in the snobbish XVIe Arrondissement—supposedly to discuss her "good works"—instead of a wretched woman to whom he had brought the proceeds from some of his theological books, there would never have been a scandal.

Jean had always felt sympathy for the unfortunates of the earth; for a time he even celebrated a mass for homosexuals. He tried to help prisoners, delinquents, young people in distress, and prostitutes. He had no bourgeois prejudices. I would have been happy for him if, as people suggested at the time, he had come to know the pleasures of the flesh at the end of his life. For me there is no conflict between physical love and the spiritual life—in fact it is the contrary.

I deeply admired the way he died, and could not help thinking of those martyrs whose spirit rises straight to Heaven under a cloud of infamy and among the jeerings of the crowds.

Like a true saint, he died an object of scorn and disgrace and the laughing-stock of an evil-minded and spiteful society; but that was so much more appropriate for him than lying in state in the echo of funeral orations amidst the catafalques of Notre-Dame. I lived near Rome during the last years of my brother's life, and people connected with the Vatican circulated stupid rumors according to which I had come only to impede Jean's chances for the papacy; the clergy obviously thought of me as a notorious renegade. People would sometimes get us confused and some critics even attributed my book *L'Erotisme divinisé* to Jean, saying: "It is common knowledge that Jesuits are notoriously open-minded, but this is going a bit far. . . ." My brother showed the world that, far from being a result of our beliefs and actions, scandal is the work of gods who care nothing for that jumble of pious rules of conduct and so-called infallible truths they seem to represent for so many people.

From the point of view of the Hindu religion, which welcomed me among its members, there is nothing reprehensible about my style of life or my way of thinking. This is not true of the Christian Church which considers me a heretic, a pervert and an immoralist—a strange contrast between two worlds that claim to help man in his search for the divine.

Catherine, my best friend and ally since childhood, was two years younger than I. For my mother, daughters did not really count, which was odd considering she had dedicated her life to the intellectual training of young girls. Catherine spent some time in a convent, where she was forced to wear a long shirt reaching down to her toes every time she took a bath. She suffered deeply from my mother's apparent indifference. She had a lovely voice, but her talent for Romantic lieder, of course, was never encouraged.

When she was still very young, Catherine married a friend of Jean's called Georges Izard, a graduate of the elite teachers' training college, the Ecole Normale Supérieure, who later became a well-known attorney. I was quite horrified by this marriage. In her discreet way, Catherine had always staunchly defended me in the hostile family circle. Although we were very close, I had no inkling of Cathe's plans. I lived in a totally unreal world.

When Catherine married, I felt that she had betrayed me and practically stopped seeing her, which made her very unhappy. Yet when the war was over and I returned to France after many years in the Orient, it was to my sister that I turned for shelter. Catherine and her husband welcomed me with great kindness, though with some reserve, and helped me readapt to the Western world.

Catherine perfectly illustrates the role a woman can play in society: self-effacing, completely devoted to the man of her choice, his supporter and his friend no matter what happens, no matter what he does. She is the key to his success, the heart of a family circle where children and grandchildren can find each other with ever-renewed pleasure. Her home also serves as a social center where a pleasant and intelligent hostess can do so much to advance her husband's career.

Georges was the son of a schoolteacher in Béziers. He had met my brother Jean at the Ecole Normale. Neither of my parents did anything to help the young couple materially, which made the first years of their marriage very difficult. Georges, an ambitious left-winger, clever in his dealings with people and a gifted public speaker, made a brilliant career for himself in the field of law. In a famous trial he ardently defended the Soviet dissident Kravchenko, who was considered by all the left to be a traitor for having dared to denounce the gulags and the repressive tactics of "Saint" Stalin. In his sumptuous apartment on the Boulevard Saint-Germain and in the huge estate he had bought in Morsang, near Corbeil, Georges presided over a circle of friends who liked to discuss literature, the arts, and politics (left-wing, of course). Catherine was a pleasant, unaffected, but wonderfully skillful hostess and seemed quite unaware of the secret motives of the men who assembled around her. When Georges suddenly died in 1975, she was completely lost and bewildered. The loyal group that had met each week at her house vanished into thin air, and she suddenly found herself abandoned by most of those "friends" who had once seemed so close. People still speak of her with affection and admiration; but politicians always have ulterior motives and cannot afford to associate with those who do not serve their ambitions.

In India, where marriage is a reality and a sacred bond, widows often commit suicide after their husbands die. Catherine could easily have done the same. She has not learned to survive the man she loved and supported; the inner spring that might have enabled her to find a new interest in life is worn out. When she appears in society, she hides her sadness and sensitivity beneath a thin veil of artificiality; rarely does one see a trace of the daring and vivacious young girl she used to be. When Zaher, the deposed King of Afghanistan who had lost everything in life—family, fortune, glory—saw her again after many years, he said: "I can hardly recognize her. She seems a different person." He had been very fond of Catherine in her adolescence, but could not see through the slightly stiff and polite exterior masking the vast desert and emptiness of her soul once the great love and meaning of her life had gone forever.

François, born three years after Catherine, was our mother's obvious favorite: she never did anything to hide the fact. He was a violent child and got everything he wanted by making scenes. We were never friends. He became a successful banker and married a beautiful woman whom he later divorced. They had two daughters: one of them, Sophie, is a very charming girl, and she and I have grown quite close. François died tragically. He woke up after an operation and, finding himself attached to his bed, got into such a rage that he broke his stitches trying to free himself and died of a hemorrhage.

Then came Louis, the youngest son in the family. He was a mild and gentle boy, a bit of a poet and dreamer. I never knew him very well, but he was very sweet to me. I have always been a subject of contention in my family, between those who were on my side and those who were not. Louis was born during the First World War. He married young, became a Navy officer and an airplane pilot. In 1940, when he was about twenty-four, he left for London to join General de Gaulle. I later learned from British friends that the General, who had the greatest confidence in Louis, has sent him on a secret mission to warn the authorities in Algiers of the projected Allied landing. This useless and foolhardy venture was judged unacceptable by the Anglo-American commanders, who always kept a close watch on de Gaulle's activities: they regretfully blew up the airplane the moment it took off. A former de Gaulle associate, who later became a diplomat, assured me that the story was untrue. The fact remains, however, that the airplane was destroyed by the British DCA. There had to be a reason. The General never felt any remorse or regret for having caused the death of his loyal and devoted supporter: that was not his style. Military men measure their victories by the numbers of dead. But de Gaulle was disappointed by his failure and unconsciously expressed his frustration by a marked hostility towards our family, as I later had occasion to note. It was many years before I heard all the details of the tragedy. I learned of Louis' death through a Free French review published in Delhi: a poem had been dedicated to his memory. The review had been forwarded to me in Almora, a small Himalayan city where I was convalescing at the time. Louis left a son, the only one of his generation to carry on the family name.

The youngest in the family was Marie, a lovely girl full of charm and fantasy. We called her Minette.

From a very early age, Minette showed a marked interest in boys. I could never understand my mother's attitude: perhaps in allowing her daughter to behave as she did, she was unconsciously satisfying a frustrated side of her own nature. When Minette was fifteen, she had an affair with a ski instructor. Mother found the boy charming and pretended that her daughter's *rendez-vous* were perfectly innocent. Christine, a young teacher who looked after us, tried in vain to warn my mother, who refused to take her seriously and sent her about her business—I was going to say, to the devil. Minette had many romantic attachments, and when this threatened to produce a concrete result, my mother did not hesitate to get rid of it. For any other woman such an action would have been strictly forbidden, but our family honor and the glory of God were more important.

Mother finally decided to lay down the law and arranged a marriage between Minette and a businessman, whose incompetence and bad management caused the loss of a large part of the family fortune; in this way my mother succeeded indirectly in disinheriting all her other children. Minette had several children of her own. She was a sweet and pleasant girl, always very affectionate with the calm and distant brother who had escaped the family tyranny. For a while she was under the influence of a false guru who encouraged her to take psychedelic drugs; she claimed that she could fly out of the window and float around the Eiffel Tower. This charming, uncalculating girl had never been taught to face the problems and realities of life.

Minette and I had a great deal in common. By nature she was mystical and sensual, always searching for that delicate and mysterious link between earthly love and divine reality. She was courageous, enterprising, and talented, and sang with realism and poignancy; but she never met anyone who could understand or guide her. I alone could have helped her escape the stifling, self-righteous family atmosphere through other means than despair; but she was not yet fifteen when I fled Europe, and when I returned twenty years later, she was already—physically as well as morally—a broken woman. Catherine tried to come to her aid, but could do nothing for her. Perhaps, if I had tried, I might have helped her get back on her feet and brought her out of the rut she had let herself slide into through a complete misunderstanding of herself; in the hypocritical Christian atmosphere she lived in, there was no way she could know that her inspired Bacchanalian nature was really a thing of beauty. But I never did find the courage: my visits to France were always brief, and after all those years in the Orient, it was already difficult enough for me to adapt to the West. I was deeply disturbed by Minette's dissolute appearance and the depressing environment she had escaped into. She had become a pitiful creature, lost in a vapor of alcohol. She died a few years later in a agony of suffering. Perhaps I could have prevented her from sinking so low, helped her at least to catch a glimpse of the luminous and sacred path the gods had meant for her to follow but which remained forever closed to her. Minette's affection and admiration for me were very touching—quite different from the attitudes of my other brothers and sisters, who never showed anything more than the cautious benevolence befitting the "black sheep of the family," as they liked to call me. In spite of the honors and respectability I had earned during my years in the East, my brother the cardinal and my sister Catherine never made the slightest gesture to help me along: I met their closest friends through other people. I was neither shocked nor surprised by their behavior. The paths they had chosen forced both of them to frequent circles in which certain ideas—the most questionable in fact—could not be put in doubt. I was unpredictable, therefore potentially dangerous. But now I belonged to a completely different world, and my former life, that of my childhood, was like a half-forgotten dream that had nothing to do with reality. The dramas and passions in the lives of these people left me relatively indifferent.

MADAME LEFER DE LA MOTTE

Madame Lefer de La Motte was a Spaniard and a woman of remarkable intelligence. Passionate and probably somewhat mystical by nature, she had been Mother Superior to the religious order of the Oratorians. She was very free in spirit— and possibly in body as well—and had been accused of wearing civilian clothes and travelling with young men with whom she shared adjoining rooms in hotels. These were only rumors, and I never looked into the matter—it did not really interest me. Madame Lefer was condemned by Rome and forced to abandon her order. She became a kind of guru and lived among artists, writers, and poets. Several nuns from her order, including my aunt Marie, followed her into civilian life.

My godmother, the Baronne Pierard, had sold her vast park in Neuilly, but kept an enormous house with magnificent gardens on the Boulevard d'Inkermann, right across from the Lycée Pasteur. She was a fervent disciple of Madame Lefer, who moved into her house and soon began to hold court.

My father, a young Romantic poet at the time, had just left Britanny and landed in Paris like a bird fallen out of the nest. He was well received by this free-thinking and quasi-religious group, which then proceeded to convert the infidel and get him baptized. It was there that he met my mother, a brilliant young student. They were both passionate *dreyfusards* and violently opposed to the injustice, anti-Semitism, and dishonesty concealed behind so-called military honor and the "best interests" of the country. Madame Lefer arranged the marriage. At first the young couple lived in a small apartment in Neuilly. Madame Lefer and the Baronne Pierard were respectively chosen as godmothers for Jean and me. Madame Lefer then lent my parents a small ten-room pavilion which abutted her enormous house and had a small garden of its own.

My father had a magnificent study with stained glass windows and a wooden staircase that reached the highest bookshelves. He sat enthroned on a medieval chair behind a table whose feet might have been designed by the renowned nineteenth-century architect Viollet-le-Duc and represented griffins with their tongues sticking out.

We lived in this house until the beginning of the First World War. It was there that Catherine, François, and Louis were born. I vaguely remember the comings and goings of the doctor at the time of François' birth, and also the scene of the telegram announcing Uncle André's death, in 1914.

From time to time I would visit my godmother. She was very beautiful, always in black, and covered with fine jewels; a long white ringlet curled down her shoulder. As I approached her from a distance, I could see her reclining on her chaise longue on a small platform at the end of the gallery, a kind of greenhouse whose windows were decorated with painted lilies and purple irises. The wooden floor was so smooth and shiny that I was always afraid I would slip and fall.

My brother Jean was an habitué of Madame Lefer's group; he was probably attracted by her free Christian views, so different from those of his Jesuit instructors. Many strange people could be seen at the house on the Boulevard d'Inkermann: Anael Alastaire in his floating silk robes, young writers like Robert Honnert and Marcel Angagneure, a certain Abbé Courtade, and many other well-known personalities of the time whose names I did not know. I met many of them later, in other circles. In this environment, Jean came in contact with a fashionable group of intellectuals who were preoccupied with problems of Christianity. He met such writers as François Mauriac, Maurice Sachs, and Max Jacob, who, though not part of the group, were experiencing a similar conflict between religion and morality.

No attempt was ever made to make me part of the group. I was not preoccupied with religion or moral conflicts, so they did not find me interesting.

When the Baronne Pierard died, Madame Lefer and her

group abandoned the Jugenstyl for neo-Gothic and moved to a sort of manor house near Douarnenez, in Britanny, surrounded by many beautiful trees. I occasionally stopped there on my way back from Locronan, or when I went bathing on the beach of Ris. There was a large dining room with frescoes on the walls, representing aquatic scenes with fishes. I liked the conventional style of painting very much, but everyone around me said it was terrible; I could not understand why. But it did not really matter to me what they thought. I was not interested in the opinions of adults.

Madame Lefer was a generous and a very modern woman. She organized a pioneer group of volunteer social workers and sent young women from good families to visit wretched people in poor neighborhoods. She bought a hotel on the beach of Ris near Douarnenez and created the first holiday camp for underprivileged children. The famous Professor Reilly of the Pasteur Institute, one her most faithful habitués, volunteered his services and spent the summer months taking care of the children.

SAINTE-MARIE

Shortly before the First World War, my mother, with the help of various patronesses, bought a large convent in the middle of a great park, on the Boulevard Victor-Hugo in Neuilly. It had once housed Augustinian nuns. Under the auspices of Pope Pius X, with whom she apparently enjoyed a direct and informal relationship, she founded a new religious order for women teachers in civilian costume. This order, called Saint-François-Xavier, had been set up as an association in order to get around a prevailing law barring the formation of religious congregations on French territory. Soon afterward my mother established the Collège Sainte-Marie, which was attended by most of the young girls of the Catholic *haute-bourgeoisie* of the time. It was an excellent business venture: the teachers, who held the highest degrees, were not only unpaid but often brought along their dowries as well.

The funds for this enterprise were provided by a large conservative and Catholic organization represented by a group of lady trustees. I was always hearing about Madame

Schneider of Le Creuzot and her daughter, the Comtesse de Fels. My mother would get quite excited describing the lively board meetings and claimed that she always had the last word.

Sainte-Marie played a relatively important role in French cultural life. My mother inspired both admiration and fear; the young ladies of good family who were educated at Sainte-Marie either worshipped or hated her.

In 1916 or thereabouts, my family moved into what had once been the chaplain's residence. It was a rather pretty house with a private garden, separated from the main building by a small door. My mother lived only a short distance away from her office, which saved her a great deal of time. Meals were brought in from the school kitchen, so the housework required of our two Breton maids was reduced to a minimum.

My father must have found this arrangement very inconvenient. He had no rooms of his own in which to work or entertain and could never invite anyone. As a result he ate out most of the time and held meetings at a *brasserie* on the Place des Ternes.

The presence of a red devil within the convent walls did cause some problems, however. One day, during a board meeting, the Comtesse de Fels voiced her objections to this left-wing commoner's intrusion into such a holy establishment. My mother supposedly replied: "My husband may be of humble descent, but *my* ancestors, the Princes of Clamorgan, are buried around the church of Valognes. Where, may I ask, are the ancestors of Madame de Fels?" The matter went no further.

I remember being taken down to the cellar with my brothers and sisters in 1917, during the bombings of "Big Bertha," the Germans' famous long-range cannon. We had a wonderful time, but my mother, who preferred risk to discomfort, refused to join us.

CHRISTINE

My mother's congregation included a large number of young women teachers with university degrees.

In order to help out their Mother Superior, some of the girls would take turns looking after her children as well as the household. One of them was sent with me to the country. All during my childhood there was always a young girl to take care of me and teach me Latin. It must have been a great trial to them to be sent so far away, alone with a delicate and sometimes difficult child, but they performed their task with great patience and devotion. Among them I remember Geneviève Standaert, a Belgian girl who shared my passion for raising animals. She helped me build a chicken house in the Neuilly garden, where I spent a great deal of time looking after my brood.

Suzanne Mongin was a native of Champagne. I spent several very happy winters and springs with her in a closed-down convent in Saint-Loup-sur-Aujon, near Langres. I was twelve years old. It was wonderful to have so much space all to myself and wander freely around the empty chapel, the ice-cold corridors, or the abandoned parish garden; I was even allowed to ring the noon Angelus. There was a small enclosed orchard where primroses and daffodils grew in the springtime; the old walls were covered with flowering sweet-alyssum. I lived with Suzanne—whom I called Suze—in a large room, once the chaplain's, where a pot-bellied stove helped us fight against the cold. At night, I would climb into a very high bed and snuggle underneath a large red eiderdown. Before bedtime, the sheets were heated with warming pans or a wooden construction with hot coals in the middle called a *moine*; a kitten would curl up beside me. In the daytime we used foot-warmers. In the lower corner of the convent grounds was a farm run by three former nuns, for the order still owned a great deal of land. They made hay and planted potatoes. There were enormous barns filled with mysterious machines, all in various states of disrepair. There was also a flock of sheep tended by a half-witted shepherdess, and an old gelding called Pierrot that I was sometimes allowed to ride, though I always ended up hanging by its neck. I could not understand why they called it a gelding: "Why is he a gelding?" I would ask. "Because his parts were cut off." "What parts?" "You ask too many questions."

We ate our meals in a large smoky kitchen where cheeses were laid to dry on shelves beneath the beams. A large, stocky woman who bore the poetic name of Eugénie Paintendre [soft bread] Jobert was in charge.

Other years, I would stay with Suze's parents. Her father had once been a printer, and owned a house behind the cemetery. For the first time in my life I had a piano all to myself and spent long hours going through scores and discovering the enchanted world of music. In those days I used to worship the Moon and prayed to it in my room at night. I had invented a whole ritual. I prostrated myself before the divine and wondrous star, laying down offerings. I made a small altar with a picture of the moon upon it so that I felt protected even in the daytime. I would peer at its mountains through a telescope, with visions of the Lake of Dreams and the Sea of Serenity floating in my mind.

Christine, a young girl of great beauty and superior intelligence, came from a family of Breton fishermen. Her dark hair, which she wore coiled around her head, was as long as Isolde's and went all the way down to her feet. She had been a brilliant student, then left Brittany and came to Paris to pass her examinations under the sponsorship of my mother, who promptly took her into her school.

Christine appeared in our midst when I was about fourteen. She was ten years my senior, knew a great deal about Grecian art and culture, and was passionately interested in ancient Greek and Roman sculpture as well as art in general. Her freedom of mind, her philosophy and vision of the world were far closer to Homer, Sophocles, and Virgil than to Saint Paul. Christine became my friend, ally, and defender both within my family and the Sainte-Marie community, where everyone loved to gossip about the Daniélou children—especially me, for I was already considered a somewhat dangerous character. It was with Christine that I began to visit museums and discovered Monet's *Water Lilies*, Van Gogh, and ancient Greek sculpture—a whole world of art that I had never heard mentioned in my family circle.

After I left home, Christine continued to visit me several times a week. Meanwhile my mother had put her in charge of Minette, which caused Christine a great deal of anguish. She did not know whether it was worse to betray the daughter or the mother, who rebuffed her suggestions of prudence in regard to Minette. Christine often used these flare-ups as an excuse to come and visit me, which somehow made up for the excessive freedom accorded to my sister.

My father took a great fancy to Christine. He called her a druidic priestess and wanted her to work as a secretary in his ministry; their common Breton heritage made him feel very close to this very beautiful young girl. Christine found herself faced with a delicate situation that might have become dramatic had she not resolved it with infinite tact, gentleness, and propriety. In fact it was I whom she was most attached to, and she always remained true to her affection.

During my first visit to Shantiniketan, the Indian poet Rabindranath Tagore had asked me to find someone to run the women's division of his somewhat fanciful university. Christine, by then, could no longer bear the atmosphere of Sainte-Marie. With the help of my friend Raymond Burnier, of whom I shall speak later, I managed to spirit her away. One day, without the slightest warning, she disappeared from the convent and never came back. A handsome wardrobe had been prepared for Christine by one of our couturier friends, who also fell in love with her, and in 1935 she found herself aboard one of those magnificent Italian ships that used to travel from Genoa to Bombay via the Suez Canal.

At first Christine felt completely lost in this strange Oriental world of which she knew nothing, not even the language. But she soon adapted to her new life, perfected her English, and learned to speak Bengali extremely well. The old poet Tagore worshipped and admired her.

Christine remained in Shantiniketan for several years and only left after the poet's death. She taught for a while at an English school in Darjeeling, in the Himalayas, then became director of Calcutta's Alliance Française and Cultural Center.

Christine developed a great interest in Indian culture, music, and painting. Thanks to her, the Alliance Française became not just a French language school and a place where official envoys could give their boring lectures and mediocre concerts, but an important Bengali cultural center. She became great friends with Lady Ranu Mukerjee, wife of a powerful industrial magnate and director of the Academy of Arts, later president of the Alliance.

The modest rooms of the Alliance Française became Calcutta's principal cultural center, where Bengali artists, writers, and politicians could get together and meet foreign visitors. Meanwhile the sumptuous quarters of the British and American-run organizations remained empty and deserted.

Christine's sweetness, hospitality, devotion, and brilliant though unassuming intelligence won her the friendship of all the important people who visited Calcutta during those years, including the film-maker Jean Renoir, Alexandra David Neel, various diplomats, writers, Indian ministers, and French and English public personalities. Her friends always remained true to her even after they were promoted to more important posts. After she retired, she returned to Paris and became a powerful *éminence grise* in various ministries. Renoir, who remained in correspondence with Christine until his death, at a loss to describe the contrasts in this multifaceted personality that was both stubborn and self-effacing, modest and widely cultured, daring and whimsical yet capable of unlimited devotion, could only say, in his Parisian jargon: "Christine, elle est bidonnante." ["Christine, she's something else!"]

Christine often came to see me in Benares. When Raymond and I went to Calcutta, we used to stay in her large apartment on Park Street. It was open on all four sides and had very little furniture, which allowed a light breeze—so delicious in the warm and humid Bengali weather—to circulate freely through the rooms.

Young people in need of counsel and support were often sent to Christine, who always seemed able to find a practical yet very human answer to their problems. She unfailingly knew when to make a discreet recommendation, and people never refused to help her protégés.

The friendship that had bound me to Christine since childhood always remained strong and free of shadow. Her stubborn and courageous Breton nature helped her to overcome the difficulties of a relationship that must have been extremely frustrating to her. She accepted my friends without the slightest trace of resentment.

In 1982 Christine suffered a heart attack. I immediately went to visit her in the hospital and promised to return the next day. But as I was passing through the door she raised her hand in farewell, a gesture customary among sailors' wives in her native land of Britanny. She knew that we would never meet again.

On Friendship and Love

From my early childhood, animals were much more important to me than human beings.

All my life I have felt very close to plants, birds, and all other living things. The first friends I ever made were cats, dogs, mice, and squirrels. I never saw any real difference between people, plants, and animals: it always seemed to me that man's claim to a "soul" setting him apart from other creatures was stupid and impious. Whenever I painted landscapes, I felt in perfect communion with the soul of nature; I would speak to it, listen to its message, and try to transcribe its beauty and feelings. Trees and plants have always been like people to me. I have formed deep mutual attachments with animals; even when they do not know me, they approach me without fear or hostility. When I left the old convent of Saint-Loup, I was not allowed to take along the kitten that liked to cuddle up beside me under the red eiderdown. After I had gone, it just lay in front of the door and died. I felt very guilty for having abandoned it. When I was a child I was surrounded with birds. In Neuilly, I had a small corner of the garden all to myself and a windowed lean-to where I raised my chickens: lively White Leghorns, sturdy, golden-brown Rhode-Island Reds, and fanciful and rustic Faverolles. At various times I also had rabbits and dogs. I once brought back two squirrels from Auvergne, and gave them the poetic names of Sylvain and Urlande. They scampered around the house and were thoroughly misbehaved. They made their nest in the library, inside a rare and luxuriously bound edition of the complete works of Voltaire: they had hollowed out the insides of the volumes so cleverly that, from the outside, no one noticed any difference. There was a dreadful scene. I was told to put my squirrels in a cage, but they were so miserable that I finally carried them into the woods and gave them back their freedom, for which they probably had little use.

I was raised strictly by women—not the ordinary kind one meets in society, but young nuns who were supposedly asexual. I was quite astonished to hear boys talking about them as potential sex objects; such an idea had never even crossed my mind. This is perhaps one of the reasons why I have always felt embarrassed when a suggestion of sex intruded upon my relationship with women I appreciated for their friendship and intelligence.

With certain women I find it quite easy to establish a relationship of affection and trust, a sort of romantic complicity. But the moment I sense an intention to go on to more physical gestures, my instinct always rebels. I am not programmed for such things. Some people, I believe, feel the same way about homosexual acts.

I love the company of mature women, their good sense, devotion, and protective generosity—in other words, their maternal qualities. Some women have been loyal and precious friends to me. But I am terrified of the hard, egocentric, self-interested praying-mantis types who use their charms to capture men. I am not at all drawn to this kind of woman.

In human relationships one sometimes feels an element of attraction, affinity, and vague sensuality, which, in some cases, can be fulfilled by acts of sex; it has something to do with hormones and chemistry, procreation, and natural selection. The important thing is to follow one's instinct.

Women are far less bound by theoretical systems than men. It is easier for them to go beyond the limitations of words and so-called logical reasoning, the kind of rationalism that is closed to anything of a transcendent nature. They seem to be intuitively closer to Einstein than to Euclid. In my search for "other" realities, I have often found women more subtle, less dogmatic—in other words, more intelligent and open-minded than men.

I had my first romance during a winter in Arcachon, when I was ten. Mercedes de Gournay, a disciple of Madame Lefer de La Motte, found me charming and was always trying to lure me to her house, where she would kiss and caress me. She had a beautiful fur blanket that I loved to curl up in. I was quite flattered by her attentions and allowed her to kiss me, but I stayed on my guard and never really responded to her feelings. I also had a tremendous crush on a fourteen-year-old boy who happened to be "a Protestant," which added a sacrilegious flavor to my passion. I teased him continually in the hope that he would at least deign to beat me. He wore knee-length coal-gray trousers that had a nice tweedy smell.

When I was about fifteen, my mother decided that a pilgrimage to Lourdes would do me a world of good. She entrusted me to my uncle Paul, the canon, who was escorting a group of boys from one of his church-run organizations. The train was packed with pilgrims, the journey interminable. The boys were very disagreeable. Uncle Paul, as usual, wasted no time in cutting me down. As I was exclaiming before the magnificent Cirque de Gavarnie, in the Pyrenees, he said: "You speak like Monsieur Perrichon"—Monsieur Perrichon being the classic bourgeois traveller in Labiche's famous play. My feelings were quite hurt. I refused to go to any of the masses or to wait endlessly near the waterfall hoping for miracles to happen. I preferred to spend my time with a girl who sold devotional articles. She lavished gifts upon me, which I found very agreeable, and cried when I left. She wrote me several passionate letters. But mail trains are speedier than passenger trains, and when I got home to Neuilly, her letters had already been opened. I was forced to send back all the gifts she had given me. After this I was considered unredeemable, a lost soul. I have never been able to understand my family's indignation over this affair. Their innuendos struck me as vulgar and gross; I was also very sorry to lose my friend's little gifts.

One summer when I was about fifteen, my father rented a house in Camaret and borrowed a small sailboat for me to use. I would spend long hours sailing about the sea. I was very fond of the sailboat and hated for anyone to accompany me. My mother had invited one of her Breton students, a rather beautiful young girl of twenty-five who paid me far too much attention. She would insist on sailing with me and, once we were alone, would press her body against mine and put her arms around my neck, which thoroughly repelled me. I soon learned to manipulate the rudder so that the boat would suddenly change course and cut obliquely across the waves, which made the poor girl terribly seasick. By the time I triumphantly reached the port, she was in a dreadful state, her face a greenish hue. She soon gave up pretending that she loved sailing on my little boat.

When I was living in my small Paris studio on the Boulevard Gouvion-Saint-Cyr, a young Jewish girl who lived in the same house tried repeatedly to seduce me. She was rather fat and wore a pearl around her neck, which she considered a bad luck charm. With disarming naïveté she would tell me: "I'd like to be rich enough to force you to make love to me!" I was certainly not held back by any scruples, I was very poor, and I really did enjoy the company of women; but female sensuality terrified me. Later she married a painter and tried to see me again, but I did not respond. I was sorry about this, for I really liked her and wished we could have remained friends.

When I was in America, a tall, wiry, and ugly girl called Anne, who looked rather like a horse, tried several times to lure me into her bed; she nearly succeeded. Then there was Stella, the German professor's wife; our romance broke up her marriage.

In India I made friends with a young woman musician, a former disciple of Gurdjieff's, who very devotedly helped me in my work. She was an excellent pianist and we often played music together, but a certain tension between us made our relationship rather awkward. She followed me to Pondicherry and ended up marrying a pseudomystical Indian. The marriage, I think, was not a success, and her life was difficult and unhappy. This made me very sad, for I sincerely liked and respected her.

I met Marion in Budapest. She was an American of Hungarian origin, married at the time to the famous Hollywood director Otto Preminger. From the first day we met, Marion was consumed with a violent and completely unreasonable passion for me. She was intelligent, beautiful, and elegant, but terribly Balkanese. Everywhere I went she appeared unexpectedly, armed with her flaming passion. I left without leaving a forwarding address, but in vain. One day, as I was getting off the plane in Los Angeles, where Jean Renoir was awaiting me, I saw Marion on the runway holding an enormous white lily which, to everyone's astonishment, she then proceeded to offer me. Little by little, my long trips to India and my total silence wore out her passion. In the end, Marion gave up on me. She got divorced and soon married another man, who I hope was able to satisfy her fiery temperament.

I would never have become the man I am or done the things I have done had I not enjoyed the advantage of preferring love in the masculine. Even as a child I was aware of it and I never felt the slightest doubt or anxiety about this peculiarity in my nature: I seemed to know that this was one of the basic factors that would allow me to accomplish my destiny. All my life I have been surrounded with youth and tender friendships. I have always worshipped physical beauty. Hindus say that gods are perpetual adolescents. For me, the glorification of love has always been inseparable from my sense of the divine.

For certain Christians, the important role that is given in these memoirs to human affections and erotic encounters may seem to run counter to the pursuit of a spiritual life. With the passing of time I have come to understand that the state closest to godliness is to be found in love of divine creation, the beauty of the living body, and the intensity of happiness and pleasure. Christian masochism does not lead to wisdom, but to cruelty, inhumanity, and hypocrisy.

A NEGATIVE EDUCATION

My mother was always talking about forming human beings, moulding characters, influencing people. During the unhappy years of my adolescence, confined within a puritanical and bourgeois family, I had only one goal: to escape my mother's influence, which I felt to be an evil force, destroying any individuality or potential genius.

In my isolation, deprived of friends, human relationships, and social life, surrounded by those asexual shadows of womanhood at Saint-François-Xavier who graciously looked after me, I sought refuge in seminal rites of sacrifice—elaborate and intense masturbatory games which, in retrospect, suggest a precocious Dionysian instinct, but seemed at the time the only way to escape my mother's influence.

Whenever I spent any length of time in Neuilly, I was allowed as a special favor to take classes at Sainte-Marie, which was of course a girl's school, but I never spoke to any of my classmates: they seemed silly, ugly, uninteresting. Later, when I was sent—also by special favor—to Sainte-Croix, I found myself among brutal, terrifying boys who knew that I had studied "with the girls" and teased me unmercifully. I never made any friends there and remember those periods at Sainte-Croix as months of terrible anguish and fear. On one occasion only, a lay history master silenced a few boys who were jeering at me while we were climbing the stairs to class. I was surprised and quite touched. I did not expect any sign of humanity in that foolishly Christian milieu.

I had spent most of my childhood in the country and did not know how to deal with the real world; in fact I had not been taught anything at all. I had no idea how to behave at table, how to kiss ladies' hands, say thank you, or carry on polite conversations. I was a little barbarian—a very amusing and whimsical child, it seems—but I had to learn to deal with social situations without any help or counsel, which is never easy. My poor health, my inability to pursue serious studies, my total lack of interest in intellectual or religious matters completely ruined any plans my wise and inspired mother might have laid out for me. By the time I was fifteen, I had grown so tired of my physical frailty that I began to do gymnastics and take part in sports, although such activities were looked down on by my family. I got myself a racing bicycle and became a member of the Racing Club; I also went on camping and canoeing expeditions. Some of my exploits were written up in the newspapers: in 1926, for example, I travelled along rivers and canals by canoe, from Paris to Brittany, with a Russian boy called Vadim de Stavraky, the son of a refugee my mother had found starving in a Parisian slum and taken under her wing. By the time I began to study classical ballet and floor acrobatics, I had grown strong and muscular and no longer had health problems of any kind.

When I was a very small child, I had an excellent memory

and could learn things quickly and easily, but in my own particular way and according to my whim. My critical faculties rebelled whenever I was forced to absorb oversimplified concepts. The kind of dogma according to which two and two make four was only acceptable to me once I had figured it out for myself and acknowledged it to be true. A cat and a mouse do not add up to two cats or two mice, but to a fat cat. Because of my critical turn of mind, I was soon considered unfit for study. I learned to read when I was four years old, and found it so easy that, to amuse myself, I practiced reading upside down, top to bottom, every which way. One day, before witnesses, my mother came to check on my progress. As a joke, the book was handed to me upside down. I can still remember that idiotic book and the childish poem I was asked to read—a feat I performed without the slightest difficulty:

Ah! Ce portrait de l'oncle Jules!	Ah! That portrait of Uncle John!
Quel travail! Le voici fini.	What a chore! At last it's done.
Quelle heure est-il à la pendule?	Now, what time does the clock say?
Quoi! Douze coups. Il est midi.	What! Twelve strokes. It's now midday.

Everyone laughed and made fun of me. I obviously did not know how to read and had learned the book by heart. No one gave me a second chance, or asked me to read another passage right side up. I was sick with embarrassment and have remained bitter about the incident to this day. I can still see the scene in the dining room of the house we lived in before 1914. It seems like only yesterday.

I found it very easy to memorize things that interested me: I can still recite entire chapters from Jules Verne and all kinds of poems. My memory is cluttered up with a jumble of useless things. Children's capacity for memorization in the Western world is hardly used to advantage. In India not only do they learn the dictionary by heart, but Sanskrit grammar, in verse, and all the texts of the *Upanishads*. During my adolescence I learned English with great ease: it was Turner's language, and he was my favorite painter. Later I grew very fond of my Italian teacher—who also fancied me—and, in the space of two years, learned Italian so well that when I passed my *baccalauréat*, my examiner thought I was Italian. With my knowledge of languages and certain points of mathematics and physics that had caught my interest, I passed the first part of the *bachot* with the highest honors, a *mention très bien*. My mother's only comment was: "Isn't that typical! Examinations are all the same, just a question of luck!" I swore that I would never pass another examination as long as I lived, and I never have. All the university titles and honors that I received later in life were offered to me on the basis of my work and research; I never went out of my way to obtain them.

Even when I was very young, I always made a point of scorning "intellectuals". It seemed to me that people only wrote books because they could not express their ideas through drawing or music. Because of this I was considered a simpleton. Whenever I tried to take part in serious discussions, I was promptly put in my place.

All the things I have ever learned I discovered on my own. As a result, my general knowledge is erratic and filled with enormous gaps, and my approach to most forms of learning has always been unconventional. Many years later, in the corridors of the Académie Française, my brother-in-law Georges Izard said to Pierre Gaxotte: "Who would ever have thought that Alain would become an intellectual and a scholar?" "You misjudged him completely," answered Gaxotte, who, even in my youth, had shown interest in me and encouraged me to write.

CHAPTER THREE

The Arts

In 1920, while spending a holiday with my mother in an isolated hotel in Croix-de-Cavalaire where she was recuperating from a long illness, I discovered painting. I was thirteen at the time and had never been taught drawing or gone to a museum. Someone had given me a box of watercolors to keep me busy. My first attempts at painting were quite satisfactory and I got into the habit of going out on long walks every day to paint landscapes. I discovered the abandoned village of Grimaud, a small port called Saint-Tropez, various deserted beaches and capes, several beautiful villas with magnificent gardens, and a small cabin where lived two lady friends who grew flowers in their yard.

The discovery of painting was an important event in my life. I had found a way to commune with the beauty of the world in a language that expressed feelings better than any words can do. Through painting it is possible to analyze a landscape and reveal its secret. For me, the act of painting soon became a sort of ecstatic semi-conscious rite, and it has always remained so. I would let colors and shapes express themselves through my paintbrush, which seemed guided by a force other than my own. While I painted I would talk out loud, asking the colors what they really were, for they are never quite what one thinks: the sky is never blue, the grass is never green—they are subtle combinations of mysterious and unexpected hues. Through the medium of the painter, the landscape or model expresses its true nature. One can never touch up or perfect the product of such direct communication without destroying the poetry or betraying the model. The more systematic type of composition that I, like most artists, later practiced has nothing to do with this kind of experience: the first drafts of a painting are always more alive than the final version.

The act of painting caused me such intense emotion that the landscapes have remained forever engraved in my memory. I have painted hundreds, perhaps even thousands of water-colors, and though I remember nothing of the circumstances, the places, or the people involved, each scene remains as vivid in my mind as the memory of a first kiss or the raptures of love.

This solitary and passionate apprenticeship, as was later the case when I became involved in music, left me in a state of total bewilderment before the works of the masters. Most of the time they seemed to perceive nothing more than the exterior quality of objects, and had no sense of their magic. There were exceptions, of course, and some artists I really did admire, but my judgment was based on criteria that had nothing to do with genre or style. So few paintings seem to possess a soul. A few years later I discovered Van Gogh, then Turner. In 1924 I went to London and spent my entire visit at the Tate Gallery, where most of Turner's works can be seen. My only other memory of the trip is the waxy smell of the house I was staying in. I was also very moved by certain paintings by Corot, Blake, Monet, but I hated Cézanne. The human figure is something quite different, for an erotic element then comes into play. I used to collect photographs of Greek statues; I was in love with Botticelli's *Mars and Venus*.

No one in my family was the least bit interested in my painting. As time passed, my collection of oils and watercolors grew larger and larger, but most them have been lost.

When I went to college in America a few years later at age nineteen, I was quite surprised to find professors and town people willing to pay good prices for my watercolors; I was also asked to illustrate the students' yearbook.

Later, in Paris I had a few shows. My exhibition at the Galerie Castel in 1937 was in fact quite successful, which rather surprised me, my style being entirely different from the cubism then in fashion.

Then I went to live in Asia. I have never stopped painting nor ceased to experience a symbiotic communion with landscapes. I have also painted a few good portraits, including one of Rabindranath Tagore, which was well received and can still be seen in a Calcutta museum dedicated to his memory. When I returned to Europe after the Second World War, I had to abandon painting, but took it up again in a different spirit after I left the Institute of Music in Berlin and found more time for myself.

Like all proper children, I was given piano lessons from the age of ten. My teacher was a lady who had won a prize at the Paris Conservatory. Her name was Mme de La Vieuxville, and it was rumored that her husband had gone berserk in the bridal carriage right after the marriage ceremony. I have always felt that it was one of those stories that people tell children in order to conceal the real truth. My lessons were few and far between, for I only lived in Neuilly for short periods during the spring and autumn. In the winter I was sent off to the country for my health, following the medical superstitions of the time. I never had to sleep in a stable, however, that kind of treatment being somewhat out of date. In the summer the entire family went to Britanny to stay in our house in Locronan, where there was no piano. In Neuilly I would run to the piano whenever I had the chance; such opportunities were quite rare, however, for the sound of a child practicing is always exasperating for everyone.

It was during those winters in Saint-Loup-sur-Aujon, while I was staying with the old printer, Suzanne Mongin's father, that I was finally able to work alone and uninterruptedly for months at a time. There was an old but quite good upright piano in a small room filled with musical scores where I discovered Chopin's Etudes, Liszt's *Années de Pèlerinage*, Schumann's *Variations Symphoniques*, and Schubert's Impromptus. Some of those pieces have remained associated in my memory with certain landscapes, light effects, poetic emotions, and clandestine readings. I had never been taken to a concert, and people had no records or radios in those days; I had never heard a pianist and there was no one to give me advice. My understanding of music was a strictly personal experience: I felt it as a living thing, an emotional projection of myself. For this reason I later found it very difficult to enjoy listening to pianists, though there were some exceptions—Cortot and Rachmaninoff in particular; I found most of the others revolting. The most famous pianists, it seemed to me, did not understand what they were playing. They would go through the most moving passages without seeing anything at all, completely oblivious to the accents of musical emotion that are expressed through certain pauses and ornaments; they seemed to have no sense of the composition's movements and rushed through the musical landscape as blindly as a herd of stampeding elephants.

When I was about sixteen, my father brought home a famous musician so that he could listen to my sister Catherine, whose voice was quite lovely. She sang some Schubert melodies while I accompanied her on the piano. The eminent guest listened to us very attentively, then took my father aside. "Your daughter has a lovely voice," he said, "and would benefit greatly from singing lessons. But the one who really impresses me is your son: he is exceptionally talented and should pursue a career as a pianist."

After he left, Father seemed quite happy, but my mother was adamant: "It's unthinkable! My son a musician, climbing on the stage!" As usual my father said nothing. I was given no teacher and the piano became more inaccessible than ever.

When I was a child my voice was very pure. I loved to sing, and my sister and I would go through the repertoire of the time: Fauré, Reynaldo Hahn, Duparc, Chausson, and of course Schumann's lieder. I used to sing in the chapel of my mother's school, and she was deeply moved by my angelic voice as it sweetly rose towards God. Sometimes, it seems, it rose too high, and I would upset everyone by singing the motets at such a pitch that the choir could not follow me. Once, during a *Cor Jesu*, the choir finally gave up trying and suddenly stopped, while my solitary voice soared up to the chapel vault. These athletic victories gave me a great deal of satisfaction. Sometimes I was asked to sing at home; people found my voice quite ravishing. Then, when I was about thirteen, my voice began to change. No one told me that this was a passing phase and that I should be careful not to force it. I heard nothing but insults: "Alain, be quiet! It's awful!" It was a terrible letdown and I was in despair, like an aging actor who suddenly finds it impossible to get a role: one day he is an idol, the next an object of contempt, "that bloody bore!"

Later my voice improved and became a light baritone, almost a tenor; but I had overstrained it during the "breaking" period and it remained fragile thereafter.

When I was twenty I went to see Charles Panzera, who agreed to give me lessons. After a short time he told me: "There is nothing that I can teach you, except perhaps in voice projection." I noticed that, unlike his other pupils, I was allowed to sing his own repertoire. This deeply sensitive musician seemed interested in the way I experienced music. He gave me a signed photograph of himself with an inscription that mentioned "the great artistic emotions that have brought us together." Panzera was aware of my difficult situation and my family's hostility towards music. When I was practicing the famous aria from the opera *Véronique*, he complimented me with a smile on the artistic conviction with which I sang the lyrics "'Tis *good*, believe me, to have a family."

Then I left for the Orient and completely lost touch with Western music. Little by little I was initiated into an astonishing new world—the music of India. But although it was very different from Western music, the two styles remained separate and distinct in my mind and I never tried to mingle them. Musical systems, like languages, do not mix; but one gradually becomes aware of the resemblances between them, not in form but in evocative power. On a certain level they may seem to have nothing in common, but a *râga* can express the same feeling, the same vision of the world as a Beethoven adagio or a movement in a Chopin sonata.

When I was very young I wrote poetry. I have always had a sharp sense of language forms, which later facilitated my work as a translator. All of my poems have been lost, but I vaguely remember a few stanzas I wrote when I was twenty:

Matins tristes d'Anvers pleins
  d'ombre et de clochers
Désespérément plats, tièdes et
  saturés.
Immense troupeau bleu d'oiseaux
  changés en pierres
Qui sans jamais pouvoir regarder
  en arrière
Sentent le vent marin qui entoure
  leurs yeux
De ses replis stridents, amers et
  douloureux.

Melancholy mornings of
  Antwerp, filled with
  shadows and steeples,
So desolately flat, sodden and
  warm;
Great flocks of blue birds
  turned into stone
That never can look back,
But feel the sea breeze biting
  their eyes
In sharp and strident pleats of
  pain.

Or again:

Et quand je t'ai revu, paré de clair
  de lune
J'ai su que tu ne savais pas que je
  t'aimais.
Et je n'ai pas osé dire mon
  infortune,
Tu eus peut-être ri. J'ai cru que
  j'en mourrais.

When I saw you again framed
  in the moonlight,
I knew that you knew nothing
  of my love.
I dared not tell you of my
  sorrow,
You might have laughed. I
  thought I should die.

I have always felt that English was a wonderful instrument of poetry. When I was studying at St. John's College, the English professor sometimes read my poems out loud in class; he thought they were excellent literary models. Unfortunately I have lost them all.

I spoke English quite well. It is a rich and subtle language, and I have used it in many of my books. Nevertheless, when I was living in Benares, I deepened my knowledge of the poetic language with the help of a young English poet, Lewis Thomson, who taught me how to make better use of its more archaic Saxon terms rather than the latinate vocabulary, which has so much less character.

This was of great help to me when I translated Indian texts into English such as *The Ankle Bracelet*, a third-century epic romance written in Tamil.

Birds' songs are ended now
The ruler of the day has gone
Unending tears are tedious for pretty eyes.
Maid whose tresses are decked with flower buds!
Tell me, does this maddening twilight come
From the country where the absconder lives?

I translated this text into French as well, under the title *Le Roman de l'anneau*:

Le chant des oiseaux s'est éteint.
Celui qui règne sur le jour a disparu.
Mes yeux s'ennuient à verser des pleurs incessants.
Jolie fille aux cheveux entremêlés de fleurs,
Dis-moi!
La lueur de ce crépuscule qui me rend folle
vient-elle du pays où vit le déserteur?

I also translated from Sanskrit and published some charming seventh-century court plays by King Harsha.

I had refused to prepare the second part of my *baccalauréat*. Since it was already an established fact that I was no intellectual, why go through the bother of pretending to do "serious" studies? Since I appeared to be "an artist," my mother decided that architecture was the proper and respectable career for me. And so, in 1925, I enrolled in the Ecole des Beaux-Arts, Paris's famous school of art, and entered the studio of a political friend of my father's, the architect Lemaresquier.

My mother's prime concern had always been to preserve her children's purity, and I had grown up completely isolated from the real world. With the most perfect naïveté, she threw me into an atmosphere of utmost vulgarity where obscenity was the rule. The boys would publicly "screw" the girls on the table tops; most of them had venereal diseases; the toilets were filled with greenish wads of cotton; the filth was indescribable. But these shameless fornicators were a great deal nicer than the virtuous pupils of the Collège Sainte-Croix who had caused me so much grief. They made fun of me because I was so naïve, but were never unkind.

The teaching of architecture at the Beaux-Arts, with its emphasis on drawing, Greek capitals, and plans of Renaissance cathedrals and villas, was strictly mechanical and very different from a simple aesthetic approach. My instructors considered Palladio a model of perfection, but I thoroughly detested his colonnades that supported nothing, his pediments that only pretended to be connected to roofs, and his weighty architectural style that used elegant Greek and medieval solutions to structural problems as strictly decorative devices. In those days, people were only beginning to think of a modern style of architecture with logical solutions, entirely free of Palladio's weighty heritage and overelaborate pomp. Even Lemaresquier, who had just built the Gare d'Orsay in Paris, was making some uninspired attempts at *modern style*; genius, however, was something he could do without, for he got all his state contracts through his powerful political friends.

I felt very uncomfortable at the Beaux-Arts, where one only seemed to learn from one's own efforts. The utilitarian function of architecture in those days, and all its decorative bric-a-brac, left no room for the freedom of expression, sensitivity, and imagination that could be found in painting or music.

Many years later, when I studied the architecture of Hindu temples, I grew interested in the symbolic diagrams of medieval cathedral plans, a very basic subject I had never even heard about at the Beaux-Arts.

As soon as I had the chance, I left the Beaux-Arts "bordello", without a twinge of regret.

I was greatly attracted to dance, which allowed me to exteriorize musical feeling as well as indulge in the narcissistic dream of displaying my physical harmony. In the Christian world, dance is the only domain in which the human body can be worshipped and glorified; sports, in those days, did not have the spectacular element they have now. When I was fifteen, I was already making attempts at interpretation and doing rigorous flexibility exercises. When I showed some of these efforts to my friends, they encouraged me to perfect my technique. As soon as I had the chance, I went to see all the ballets that came to Paris. I saw the Russian and Swedish ballets, but also performances by the German school, Laban, and Mary Wigman.

By a stroke of luck, the daughters of Bronislava Nijinska happened to be students at Sainte-Marie. My mother found this lady not only respectable but quite famous, which counted for a lot, so she made no real objection when her unpredictable son went off to find Nijinska. I was already twenty, which seemed a bit late to begin a career in dancing. Nijinska, however, took an interest in me and sent me to Legat, Nijinsky's famous teacher, who was giving classes at the Wacker Studios on the Place Clichy. Later, during my brief stint in the Navy, I was transferred from Toulon to Paris and immediately reenrolled in Legat's class. It was a period of very intense work. Within a few years I acquired quite a good classical technique: my double spins in the air were impeccable; my *entrechats-six* easy and fluid, and my *jetés battus* quite elegant. Outside of class, I practiced to the point of exhaustion for several hours a day. I also took classes in acrobatic dance at the Saulnier Gymnasium in Montmartre, along with the girls from the famous quadrille at the Moulin Rouge. The atmosphere there was wonderful, the people infinitely kind and helpful towards one another. I learned to respect the profoundly human qualities of those so-called lost women, so different from the frustrated and perfidious young ladies of good society who had always terrified me, or those enigmatic *demoiselles* who flocked around my mother.

I attracted the attention of a Rumanian dancer, Floria Capsali, who later became ballet mistress at the Bucharest Opera. She promptly hired me as a partner, and we gave many recitals together; we also performed in several elegant nightclubs. I then found another partner, an Englishwoman called Marjorie Daw, who had a brilliant technique. We gave several music-hall performances. On one occasion, my brother Jean came secretly to Brussels to see me dance at the Summer Palace. Marjorie left on a tour of England but I was unable to obtain a work permit, so our collaboration came to an abrupt end. During those years I used various stage names.

All these experiences were very interesting but had very little to do with my own personal conception of dance, which I felt to be a dynamic response to the soul of music. In classical ballet, dance movements often seemed to be superimposed on musical themes, which were then modified to fit the steps: it looked more like gymnastics than art. I did not like Legat's choreography. I began to create my own dances, in which movement was a direct response to musical feeling. I gave a few recitals and attracted many admirers. Three men who hardly knew me—a doctor (son of the painter Carrière), a journalist, and the director of an industrial company—offered to pay for costumes, concert halls, etc. A number of photographers took series of pictures of me; a famous painter, Arthur Grünenberg, made sketches of several of my dances.

On one occasion I danced a fragment of Honegger's *l'Amphion* in a recital at the Cercle Interallié organized by the Comtesse de Pange. Jacques Copeau, the famous actor and theater director who was supposed to follow my act with a recitation of poetry, was standing in the wings during my performance and heard me pronounce the few words written in Honegger's score. He was so outraged that anyone should dare utter even a simple sentence at a recital in which he was also taking part that he left in a great huff. The poet Robert Honnert, who recited badly, had to replace him on very short notice. At the same recital, I wore a scanty costume—a kind of Cretan-style loincloth—for Gluck's *Danse des Ombres*. Two respectable ladies who were sitting in the front row exclaimed: "We can't possibly watch this from so close up!" and conspicuously moved three rows back.

A German opera company had invited me to choreograph a ballet for the *Contes d'Hoffmann*. I refused the offer, not feeling mature enough to take on such a responsibility. On subsequent visits to France I continued to give recitals, several of which I performed with the Javanese dancer Suyana, who had returned with us from our first trip to India. During a recital in Budapest, I sprained my ankle. In the end India prevailed, war was in the air. My career, which had begun so well, gradually came to an end. I had to give up dancing.

During this period of my life, I became acquainted not only with Nijinska, Legat and his wife (who both left to live in London) but also with Karsavina, Preobrajenska, Spessivtseva,

Maximova, Rolf de Maré, Mary Wigman, the Sakharovs, Pe-
retti, and Balanchine; also with the musicians Max d'Ollone,
Henry Sauguet, Reynaldo Hahn, Nicolas Nabokov, Georges
Auric, and Francis Poulenc. Many of these remained my good
friends. Reynaldo Hahn sent me one of his ballet scores in the
hope that I would use it for a dance. Max d'Ollone sent me a
copy of his ballet *Le Temple abandonné*, inscribed with the following words: "To M. Alain Dunoeli [my stage name at the time],
who breathes life into Ancient Greece, in the hope that some
day he will be the incarnation of that god." Later, after one of
my performances, he added a second inscription, "To Alain,
who did become that god, with the affectionate thanks of his
friend Max." In Legat's class I met Jean Fazil, a young dancer
from Luxembourg whose friend, a rather stern-looking
teacher, was always waiting for him outside. I was finally
introduced to this mysterious character, who later became a
famous historian and a member of the Académie Française.
His name was Pierre Gaxotte, and we grew to be very great
friends. Fazil and Pierre were a model couple and lived together in perfect harmony until they died in 1982, within a
few days of each other.

Dancing for me was a very intense experience. Through
movement I could express the deep meaning of music, feeling
it more like a good orchestra conductor than like so many of
those dancers one sees prancing about with their artificial
gestures. I practiced the art of dance and served it with passion; but little by little it grew away from me. Dancing, like all
other arts, is a hard taskmaster. A dancer must constantly
practice his instrument, which in this case happens to be his
entire body, so that it will respond effortlessly and delicately
to the wonderful fluid that music evokes within him.

CHAPTER FOUR

The Discovery of the World

AMERICA

A former French ambassador to Washington was offering a few scholarships for study in American colleges. When my father heard about it, he immediately thought of me: not only did he believe in the usefulness of languages, he also felt that, should my mother's plans for me come to nothing, he could always find me a consulate post.

As a result, I found myself aboard the old French passenger ship, the *Savoie*, which usually took about two weeks to reach New York from Cherbourg. One evening, about halfway across the Atlantic, I was having dinner at the captain's table when the ship suddenly began to vibrate violently. The captain turned pale and put down his fork, and the purser made the sign of the cross; no one else realized that the engines had been put into reverse. Suddenly there was a great crash, the ship heeled over, then slowly righted itself. All the dishes, platters, and glassware had fallen to the floor, to the great distress of the ladies, who complained about the stains on their gowns. The captain begged his passengers to remain calm and hurried out of the dining room. In the fog of the night, the liner had been impaled by a Norwegian cargo ship whose crew, we learned later, was drunk; it sank soon afterwards. The *Savoie* had a huge, gaping hole in its side, all the way down to the waterline. Many of the cabins were destroyed. The crew immediately began pumping water out of the hold, and the ship continued on its way. Two days later, we were hit by a hurricane, which also ravaged the state of Florida. The risk of high winds and waves attacking the damaged side of the ship was too great, so we changed course and for several days went southward. The passengers were no longer allowed to remain in their cabins, but had to crowd in the saloons and dining rooms and wear their lifebelts. All the furniture was overturned, including the grand piano. In the end, the crossing lasted a whole month.

Thanks to a very nice young American boy I had met at the beginning of the voyage, I had a wonderful time. We explored the entire ship—the engine rooms, the storerooms, kitchens, and pilothouse. The crew was too busy to notice us, and most of the other passengers were seasick.

Finally, very proud of our adventure, we landed in New York. Annick, a former student of my mother's who now taught in Baltimore, had come up to meet me. We took the train to Baltimore. A fat Negro train employee prepared the berths, which ran lengthways on two levels and were enclosed by curtains; there were no separate compartments. After Baltimore I travelled alone on a small train, which snaked its way through the marshy Maryland plains on countless wooden bridges, all the way to Annapolis. Nestled along the shore of Chesapeake Bay, Annapolis was an attractive little town with colonial-style houses which, in those days, could still be seen all over the South. My destination was not the United States Naval Academy but St. John's College, one of the oldest colleges in the country, which later became a famous experimental culture center.

I arrived without any luggage. The passengers of the *Savoie* had to wait an entire month before their trunks were taken out of the ship's hold and forwarded to them.

At St. John's I discovered a paradise. The vast campus was covered with beautiful old trees. The boys were friendly and pleasant and lived in attractive dormitory rooms. I was often invited home for lunch by faculty members. There was no discipline or proctoring: we could come and go as we pleased, take walks, and attend classes according to our whim. There was an excellent piano in the central hall; I would spend hours practicing or playing four-handed duets with a very talented Puerto Rican boy called Rodriguez Buxo. I painted many watercolors of the beautiful Maryland scenery and sold them at good prices to people in the town. I also helped illustrate the students' yearbook. I was considered an artist and treated with respect and high regard.

Stella, the young wife of a German professor, took a great fancy to me. We played music and took long walks together. She was always inviting me home for meals, which clearly exasperated her husband: soon after my departure, they were divorced. Stella had confided in me that she wanted to leave her husband and return to Europe. She hoped that my mother would help her find a teaching position. They probably corresponded, but my mother never mentioned it: in spite of her *dreyfusard* ideology, her religious convictions made it impossible for her to even think of associating with Jews or Protestants; in any case, she was not about to encourage a romance between her son and a Jewish divorcée.

Although I was still physically innocent in those days, I had declared myself a homosexual. All my college friends seemed to find this quite natural, and no one ever made the slightest disparaging remark. A number of boys tried to draw me into sexual relationships, but I was too shy and elusive to respond. Then came Donald. Donald was a twenty-year-old baseball player, six-foot-seven tall. One night he came into my room, took me in his arms, and refused to take no for an answer. All of a sudden I felt infused with light and an incredible sensation of pleasure ran through my body. I murmured: "There must be a God for such happiness to be possible!" For a long time I had ceased to believe in the Christian God, that severe schoolmaster who makes decrees and punishes transgressors. Oddly enough, it was in that moment of intense pleasure that a god of sensuousness, happiness, and light was revealed to me—that God of Love whom mystics write about, the God of Jalâl-al-Dîn Rûmi and Saadi, of Saint John of the Cross and Saint Teresa of Avila, of Dionysian and tantric rites. He had appeared before me once and for all; all I needed to do now was find him.

Many years later, when I was studying tantric rites in India,

I learned that certain erotic tensions can awaken the very center of pleasure, which then spreads through the body like a powerful drug. For Hindus, sensuous delight is akin to the state of godliness, the state of perfect bliss, which is why sexual intercourse is an important part of Dionysian initiation rites. The experience always awakens a feeling of divinity. It can also be provoked spontaneously by a state of extreme nervous tension, an experience not unknown to certain mystics.

Many years later my brother, who was then a high-ranking Church prelate, told me that some of his penitents had confessed to having discovered God and faith during the most blessed moments of love.

I continued to have regular intercourse with Donald and found this extremely agreeable; but the dazzling flash of light that had struck me that first night remained a unique experience.

At the end of the school year I received many invitations and could have prolonged my stay in the United States had I chosen to do so. The French consul, who was supposed to review my draft status, offered to declare me unfit for military service for a fifty-dollar fee. This would have meant deciding to live permanently in the United States, a step I was not prepared to take. I also felt that having a draft-dodger for a son would probably cause my father some political difficulties. I therefore refused the consul's amiable offer and took the boat back to Cherbourg.

At the end of each school year, short sketches were written about the students and faculty in the college yearbook. The following was written about me:

> Alain Daniélou ("Frenchie")
> "Guess if you can, and choose if you dare."
> (Corneille)
> Out of the land of romance came this temperamental artist. To be convinced of his ability and fame, turn to some of the exquisite drawings which embellish this epoch-making book. As Frenchie's work adds a sprightly touch to the practical photos of this book, so does he stand among the

Babbits of St. John's. That some of the boys do not understand and appreciate "Frenchie" is quite natural, but those who know him and his inmost thoughts find that France has really sent to us a gift of the priceless tradition of art for which she is famous.

In his portraits of the students "Frenchie" has found the "indefinable something" that is peculiar to St. John's men. He has found beauty in common things.

Though apparently young, the Frenchman seems very matured. In training, education and experience he is much ahead of the average boys of this country. He has a real appreciation for art, music, etc., and delights in amusing his classmates by displays of his skill. There will be little consolation to be found at college next fall when there is no "Frenchie" to trip lightly o'er the green or to go in raptures over a perfect feminine form.

We feel that "Frenchie" has filled a long-felt need in the life of the college. May the Gods be kind to this young artist!

REFLECTIONS ON AMERICA

American society in its early days was marked by two basic tendencies. On the one hand there were the adventurers— unscrupulous, materialistic, brutal men who later became the heroes of popular myth; on the other, emigrants from persecuted religious sects, filled with missionary zeal and vehement puritanism, who occupied the promised land without too much concern for its original inhabitants. This duality was still quite noticeable when I first came to America. Life was a wonderful adventure. A happy materialism seemed to rule the land. Money was the only claim to glory, but anyone with imagination could make a fortune. Life tended to be leisurely and pleasant because servants were easy to find; in those days, no public burdens or social programs seemed to exist. To a European eye, Americans appeared quite relaxed and free of anxiety, except in certain areas still dominated by puritanical traditions: it was considered immoral, for instance, to play the piano on Sundays or to draw one's window blinds too low.

As America grew more powerful, this strange mixture of adventurism and moral righteousness began to reveal itself in the country's foreign policy. During subsequent visits, I noticed concerns and attitudes and preoccupations regarding smaller, problem-ridden nations not unlike those of the imperialist powers of the nineteenth century—a sense of obligation, vexation, and helplessness that reminded me of what the British used to call "the white man's burden."

It is always dangerous for a nation to assume that its value system is universal. By insisting that true culture could only be French and clinging to a now obsolete language, France has only succeeded in cutting itself off from the mainstream of modern thought.

The most important centers of science and creativity today are in the United States. This is why the overzealousness of so many Americans who want other nations to benefit from their way of life can only be detrimental to themselves, in so far as they wish to serve as an example. Good intentions can only be a danger to a country whose very power and prominence in the world today calls for a dispassionate, unsentimental, one might even say a Machiavellian line of politics.

In America, like everywhere else, the proliferation of ethnic groups threatens to divert foreign policy into acts of moral opportunism that could undermine the country's ultimate effectiveness; for, whether we like it or not, the world's future lies in its hands.

In recent years, with the sexual revolution and a new concern for nature and ecology, part of America's youth seems to have gone against the flow of that country's dual tradition. Perhaps they will find a way to free themselves of its weighty heritage.

When I first went to America, I found black people extremely kind, obliging, cheerful, and unhostile. Many of today's social problems have been caused not by true blacks, but by people of mixed blood who are considered black and are completely excluded by the white society from which they partly originate. In India, Anglo-Indians have leagued themselves with Europeans and always make a point of despising "the natives." In America, the identification of people of mixed blood with blacks has falsified their values and impeded the development of a parallel black civilization founded on religious and cultural beliefs that are quite different from those of the white adventurers. In the twenties, "colored people" were not accepted in good neighborhoods, but had to live in small wooden shacks on the outskirts of towns. They were not allowed to engage in commercial enterprises or the liberal professions, except within their own restricted communities; in fact, one hardly ever saw them. It was not possible to speak to these people or go for a walk with them. Any kind of association with blacks was out of the question, except within the context of the home, if they happened to be servants. These forms of ostracism affected other ethnic groups to varying degrees: Jews, Puerto Ricans, Italians, even the Irish. When I was in college, I made friends with a Jewish boy called Kaplon. I had great fun studying Hebrew with him, and can still remember the way he read parts of Genesis with his strong Texas accent: "*B'réshith yoysoh Elohim es hashomayim vé es hohoretz. . . .*" Once, during a school vacation, I happily accepted an invitation to visit his home for a few days. I was surprised to discover the sordid atmosphere in which he lived. Certain East European Jews, living in a very closed world outside large cities, had kept traditions and habits, a style of furniture, and a rudimentary form of hygiene that contrasted sharply with the modern, aseptic tidiness practiced by most Americans.

When I returned to St. John's, I was summoned by the college president, an important and awesome character whom no one ever saw. He was shocked by my conduct. I had gone to visit Jews, which was a highly improper thing to do. He asked me not to repeat the offense.

Most of the Americans I have known who participated in black liberation movements were motivated by a more or less conscious desire to sleep with black people. This is why movements of this kind tend towards cohabitation, racial assimilation, and the glorification of interracial marriage, rather than towards a genuine respect for blackness or the acknowledgement of black people's right to move forward without losing their unique character or their particular beliefs. Antiracialism by assimilation is one of the most arrogant forms of racism.

This is why so many blacks have become Moslems. Islam offers them a respectability and a unique sense of identity that allow them to confront proselytizing white Christians on terms of equality, if not superiority.

The reins of power, in the United States, have always been held by puritans. So all-pervasive is the mask of piety that allows men to justify conquest by turning it into a crusade and to hide breaches of public trust under a cloak of virtue, that only a hypocrite or a saint can be elected to political office. All a candidate needs to do is mention the name of God in every other sentence. This does not mean that he is competent or truly virtuous.

A United States president has problems very similar to those of the pope which relate to his temporal power. A nation cannot be governed in the name of negative virtues. Prohibition was a governmental blunder of such huge proportions that the United States—the whole world in fact—still suffers from its evil effects. It gave birth to a highly efficient criminal organization that no one has ever been able to suppress: the world of gangsters.

I was in America during Prohibition and found the experience very amusing. The prime concern in life was the procuring of alcohol and sharing it with friends. Trousers were cut very wide so that flat bottles of whiskey could be carried in their inner pockets. Rich, party-giving people had to bribe the police. Corruption became general. Gangsters made so much money that they paid the Salvation Army to demonstrate in favor of maintaining Prohibition. Newspapers and government representatives were bought off for the same purpose. The entire Prohibitionist lobby was in their hands.

It is quite evident that the same situation exists in Europe today. Propaganda against certain drugs is obviously financed by those who benefit from it. A product such as hashish, which in itself is far less noxious than alcohol, is controlled by a powerful contraband organization that has made millions and given gangsters and members of the Mafia more power than ever. In the year 1985, two hundred people died of drugs in Italy; the death toll from alcohol was two hundred a day.

During the Prohibition era, a great number of people died as a result of drinking adulterated liquor. As soon as the law was repealed, the number dropped to zero.

Zaher

In the summer of 1927, I left Annapolis and the United States and joined my family in Locronan. My father, as usual, was working under Aristide Briand, who was then Minister of Foreign Affairs. The Ambassador of Afghanistan in Paris, who was preparing the coup that later propelled him to the throne, asked my father to look after his young son Zaher. My father, taken unawares and not knowing quite what to say, invited the boy to spend the summer in Locronan. When I arrived, I was delighted to find such a charming companion. Zaher was fifteen at the time. I dragged the future King of the Afghans on canoeing expeditions so frightening that he still remembers them today; once or twice he nearly drowned, but he obviously admired the daring and athletic side of my personality. My friendship with Zaher later played a very important part in my life: soon after that summer, his father invited me to pay him a visit. That was how I came to discover the Orient, to which I had never even given a thought. At twenty-one, one does not refuse royal invitations.

In Britanny I had only one friend. His name was André Gantier and he ran a canning factory in Quimper jointly with his sister. Both had handsome young male lovers. They had a lovely property filled with beautiful flowers, and the atmosphere was very pleasant. I went there often, first with Vadim de Stavraky, later with Zaher, and finally with Raymond.

Fearing unpleasant gossip and hostile comments among Britanny's self-righteously Christian citizenry, André had forced himself for a time to take a mistress, whom he saw as rarely as possible. In order to keep up appearances, this idiotic girl decided to send him passionate postcards signed Jean instead of Jeanne. The experiment was a complete fiasco and did not last long.

Like the poet Max Jacob, who also came from Quimper and

was a good friend of his, André Gantier was arrested by the Germans during the war. I never found out why. Both men died in prison.

THE NAVY

In the autumn of 1927 I was obliged to perform my military duty and joined the Navy in Toulon. Soon afterward I boarded the fleet commander's battleship *Provence*.

Toulon was then a charming little port city. There were no summer crowds, and the Côte d'Azur only came alive in winter. A small number of Parisian artists and writers would come in search of sailors, who in those days were much friendlier than they are today. I had rented a room in town where I kept my civilian clothes: it was large, airy, and bare, with Provençal tiles on the floor. While I was off-duty, I met a young Navy officer, Honoré d'Estienne d'Orves. We became very good friends and often saw each other in Paris after I got back. When I returned from the Orient, I was surprised to find a street named after him. The elegant and sensitive young aristocrat had apparently died a hero.

I was not cut out for military life and was horrified by the fate of many fine and decent boys who suddenly found themselves deprived of freedom and human dignity and subjected to the most brutal and stupid treatment. The unfortunate sailors who were caught slipping away for an evening out were locked up in a kind of lion's cage with heavy iron bars and left in the intolerable heat of the ship's hold, where there was neither air nor light. If they repeated the offense, they were sent to military hard labor camps, after which they were expected to resume their duties. Some of them never got out. But who cared anything about the poor devils, those wretched, pigheaded Breton fishermen? At night, enormous rats would scurry down the ropes of my hammock and bite my feet. The coal duties were exhausting: everything was covered with fine black dust that nearly made one choke to death. My commanding officer offered to exempt me from the more difficult chores, but I refused: accepting special treatment and abandoning my companions in misery would have been unforgivable. In a letter to my mother, I described life in the Navy. She got very worried and immediately wrote to the fleet admiral, asking him to protect her son. The admiral, fearing that my connections with the ministry might cause him problems, prudently sent me back to Paris for "reasons of health." In Paris, a medical officer of the Ecole Militaire put me on convalescent leave, which lasted until the end of my eighteen months of military service.

I had to stay in uniform and report to the medical officer once a week. There was no way I could obtain an official medical discharge, for this would have given me a right to a pension. I took advantage of my freedom and devoted all my time to dance. Every day, wearing my uniform, I went to Legat's dance class at the Wacker Studios on the Place Clichy. Everyone was highly amused by "the little sailor boy," and I became a kind of celebrity. In a milieu dominated by Diaghilev and Cocteau, sailors were very much in vogue.

ALGERIA

In 1929, when my military stint was over, the Governor of Algeria, at my father's request, offered me a grant to study Arab music. I was delighted by the idea and immediately set off for Algiers, then spent several months touring the southern cities. From the start, I felt quite at home in the Arab world. I spent long hours with musicians and the famous Ouled-Naïl dancers. I played dominoes in Moorish cafés and made a few friends—I even witnessed ecstatic *sufi* ceremonies. I frequented Moorish baths and met sheiks who, though hostile to France, invited me to their homes and treated me with kindness and courtesy. I took notes and photographs and also kept a diary. Although there was no talk of independence in those days, I soon grew convinced that French dominance over Algeria could not last very much longer. This failure was not caused by the Arabs—especially not the lower classes—for all benefited greatly from the French occupation. It was mostly due to the Administration and the French settlers, who looked down on the "natives," whatever their degree of culture, and never lost an opportunity to humiliate them or belittle their customs and convictions: the great mosque of Algiers, for instance, had been converted into a church. Even I became a victim of anti-Arab prejudice. I did not realize that my contacts with Arabs were considered scandalous, or that a Frenchman could only approach a native as a Frenchman and wearing a tie. It was unheard of for anyone to mix with these people in their cafés or their "sordid" hovels, or to wander alone in the perilous Casbah. The governor had me followed; my diaries and notes were stolen from me and sent back to Paris.

I visited several southern cities—Biskra, Touggourt, Ouargla—and took many notes on their music. In Biskra, I met a woman writer who called herself Magali and was quite interested in my painting. Finally I contracted dysentery and had to go back to Algiers to recuperate.

I returned to France with a great quantity of notes, watercolors, and photographs that are still of considerable interest to musicologists and ethnologists today. I have never been able to understand the superior attitude adopted by the French, which created such a gulf between themselves and the Arabs, especially those who were unwilling to accept French customs, prejudices or manners. Because of my obvious interest in Arab cultural traditions, I was invited to see certain things that would never have been shown to a colonist, who would immediately have stigmatized them. As a result, I had the privilege of witnessing ancient ecstatic rites of clearly Dionysian origin. The photographs of phallic rites that I took in the south are apparently unique.

The governor's report was hushed up. In his view, of course, my association with Arabs was a result of my shady morality. The report was later used against my father as a form of political blackmail. But my father never made me the slightest reproach; he only told me to be more careful in the future.

Paris in the Twenties

After my return to Paris, I worked on my dancing and singing with renewed energy. I continued to paint but, being a country boy at heart, found the Parisian scenery rather less than inspiring. I went to various art studios to draw nudes. I knew no one in the art world and nothing of Parisian life. One day, I happened to meet my brother with Maurice Sachs, the famous chronicler of Paris in the twenties. Maurice had just spent some time in a monastery and invited me to visit him. In those days he lived at the Hôtel Nollet, in Montmartre. Maurice was extremely nice to me. He offered me champagne dinners, showered me with gifts, and persuaded me to move to the Nollet, which was then the center of a certain avant-garde: among its tenants were Max Jacob, Henry Sauguet—his ballet *La Chatte* had just been staged by Diaghilev—and Jacques Dupont, whose attempts at painting were then considered a joke. Max Jacob was conscientiously making crude copies of picture postcards, and a man by the name of Pierre Colle was trying to market them. Many famous members of the artistic and literary world of the time used to gather at the Nollet. It was there that I first met Nicolas Nabokov and Georges Henry Rivière.

All these people worked very hard, without taking themselves too seriously. They did everything in fun, always looking for the novel and the unexpected, without any thought for rules or conventions. I immediately felt very comfortable in this unhostile atmosphere. Max Jacob was a delightful man, completely and disarmingly incoherent. Everything for him was a kind of game: religion, passion, poetry, life, painting. Like Maurice Sachs he had just been converted to Catholicism—a fashion launched by Mauriac—and was always very pious in the morning. He would bemoan his fate as a miserable sinner and go to confession early in the morning; then, as the day progressed, he would let himself fall into the arms of the devil. He would write telegrams to himself and receive the telegraph boy in his bathtub in the hope of seducing him. He claimed to be in love with a legless cripple. He gave me several drawings, and in times of crisis even lent me a few francs, though he was poor and rather stingy and had no hope of ever being repaid. I often saw him and sometimes, in the summer, would visit him on the beach of Tréboul, near Douarnenez.

I took art far too seriously to take part in the creative games of the time or assume the kind of snobbery that consisted in rejecting anything that seemed obvious. It was considered elegant to say that Erik Satie was sublime and Brahms and

Wagner abominable. Maurice tried to convince me that Picasso, in his cubist period, was the very height of artistic achievement and Monet, whom I adored, completely uninteresting; but he had to give up trying to correct my bad taste and, much to his annoyance, decided that I understood nothing about art. Snobbery is always fanatical. Max Jacob was always ready to contradict anything he had said a moment before. He let himself ride the shifting waves of artistic prejudice and derived great enjoyment from this. With Max there was never any need for mutual understanding: one inevitably ended up agreeing with him.

I never really made the most of my affair with Maurice Sachs: it was very difficult for me to learn anything from anyone. I knew nothing about the Parisian world or the importance of contacts and relationships, and I was not easily tamed. Maurice thought it a great joke to have caught this young savage who, though not lacking in talent or imagination, remained completely out of tune with his surroundings.

I never went out of my way to meet the fashionable people from the artistic and intellectual world of the time. I despised writers and was not at all interested in religious issues. People who tortured themselves with problems of so-called morality seemed very stupid to me; everything I heard about Mauriac— an ambiguous sort of prophet in that unbalanced world— repelled me.

One day, Maurice Sachs returned from Austria with a blond boy in leather pants. He lost interest in me and I was quite hurt. But fickleness was part of the game, and the lesson had to be learned. I remained for a while longer at the Nollet.

When I knew Maurice, he was a very slender, exceedingly elegant young man who loved to shine, go to luxurious restaurants, and live beyond his means. His religious conflicts were partly inspired by fashion and a way to attract attention. He was witty, amusing, and extremely kind. Like Oscar Wilde he needed to be the center of attraction, and fell to pieces as soon as the public eye shifted away from him.

I saw him again a few years later. He had gained a great deal of weight and had lost much of his charm and vivacity. My description of him may seem unsatisfactory, but I was very young and naïve in those days and quite dazzled by a world in which everything was new and surprising.

When I returned to Europe after the war, I was astonished to learn that Maurice had become a famous writer and had died in highly dramatic circumstances. The lighthearted, whimsical, and charming young man I had once known certainly had not seemed destined to become a tragic genius.

I did not remain long at the Nollet; I could not afford it. Max Frantel, a young journalist who had seen me dance and was interested in me, offered to let me use a large empty studio he had rented on the Rue du Cotentin, near Montparnasse. It had almost no furniture and was a perfect place to work, dance, and paint. Max would appear from time to time, always at the most unexpected moments. I used to call him the Phantom.

It was while I was living on the Rue du Cotentin that I first met Raymond and that we planned together our first trip to the Orient.

RAYMOND

Among the friends who gathered around Max Jacob was an American in his thirties who called himself the Comte de Sablon-Favier. Henry Sauguet claimed that he was a traitor and a spy, which had to be true since, as Max used to say, "he spoke the foreign tongue." He was an amiable young man and invited me to join him in Corsica, which he described with great enthusiasm. And so, in the summer of 1931, I left for Calvi. By the time I arrived, the unpredictable American had already gone back to France and was now staying in Villefranche, near Nice. I remained several weeks in Calvi, which was a charming little village in those days, very Italian. Women never left their houses, so the men used to dance together in the local *bistrots*; one often heard the sound of pistol shots in the two small hotels right outside the village. On the beaches, handsome, sun-tanned youths would wander around looking for the rare vacationing foreigner in the hope of seducing and gently exploiting him.

After painting a few watercolors of Calvi, I finally went to Villefranche and joined my American at the famous Hotel Welcome, the favorite vacation spot of Cocteau and his friends. I remained there only a short time, little knowing that those fateful few days were written in my destiny. The night before I left, a young Swiss who had just arrived had noticed me. The next day, he introduced himself to my American friend, found out that I had just left and was planning a trip to the Orient, and made him promise to arrange a meeting in Paris.

Raymond was curiously intuitive. He had just left his brother in Scotland and had raced down to Villefranche in his automobile in time to catch a glimpse of me. Without even knowing me, he immediately made up his mind that he too would go to the Orient; but, being a prudent and methodical man, he first took the precaution of having his appendix removed in Switzerland, then went on to Paris to meet me.

Without telling me why, my American friend asked me to stop by his house one morning. I suddenly found myself in the presence of a radiantly beautiful, fair-haired youth of nineteen, wearing sky-blue linen pajamas—for he was still tired from his operation. Raymond had made up his mind to seduce me and become my friend. There was no reason in the world for me to resist such a charming partner; I did not know who he was, and hardly suspected that my fate was being determined. Raymond came to live in the studio on the Rue du Cotentin, then invited me to join him in Switzerland for Christmas.

Raymond was living with his brother in a charming apartment in Lausanne that was looked after by an old housekeeper. Henry, who was two years older than Raymond, gave me a very warm welcome; the housekeeper, however, was far from amiable.

On Christmas Eve, Raymond insisted on taking me to Fribourg for Midnight Mass. We took off that night in his Chrysler convertible, which he had baptized "Choléra." Raymond came from a Protestant family but very much enjoyed "pagan" Catholic ceremonies; it would have been difficult for him to be seen at the Lausanne cathedral, and Fribourg is in another canton. I nearly died of cold in the open car as it sped through the icy night. Raymond did not feel the cold at all.

After we got back to Paris, I left the studio on the Rue du

Cotentin without any warning, which made the Phantom very angry—and quite justifiably so. I had a great many problems at the time. I was stubbornly pursuing my destiny but lacked the courage to face difficult situations, which I tended to escape by flight. In this sense, I have often behaved very badly.

Raymond and I then moved into an apartment-hotel on the Rue Saint-Honoré; my father knew the owner, who seemed rather like a procuress. I realized much later that though my father had never openly involved himself in my life, he had always been on my side—a kind of accomplice, as it were. Raymond had decided to leave with me for the Orient, and the trip to Afghanistan was all set. I received the royal invitation and the passports. We began to prepare for the great expedition. Only then did I realize that Raymond was actually a very rich man and intended to travel in style. He took a course in cinematography at a Joinville studio where one of my friends worked as a technician, then bought a superb "Debrie," a professional crank-turned movie camera that was supposed to be the best of its kind; he even had his Leica checked over by Leitz, in Germany. We were fitted out in the latest tropical fashions and even had tailcoats made for our visit to the royal court.

I insisted on introducing Raymond to my mother and told her that I would stop visiting her unless he was invited. She gave in and found Raymond charming, elegant, and distinguished—exactly the kind of young man she dreamed of marrying off to one of her daughters. What a pity to waste him on her son! She was somewhat anxious, however, and asked me: "What will happen to you if this boy abandons you somewhere in the middle of Asia?" But I was not thinking of the future and felt quite shocked by her practical point of view; the idea of introducing material considerations into matters of friendship and love seemed typical of my mother's profound amorality. I was motivated neither by reason nor self-interest. I was letting life carry me along towards a mysterious destiny that I knew nothing about, but in which I have always believed.

Raymond's family was an interesting mixture. His paternal grandmother, a Baltic baroness, had married her Swiss doctor. There were several Russians among his ancestors. His mother was descended from an aristocratic Neuchâtel family, one of those old Swiss families whose titles and castles go back to the beginning of time. She had married a penniless young officer against her parents' wishes, and died soon after Raymond's birth. Raymond probably inherited his Germanic traits from his paternal grandmother: he was very tall and fair, not at all the typical Swiss Vaudois.

His maternal grandfather had invented a condensed milk product for children called Nestlé, which became immensely popular. The family gradually found itself in control of a vast industry and an enormous fortune.

Raymond was an extremely gifted and sensitive man. He had a sharp sense of humor and always found amusing ways to defuse dramatic situations or make fun of people and their convictions. He loved to play with words and ideas; his letters were wonderfully witty.

He was also a dazzling conversationalist. We always appeared to be poking fun at everything—not because we were frivolous, but in an attempt to discredit false thinking and get to the bottom of things. We hardly needed words to understand one another. Our mutual affection and playful complicity in the face of all the vicissitudes of life led to a deep and unclouded understanding, a solid and permanent bond that nothing could ever destroy or weaken.

Raymond feared the slightest constraint on his independence. He always refused to use his talents on projects that could lead to a deeper involvement and restrict his freedom and fantasy. He was courageous, enterprising, adventurous like me, and also very clever with his hands; but he had a horror of owning furniture, objects, or houses, which are always so confining and difficult to get rid of.

The complete absence of constraint or obligation in our relationship was probably the reason why our friendship became such a strong bond, the only solid element, in fact, in Raymond's life. Unlike me, he never had an artistic vocation or any purpose to his life beyond the pleasures of love, human relationships, and the joy of being alive; but we shared a deep sense of·the subtle and divine reality of the world, which he perceived intuitively and I in a more intellectual way.

Raymond and I went many times to Switzerland together.

His father had not inherited any part of the estate, which was administered by a guardian. After he remarried, he bought a farm in Algeria, where Raymond and his brother Henry spent their childhood running through the wadis and catching lizards and snakes. When they were about fifteen, they were sent to a school in Lausanne, but the two little savages found it impossible to live this kind of life. They were given back their freedom and settled in an apartment, under the watchful eye of a housekeeper. Both brothers found it very difficult to adapt to the life of the Swiss bourgeoisie. They remained children of the bush and gave animal names to all their relatives: their paternal grandmother was "the Otter," the nearly blind old aunt "the Mole," the uncle, a doctor, "the Buffalo"; they called their father "Poussy" and their stepmother "the Queen." Henry, the older brother, ended up going off to Kenya, where he bought a vast property, adopted an African boy, and grew orchids; Raymond left with me for the Orient. Their testamentary guardian, André Chavannes, an uncle by marriage, was the presiding judge at the Court of Lausanne. At first he was quite worried by our relationship—after all I was a Frenchman, and the French are always suspicious characters, strongly mistrusted by the Swiss; furthermore, I was an artist and—what was even worse—a dancer. There was certainly a great deal to be worried about. The *bon oncle* gave me a very cordial welcome, however. He was a sensitive and cultivated man, and respected me for my independent character and my passion for art. He realized that, far from being a fortune hunter, I was in fact an excellent influence on Raymond, whom I led into my own modest and thrifty lifestyle; for this he held me in very high esteem. Never did this severe magistrate make the slightest disparaging remark about us; when Raymond and I would visit him in his home, our union always seemed the most natural thing in the world. When I first knew Raymond, he had an official mistress, a Lausanne nurse called Lil, who was ten years older than himself. Our plans to visit the Orient made it possible for him to break up this affair without too much trouble.

I visited Lausanne so many times that it soon became a kind of second home to me. Years later, when Raymond died and so many delicate problems of inheritance and legacy were raised, everything was settled with a tactfulness and compassion that exist nowhere else on earth. Raymond had left most of his fortune to a young Italian of very modest origin, yet not once did the lawyer, the bankers, or any member of the family ever betray the slightest hint of greed or conflict or make a bitter or disparaging remark; they did all they could to respect Raymond's wishes and acted as though he were still among them. No one made me feel like an intruder. And yet, as time passed, the friendly, almost affectionate bonds that tied me to that world gradually began to loosen. The Swiss mask of courtesy reappeared. I was a stranger once again.

THE AFGHAN EPISODE

"Alain has promised me that his friend the King will lend me a Rolls and a Hispano—perhaps even a camel! In any case he managed to get our diplomatic visas just before we left." (Letter from Raymond to Pierre Arnal, 17 April 1932.)

In April 1932 we went to Venice, boarded a magnificent Italian ship, the *Comte Rosso*, and took off for Bombay. During the crossing, the elegant London passengers gradually turned into colonial civil servants in khaki shorts and helmets. There were no tourists in those days. Our first contact with India was a revelation. Our taxi driver, an Indian Christian called George, showed us the marvelous tropical countryside outside Bombay and the caves of Elephanta with their wonderful sculptures. We liked George so much that we hired him as a guide, servant, and interpreter, and took him along with us when we boarded the train for Peshawar, on the Afghan border. There, after going through the necessary formalities, we rented a car and were driven to Kabul on the famous Khyber Pass road, where so many English soldiers met their death. There were no bridges and we had to ford all the rivers. But we had been too impatient: the royal limousine that had been sent from Kabul to fetch us arrived soon after we left and searched for us in vain.

We took rooms at the Kabul Hotel, the only hotel in the city at the time. It was an exceedingly modest building, fairly modern, with twenty rooms on a single floor, all opening onto a corridor; at the end of the hall were sordid toilets and showers. We were the only guests in the hotel. After a few days we moved to an Afghan house, very rustic but much cooler. The floors were covered with rugs; we were given two iron beds—a great luxury. There was also a small garden. Two sturdy Afghans served and watched us.

George did all the cooking and cleaning. After a while, a visit to King Nadir Shah was arranged. He was very cordial, mentioned all the favors my father had done for him and, seeing that we were interested in ancient cultures, suggested a visit to Kafiristan, an almost unknown region south of Pamir. I had to wait several weeks before I could see my friend Prince Zaher, heir to the throne; all the power was in the hands of his uncles, and he was closely watched. The interview took place in the Paghman gardens, twelve miles from Kabul. Zaher was surrounded by his cousins. He was very friendly, but no real contact was possible.

In those days, Kabul was nothing more than a large village of yellowish clay houses with wooden balconies. A few years earlier the former bazaar, which was made of carved wood, had burned down and been rebuilt with cement and corrugated iron. It was filled with rugs and objects made by local tribes. There were very few imported goods. No one used money or gold coins—most of the important business was conducted through bartering or, in ordinary transactions, with silver pieces called "crans" that were carried in bags.

The royal government seemed relatively powerless. The Kabul authorities were in constant negotiation with powerful tribes. Sometimes we would see groups of these armed and turbaned warriors who made the law in the provinces. The state was mainly supported by alternate subsidies from both the British and the Russian Empires, between which the king skillfully maintained a balance. People seemed to live very simply, but there were no signs of poverty and no beggars.

A few embassies could be found on the city's outskirts, in villas surrounded by high walls. They seemed quite cut off from the rest of the world, for no officials were ever seen.

Kabul is situated on a rocky and deserted plain, surrounded by arid mountains and, wherever small rivers happened to flow, verdant valleys planted with poplars. The region had once been quite fertile, until hordes of Mongolians chased away its native Gypsy inhabitants and destroyed all the irrigation canals, which were never rebuilt. Seistan, an important wheat-growing country before the Islam invasion, has become an impenetrable desert.

We waited a long time for an official permit to visit the province of Kafiristan and were finally told that the king's brother, who was prime minister, had refused his authorization. We decided to leave anyway. Raymond bought large sacs of "crans," some of which were promptly stolen. Early one morning, we took off in a royal limousine that had been officially placed at our disposal for an excursion to Djelal-Abad; from there we continued along the Chounar River until we reached the end of the road. We were accompanied by a young Afghan, Ahmed Ali, who had worked with the French Department of Archaeology and spoke good French. When he got to the end of the road, we sent back the car and announced our intention to continue our journey by mountain path to Khamdesh, the main village of Kafiristan. We hired mules to carry our Debrie, my canvases and paint boxes, as well as various supplies and a few poor chickens hanging by their legs.

Ahmed Ali found himself in a very difficult position. If he returned alone to Kabul, he would probably be hanged; but continuing the journey involved other risks. He finally opted for the latter solution and ordered two soldiers from the local guard to accompany us. Our expedition began to wind its way up a precipitous path along cliffs that rose hundreds of feet above torrential mountain streams. We did not dare ride on the mules, for the slightest false step would have sent us plunging down to certain death. The journey lasted about a week. From time to time, we passed small villages and slept on the grass outside the populated areas. The people seemed quite hospitable. For the soldiers' comfort, they would carry a bed, made of braided cord, to the middle of the village, with a blanket and a young boy. A soldier was placed on the bed beside the boy, then covered with the blanket; after a few moments' agitation, it was the next soldier's turn. Finally our small caravan reached Khamdesh, the "capital" of Kafiristan (land of the infidels), later called Nouristan (land of light). It was forbidden to mention the province's ancient name. The natives, we were told, had once been called Iluas.

These people claimed to be descendants of Alexander's soldiers. They had very fair skin, blue eyes, brown hair. No one seems to know very much about their language or religion. Until recently they still worshipped gods represented on horseback and laid out their dead on mountaintops for the benefit of wild beasts and vultures. In 1912, these Kafirs had been forcibly converted to Islam and a large part of the population massacred, so they were not overly fond of the Afghans. Kafiristan had been visited by an Englishman at the end of the nineteenth century; since then, no foreigner had ever penetrated the land. George proved himself very useful. He spoke *urdu*, an Indian Moslem language quite similar to Afghan *pashtu*, and told the local people all kinds of amusing stories about us. According to him, the two young foreigners were undoubtedly descendants of Alexander and had come all the way from Macedonia to find their brothers. Ahmed Ali and the two soldiers prudently stood by at a respectful distance.

Khamdesh was a large village perched on the slopes of the mountain. There were no squares or streets; notched tree trunks served as ladders for climbing from one terrace to another. Raymond photographed and filmed the village, its people, and its dances. I painted a few portraits and landscapes.

When we decided to return, the Khamdesh notables—who by then had grown quite friendly—offered to build us a raft. They joined together several oxhides and attached them to a chassis of intersecting timbers. On this light vessel we drifted down the wild and billowing rapids of the Chounar River, sometimes at dizzying speeds, crossing gorges so deep and so perilous that the people who lived on the opposite banks not only did not know each other but were said to speak different languages.

When we got back to Kabul we were clearly in disgrace, with no house or royal limousine. We moved back to the Kabul Hotel; I never even thought of contacting the French embassy.

My trip to Kafiristan had left me with a severe case of dysentery. A German doctor treated my illness with great efficiency and kindness and refused to be paid. I spent most of my time making large erotic drawings, which the doctor found most amusing.

It was high time we left. Our departure, however, turned out to be rather more complicated than we had expected. In order to avoid censure, Ahmed Ali had given a heroic account of his role in our expedition: he had saved us from the people's fury, for we had photographed their women, profaned nonexistent mosques, and committed various other crimes. The prime minister, in fact, had been quite right. The region we had visited was very unstable, and the mountain people hostile. Had we been massacred, the government would have been forced to mount a retaliatory attack, which would have proved expensive as well as useless.

As soon as the police learned that we were about to leave, they organized a search. George, who always managed to know everything, warned us in advance. We carefully hid all our exposed camera and motion picture film and replaced them with empty rolls—which were duly confiscated. But the police remained suspicious: a second search was to be conducted at a checkpoint right outside Kabul. George made an arrangement with an Indian truck driver who was supposed to return without cargo to Peshawar. In those days, the military authorities had only one telephone line, which worked from seven in the morning till seven at night. One evening, at seven o'clock, we hid inside the truck with our suitcases and cameras. George sat beside the driver. When we reached the checkpoint, a subordinate officer asked them if they had seen two Europeans. George answered that he had noticed them in a gray car, all ready to leave, and expected them to pass by at any moment. The officer set up the roadblock and let us go through.

We had to reach the border before the telephone went back into service. All through the night we sped wildly on the rocky road in a getaway scene worthy of an American western. We crossed the border at ten minutes to seven the next morning, exhausted and quite black and blue, but safe in British India.

Many years later I told King Zaher the entire story, which he found very amusing. In the meantime, Ahmed Ali had made a fine career for himself and become director of the museum: his highly exaggerated account of our expedition to the mysterious region of Kafiristan was one of his greatest claims to fame.

We gave our film to a technician from Nice who had been recommended by friends. It made a very interesting little documentary.

Georges Henry Rivière, the famous ethnologist, put together a large exhibition of Raymond's magnificent photographs, which can still be seen at the Musée de l'Homme, Paris's anthropological museum; he also organized a showing of the film at the Trocadéro. Since we were leaving Paris again, the technician who had prepared and edited the film offered to circulate it. When we got back, the man had disappeared. I never found out what happened to the film.

CHAPTER FIVE

First Contacts with India

"We shall go wherever Alain finds a civilization that pleases him and bodies that caress themselves in dance; where work recaptures all its beauty, and time its eternal form." (Letter from Raymond to Pierre Arnal, Kabul, 16 June 1932)

From Peshawar, a picturesque bazaar filled with Moslem tribes from northern India, we travelled down to the plains in strange trains without corridors. Each of the large compartments was equipped with four beds, a toilet, and a shower; we had to carry our own bedding. First-class compartments were reserved for Europeans, second-class for missionaries and wealthy Indians; Eurasians travelled in what was called "intermediate class," and third-class compartments were filled with Indians crowded together like cattle. This new type of caste system was far more humiliating than the Hindus'.

Indians always travel a great deal, and the discrimination practiced on trains was one of the most disagreeable aspects of foreign rule. We visited Lahore, Delhi, and Benares, and finally arrived in Calcutta. George went back to Bombay.

Calcutta, the former capital of British India, was built in the eighteenth century by the East India Company on the banks of the Hooghly River, one of the branches of the great Ganges Delta. When I first visited Calcutta, it was a peaceful, airy city with large colonial villas surrounded by beautiful flower gardens. In the middle of the city, several imposing structures were grouped around the Maidan (the plain), a vast park with beautiful trees, perfect lawns, and several horsepaths. In the middle of the park was the famous Victoria Memorial, an enormous white marble pantheon that resembled the Sacré-Coeur in Paris and looked quite incongruous among the sacred mango and fig trees. In spite of this, the monument could be quite poetic in the moonlight or floating above the mists of dawn. The Indian part of the city, which stretched endlessly towards the north, was a web of tiny streets and buildings, a mixture of large residences and shantytowns intersected by wide, ill-kept avenues.

We moved into the Grand Hotel, where the rooms looked out upon the Maidan and the heat was alleviated by slow, silent fans. Soon after we arrived, while we were out for a walk, we ran into Haren Ghosh, an elegant Bengali I had met in Paris when he was managing Uday Shankar's dance troupe. He promised to visit us the following morning. Haren arrived just as we were sitting down to breakfast in the hotel's large, empty dining room. We asked him to sit with us for a few minutes. The waiters refused to serve us, claiming: "The gentleman at your table is not in proper dress." Haren was wearing a very elegant and quite impeccable Bengali costume. We immediately got up, asked for our bill, and moved out of the hotel. Haren Ghosh wasted no time telling his friends what we had done, which opened our way into Indian circles.

We moved to another hotel, the Great Eastern, which was hardly any better. But the gesture had been made, and that was the most important thing.

The attitude of the British was rather curious. They were always very correct and even quite cordial towards Indians in their official dealings with them or in the military world. Indians occupied very high positions in the Army and the administration; but in everything that concerned private life, clubs, hotels, railway cars, and residential areas, segregation was very strict and often took disagreeable forms. People said that this attitude was relatively recent, dating back to the opening of the Suez Canal. Until then, British public servants had always come without their wives. They would take Indian mistresses, sometimes wore native costumes—which in those days were more comfortable than European outfits—and participated in the life of the country. On Sundays, the high officials' concubines, called "bibis," would ride through the Maidan in open carriages; sometimes they even appeared at receptions. After the opening of the canal it became far easier to travel. British officials began to bring their families and lived in special quarters reserved for Europeans. Some of the Englishmen used to say quite wistfully: "The *mem-sahibs* [English wives] will make us lose the Empire."

During my first visit to India, I once saw a sign in a British club north of Calcutta which said: "Members of the club are requested to refrain from shooting at natives across the river during target practice." This kind of thing did not make communication very easy.

We met the German Consul, a very cultivated man called von Ow, who was a great connoisseur of sculpture; Raymond made a series of photographs of his collections. The consul got into trouble for driving around at night and stealing stone images the village people placed beneath the sacred trees. He left India just before the war, which was a great mistake: like many German aristocrats he hated the Nazis, and he was eliminated soon after he got back.

The French Consul was a nice, friendly man who lived with a very fat girl; among her many charms, she was Belgian and one-eyed. He insisted on taking her to receptions, but everytime he did this, the British Governor—pretending not to see her—would turn towards his aide and ask, in a very loud voice: "Who is this person?" They were replaced soon afterward by another consul called Dubois whose wife was a tall, redheaded German with pleasant, unaffected manners. Both of them spent the war in a camp near Darjeeling. Consular posts in Calcutta were not very popular in those days, but the situation changed after India became independent.

In later years, I visited Calcutta many times. At first we used to stay in Tagore's enormous house, which made our contacts with Westerners very difficult. This problem was resolved after Christine became director of the Alliance Française and invited us to live in her own apartment on Park Street, in an elegant neighborhood. I never went back to a British hotel.

Two tragic events completely transformed the character of

Calcutta. First there was the great famine. During the war, the Japanese occupied Burma and threatened to take eastern India. In order to discourage a possible invasion the Indian government cut off all food supplies headed for Assam and East Bengal. Millions of starving peasants swarmed into Calcutta, digging into garbage cans and dying in the streams. The Brahmaputra-Ganges Delta, forming Bengal (today called Bangladesh), became very dangerous to cross because of various epidemics, and the Japanese abandoned their plans of invasion, which they found far too costly. In the city, well-fed Europeans, who were never subjected to food rationing, would walk with disgust over the skeleton-like forms of men, women, and children, as they hurried on to their clubs and official dinners.

The second invasion took place when India was partitioned. East Bengal was declared a Moslem zone and given over to Pakistan. The Hindus, who made up half of the population, were pillaged and massacred. Millions of terrified refugees swarmed into Calcutta, which had remained Indian. Various attempts were made to gather and feed them, which proved an impossible task. Padmaja Naïdu, a wonderful woman who became Governor of Indian Bengal after independence was declared, told me with despair that eight thousand refugees flocked into the area each day and that there was no hope at all of ever feeding them or finding them work. All the most fertile regions had been given to Pakistan, and India was left without any sources of supply. Calcutta never got over this invasion and has remained a frightening city, teeming with beggars.

Haren Ghosh met a tragic end. During the riots organized by the British to prepare for India's partitioning, a group of Moslem fanatics entered his apartment. He was talking on the telephone to a friend who helplessly witnessed, from afar, the entire scene of Haren's murder and agony.

Uday Shankar

After our first meeting with Haren Ghosh, he took us to a large house in the Indian part of the city where Uday Shankar worked with his troupe. I had already met Uday in Paris with his French partner Simkie, who had been trained in Indian dancing. Uday's younger brother, Ravi Shankar, was then fifteen years old and working on his dancing and music.

Uday had had a rather interesting career. The son of a high-ranking Bengali official, he had come to Paris to study painting. Pavlova, who was trying at the time to create an Oriental ballet, took an interest in this boy who knew nothing about dance but had a great deal of imagination. He helped choreograph the ballet, which turned out to be very poor. It was here that he met Alice Boner, a Swiss woman from Zurich who had inherited a large fortune in industry. Alice took an interest in this very handsome Indian youth and decided to take him back to India so that he could devote himself entirely to dance. Alice was a beautiful woman of about thirty-five, tall and stately, haughty and strong-willed. She rather reminded me of Juno. She was also quite a good painter. She began to track down any surviving evidence of Indian classical dance, which was very much looked down on in Anglo-Indian cultural circles as were all the other traditional arts.

Alice was the first person to discover the great art of Kathakali dancing, which still existed in a few forgotten villages in the state of Trichur in Kerala, in southeast India. She encouraged a local poet called Vallathol to bring together the best of the surviving masters of this remarkable art, and helped him found the Kerala Kala Mandalam, the famous school of Kathakali, in the village of Chiruthuruthi. The school later became one of the greatest glories of India. It was she who discovered, helped, and supported the two splendid Bharata Natyam dancers, Bala Saraswati and Shanta Rao; she also knew many musicians, especially the famous Alla ud din Khân.

At her suggestion, Ravi Shankar decided to study music seriously and spent several years working with Alla ud din in the small central Indian city of Maihar. I went to visit him several times and followed his progress with great interest, as well as the work of Alla ud din's son Ali Akbar. Ravi Shankar later married his master's daughter, also a remarkable musician. Alice's prime goal was to create a ballet for Uday Shankar. Her efforts to discover the sources of Indian dance resulted in an adaptation of classical art to modern theatrical conceptions, a kind of "mishmash" that eventually led to a contemporary Indian ballet of questionable value.

Alice's most interesting contribution was in the domain of costume. Indian dancers traditionally wore very heavy outfits. Inspired by ancient frescoes and medieval sculptures, Alice designed costumes, necklaces, jewels, and trinkets that revealed as much as possible of her handsome dancer's body. What passes today for the traditional costumes of Indian ballet was in fact invented by an artist from Zurich.

Alice put together a dance company that became successful in Europe, America, and even Asia. She managed the company, negotiated contracts with impresarios, supervised rehearsals, and designed costumes. The modernistic orchestra that accompanied the ballet was abominable. Alla ud din once went on tour with the company but was so horrified by the orchestra's musical arrangements that he soon gave up and left.

One day Alice decided that she had had enough. She abandoned the company in the middle of a tour and went back to India with a young Bengali lawyer called Montu Mitra, who remained her loyal companion for many years and died in 1975. Alice settled in a small house in Benares, a few hundred yards away from the palace of Rewa, where Raymond and I went to live soon afterward.

While living in Benares, Alice grew passionately interested in the aesthetics and symbolism of Hindu architecture and sculpture, which led her to the study of ancient texts. She collected a large number of manuscripts, but since she knew only a few words of Sanskrit, she enlisted the help of a few Indian scholars to translate them for her. She discovered unknown treatises of exceptional significance and, many years later, published some of these texts as well as her internationally famous studies on the architecture of temples, the best-known being her work on the construction techniques of the gigantic temple of Konarak.

Alice was my neighbor in Benares for many years; Raymond and I were the only other foreigners living in the city at the time. She trusted Raymond because he was Swiss, but seemed to have great doubts about me. By then I had become completely integrated in Hindu life and spoke and wrote the language fluently. Alice basically remained a European with a great interest in India. She never wore a sari and always insisted on sitting with the men at receptions and concerts. She was quite critical of certain aspects of Hindu society and not at all afraid of shocking people by refusing to observe customs she disapproved of.

Alice felt very much at ease in the modernized Indian society of New Delhi among people like Nehru and the great Indian industrialists who patronized the arts. Oddly enough, she knew hardly any English people, whereas I, in spite of my shocking behavior, found many real friends among members of the Viceroy's circle.

Later, when I returned to Europe and began to act and look more like a Westerner, Alice sought me out and we came to like and trust each other.

After Alice abandoned Uday Shankar, he was rescued by a rich young American woman, Beatrice Straight, who later made her career in the theater. Beatrice's mother's second husband, Leonard Elmhirst—whom I shall speak of later—was an English agricultural engineer and a very good friend of Tagore's. Beatrice financed Uday Shankar's dance company for a time, then decided to help him establish a cultural center in the Himalayas. She bought a magnificent estate near Almora that had once belonged to an order of Catholic nuns. The scenery was marvelously beautiful, but the rainy season was long and the winters harsh. We had rented a summer house in the same area. Beatrice built several studios and went to a great deal of expense hiring well-known masters from southern India. But the climate and altitude did not suit these elderly men, who were accustomed to the gentle tropical climate of Kerala. The discipline of dance hardly helped matters, and two of the masters died of heart attacks. But there were also other problems. The students and members of the dance company grew very bored living in such poetic solitude; they were also in very close contact. Several undesired future pupils were brought into the world. There was a great scandal. In the end, the center was formally disbanded. Beatrice went back to America, and Uday Shankar returned to Calcutta.

Shantiniketan

Raymond passionately admired Rabindranath Tagore's *Gitanjali*, a collection of poems written in English, as well as Bengali, which had been translated into French by André Gide under the title *L'Offrande Lyrique*. I knew almost nothing about this poet: anything connected with Gide was considered taboo in my family. When Haren Ghosh offered to take us on a visit to the school that Tagore—who hated all schools—had created in the middle of the country, Raymond was overjoyed. We took the train to Burdwan, were jostled over bumpy roads and river fords in a primitive vehicle, and finally reached Shantiniketan (the abode of peace). We were very cordially welcomed and taken to the guest house, a somewhat dilapidated old colonial building with a portico, wrought-iron balconies, and large empty rooms that opened out in all directions and were swept by a gentle Bengali breeze.

The day after we arrived, the poet asked to meet his new visitors. He normally lived in small hermitages he had built on the property for his own use, but also had a large official residence decorated in a rather charming pseudo-Indian style he had created himself. It was here that he received us. We entered a enormous room, a kind of covered verandah supported by large square columns, which had no walls, doors, or windows and opened out onto vast gardens. The poet wore a flowing Tibetan robe of brown wool and had a long, meticulously groomed white beard. A very spicy Bengali meal, which we had to eat with our fingers, was brought to us on silver trays. The poet was surrounded with doe-eyed young girls, silent, attentive servants, and a host of admirers: he reminded me of the Sultan of Baghdad in one of the *Arabian Nights*.

The venerable poet talked with us for a long time and probably found us quite entertaining. He told us that we could stay as long as we wished, which was quite unusual. According to the rules, visitors were not supposed to stay longer than three days.

The school was on a vast property planted with beautiful trees, located in a semiarid region near the Bihar border. Teachers, artists and friends lived in small pavilions scattered all over the grounds. There were several large buildings, including a dormitory for boys, a girls' residence, a well-stocked library, a Chinese studies center, a dining hall, a school of art, dance, and music. All the classes were held outdoors. Each teacher had his own tree, a large mango tree or a shady *banyan*. The students sat on the grass around their master. They went to classes when they felt like it. There was no discipline of any kind and no one was ever punished. The boys played all sorts of practical jokes, which amused the poet enormously; he was always on their side and against the teachers and school regulations. The girls were watched more carefully—in India, the virtue of women is no laughing matter. Some of the boys had invented a game that consisted in seducing visitors, men or women and stealing one of their belongings—a scarf, a cigarette case, etc. Then they would offer it as a gift to the next person they seduced. The inevitable followed. A Parsee lady would confront a visiting English poet: "Ah, so you're the one who stole my scarf!" The victims were far too embarrassed to reveal the real criminal. When Tagore heard these stories, he would look very grave but was secretly delighted.

With the students' help, Tagore produced his own plays. He always acted the role of a wise man or king. He also wrote songs; all his poems, in fact, have melodies. He often drew inspiration from *bhatiyalis* and *bauls*, the famous songs of Bengali boatmen and wandering monks. Each morning he would hum a poem to some of his disciples, who transcribed the words and melody in Bengali notation. I translated and transcribed a number of these musical poems, several of which were published by Ricordi in France.

Many years later, in 1947, when India became independent, the poet expressed the wish that one of his songs be chosen as the national anthem. When independence was declared, his son Rathindranath asked me to orchestrate two songs, "Jana Gana Mana" and "Bandé Mataram." I prepared the orchestration and made a quick trip to Paris to ask my old friend and master Max d'Ollone to check over my work. We rapidly composed arrangements both for orchestra and brass band; as a result, "Jana Gana Mana" became the national anthem, and "Bandé Mataram" the national song.

Shantiniketan was the only place in the entire country

where Europeans could meet Indians on an equal footing and in an Indian—though not traditional—atmosphere. The poet belonged to a reformed sect founded by his father called the Brahmosamaj, and rejected the taboos that made contact with Hindus so difficult. His visitors came from far and wide—poets, writers, artists, philosophers, and scientists. The most famous Oxford professors visited; Sylvain Lévy, the best-known Indianist in France, often stayed at Shantiniketan. In many ways the education offered at the school seemed rather absurd, but it certainly freed the children from any kind of inferiority complex. Out of it came a great number of famous people who played key roles in India after it gained its independence, including Indira Gandhi. Nehru and Gandhi made frequent visits to the poet, but Tagore loathed Gandhi, whom he considered false and ambitious; he feared his political role—and rightfully so, for it led to the partition of India.

Tagore came from a family of landed gentry. He owned vast tracts of land in the region that is now called Bangladesh. This aristocrat, who was very well versed in British politics, believed that the English would eventually have to leave India and that the matter should be settled in a gentlemanly way, without fanaticism or uncontrollable mass uprisings. Unfortunately, no one listened to him.

The schoolboys often used to come and chat with the visitors. Raymond took a large number of photographs, and I painted many watercolors and portraits, including one of the poet that was very well received and can still be seen in Calcutta. We would take long walks with the boys and go swimming in the ponds. Not far from the school were a number of Santal villages inhabited by pre-Aryan tribes who often celebrated feasts, with boys and girls dancing through the night. Some of the students from Shantiniketan would pursue Santal girls and rape them in the fields. No one in the school seemed to mind, for the Bengalis considered the tribes savage.

At Shantiniketan there was a model farm run by the poet's son Rathindranath, a man of great charm and refinement who loved to fix things and do odd jobs. The farm had been created according to the poet's ideas by an English agronomical engineer, Leonard Elmhirst, who later set up a similar establishment and a cultural center in South Devon, England. This institution, called Dartington Hall, once played a very important role in English cultural life. It was a center for agronomical experimentation, art, and culture, as well as a residence for musicians, painters, and writers. Agriculture and culture were united according to a very romantic human ideal. As for the model farm, it suffered a number of magnificent fiascos, after which a new plan was devised: instead of "teaching peasants new agricultural methods," it was judged preferable, both at Shantiniketan and Dartington, to instruct the students in the "traditional agricultural methods." The results were far more successful.

The poet organized several performances for our benefit. He also asked me to dance for him, which I did to the accompaniment of recorded music.

We stayed at Shantiniketan for two months, then decided that it was time to leave. Tagore urged us to return very soon and entrusted me with two missions: to seek out his friends in Europe in the hope of obtaining funding for the school, and to bring back some colored inks he needed for his paintings. He used the ink I brought back to the end of his life; the bottles can still be seen today in his study, which has been left intact, like a museum. Raymond persuaded Suyana, a young Javanese from a noble family, to accompany us. He had been a dancer in the palace of the Sultan of Solo, then gone to India to pursue some vague studies. He was now quite bored with the school, so we took him along with us. Before going to Europe, however, Suyana had to see his family. We accompanied him on a very interesting trip to Rangoon, Kuala-Lumpur, Penang, Singapore, and finally Batavia, Buru-Budur, Solo (Surakarta), and others parts of Java.

In Batavia (now called Djakarta), we had to stay in Chinese hotels because Suyana was not accepted in European establishments. The Chinese hotels were odd-looking constructions with only one floor and a central corridor. They were dead silent and always seemed quite deserted. There was no furniture besides the iron beds, but everything was impeccably clean.

It was in Solo that I first heard the magnificent traditional music of Java, which was completely unknown in Batavia but still retained all its beauty and refinement in performances at the sultan's court.

The rainy season had just ended. The mountains, with their terraced rice paddies climbing all the way to the top, seemed carved out of crystal.

Both Suyana's father and his master, who was director of the sultan's personal ballet, gave him permission to leave with us for Europe. And so, after a few weeks' stay in Solo, the three of us left for Singapore and from there took an English ship of the Peninsular and Oriental Company bound for Ceylon, Aden, and finally Marseilles.

Each year thereafter, we went to Shantiniketan for a few months' visit. The poet offered us a pretty house. In 1934, when Christine arrived, she took over the management of the girls' residence. Then Gaëtan Fouquet, whom I had met through Sauguet, joined us and became manager of the guest house. Tagore was eager to give an international and intercultural flavor to his school (which was later declared a university) and was always happy when Europeans became involved in his creation. Gaëtan was an amusing man, both gentle and aggressive; Sauguet's ballet *La Chatte* is dedicated to him.

In a letter to Pierre Arnal, Raymond wrote: "Everything in India is better than ever—even Shantiniketan. I hear that Christine has built herself a reputation and Gaëtan eight new bathrooms."

Later, Gaëtan founded the pictorial review *Connaissance du Monde*, then the Club des Explorateurs lecture group at the Salle Pleyel in Paris; he also helped found the Club Méditerranée.

Finally the poet asked me to direct his school of music, which mostly taught songs—considered a form of modern music—and the basic principles of classical music. Dance, here, was a graceful mixture of styles, very pleasing to the poet but lacking a solid basic technique.

I was just beginning to study the organization of this school and thinking of ways to improve it when Raymond caught a strange illness. He suffered from terrible headaches and high fever and vomited constantly. The school doctor, a young Bengali who could only mumble a few words of English, diagnosed the illness as enteric fever; I had no idea that this was synonymous with typhoid. He suggested feeding Raymond something that sounded like "boiled water"—in fact he was trying to say "barley water." I finally decided to take Raymond to Calcutta, which meant being jostled on a bumpy road and spending endless hours on the local train. We finally found refuge in Tagore's enormous house in the heart of Calcutta's Indian city, and were visited by an English doctor who charged us a fortune. He prescribed no remedy and told me that all I could do was wait. Finally I remembered Martha, a Swiss doctor Alice had mentioned who ran a small hospital in the city. I was so exhausted when we arrived that the nurse asked me which one of us was the patient. Martha put us both in bed, gave us all kinds of injections, and Raymond soon recovered.

Martha was a remarkable woman, very small and masculine, with hair cut as short as a boy's. It was rumored that she had once removed her own appendix by using mirrors, for she did not trust the local doctors—who were happy to return the compliment. She was scorned by everyone in the profession but known to be able to cure the most desperate cases. We remained very good friends.

After a long convalescence, Raymond and I returned to Shantiniketan for several weeks, but I had to abandon the idea of running the music school. I was not really interested in what was being taught there anyway. We finally left and, after spending a few years travelling between Paris, Shantiniketan, and various other places, settled permanently in Benares, the center of India's true culture.

THE FRIENDS OF TAGORE

Tagore, who was slowly depleting his own fortune to maintain Shantiniketan, had asked me to visit his friends in Europe and ask them to suggest ways of finding subsidies for the school. The first thing we did was to create an "Association of the Friends of Tagore," which evil-minded people promptly baptized "Tagore's Darlings." We printed attractive membership cards and contacted the poet's friends, who all replied courteously and invited us to visit them. These people had very illustrious names: André Gide, Romain Rolland, Paul Valéry,

Paul Morand, André Maurois, Georges Duhamel, Salvador de Madariaga, Benedetto Croce, Carlo Formichi, and so forth. Unfortunately, Raymond and I had no idea how to approach people in industrial, financial, or governmental circles who might have been able to finance a school in India. The poet's literary friends were not in any position to give us advice. The only one who suggested anything was Romain Rolland; he thought it would be a good idea to write Mussolini, whom he detested. But how does one write to a chief of state? Romain Rolland dictated the letter himself. We received a polite reply stating that in spite of *il duce*'s sincere admiration for the poet, circumstances made it impossible for him to come to his aid.

A few years earlier, Tagore had been royally entertained in Italy; then, having passed over into Switzerland, he had been persuaded by Romain Rolland to give an interview condemning the Fascist regime. The poet, who knew nothing about such matters, innocently did as he was told. In his memoirs, Romain Rolland wrote about his meeting with Raymond and me, describing us as elegant and reckless young fops who had once gone on an expedition to Kafiristan so dangerous and so difficult that even the most hardened explorers would have hesitated to undertake it. "It is impossible," he added, "to understand the youth of today."

I never liked Romain Rolland very much. He was a middle-class *petit bourgeois*, and people of this sort often hide their complexes and selfishness beneath a thin veil of idealism that has no connection with reality. They never try to measure the consequences of their actions nor the ideas they disseminate. Although they frequently lead others to political violence that can end in catastrophe, they live in a kind of romantic dream without ever sacrificing their own comfort. Most "intellectuals" who inspire and encourage terrorist actions and brutal revolutions are frustrated *bourgeois*, never artisans or other kinds of people who know something about real life.

Gaëtan Fouquet offered to help us develop the association, but we were far too inexperienced and too occupied with our own adventures to succeed in such an undertaking. Little by little, "the Friends of Tagore" fell into oblivion. The poet never held this against us.

CHAPTER SIX

Interludes

La Montsouricière

Whenever we went to Paris, we had to find a place to live. I was still studying dance. It was, of course, impossible to ask the Phantom to lend us his studio. In 1933, after an ill-fated attempt to live in the suburbs, where Suyana—alone and forgotten—nearly starved to death, Raymond found a large two-story studio on the Left Bank, Rue de Montsouris. The building was modern and only had two apartments; the lower one was occupied by a Hungarian photographer whose red-headed German wife occasionally slept with Raymond. Pierre Arnal, whom I shall speak of later, lived with us there for three months.

Raymond hated to burden himself with furniture. The only things he brought into the apartment were the Blüthner grand piano he had inherited from his mother, a small desk, a sky-blue cupboard, and a zebra skin from his room in Lausanne. We slept on mattresses on the floor; a bed served as a sofa. We also owned a few chairs, stools, and a small table— nothing more. We hired a good-natured Alsatian woman to take care of the apartment.

Suyana often prepared Javanese dishes for our parties; other times we ordered meals from a small restaurant down the street which always sent us the same *crème-confiture*, a delicious jam and cream dessert.

Our apartment, nicknamed "la Montsouricière" after the street we lived on, soon became quite well-known. Rereading old letters from that period, I am astonished by the number of friends who came to see us there.

André Gide, who was very interested in our exotic trips, came several times with Marc Allégret to see our films and photographs. One evening a reel of film fell out of the projector, which was right over his head, and nearly killed him. Suyana always prepared him his best Javanese dishes. Gide adored litchis, which were very difficult to find in those days— he called them "angels' balls." We gave a very grand reception to celebrate Jacques Dupont's first art show. Twenty years later, when he had grown quite famous, he mentioned this to me with great emotion and gratitude; I had completely forgotten about it. La Montsouricière was also the headquarters of "the Friends of Tagore."

Two people we very often saw in those days were an extremely likeable and friendly actor called Marcel Herrand and his friend Jean Marchat, who later had a distinguished career in the theater. Marcel Herrand died very young.

A few years earlier when I was living on the Rue du Cotentin, a young singer I knew had once brought along an astonishingly handsome sixteen-year-old youth who was working as a photographer's apprentice for Manuel Frères. His name was Jean Marais; later, he became Jean Cocteau's protégé and a famous movie star. I saw him over the years from time to time. He was an unaffected, gentle boy, completely without ambition. When Raymond and I moved to the Rue de Montsouris, Jean became an habitué. He came nearly every day and got on very well with Raymond; they used to go together to an elocution course given by a certain Paupelix, then went swimming at the Chazelle swimming pool. Jean made friends with one of my cousins, a Navy officer. Soon afterwards he met Jean Cocteau and moved into an elegant little apartment at the Palais-Royal. He still continued to visit us and always remained a very charming friend. In 1939, when I was living in Benares, he and Cocteau made arrangements to visit us in our palace by the Ganges. Cocteau sent us a numbered copy of his play *Les Chevaliers de la Table Ronde* with the following inscription: "To Raymond and Alain in their faraway land where I rest beside them in spirit, with all my gratitude." Then came the war, so the project never materialized.

At the beginning of 1939, when we left permanently for India, Raymond sold Jean Marais his beautiful light brown

Matford, which he had nicknamed "le Chevreuil" [the roe deer]. It was Jean's first car, and he was delighted with it. He wrote about this charming vehicle in his memoirs, even claiming to have given it its name—which of course was not true.

In 1938 we had to move out of la Montsouricière. The piano and a few pieces of furniture were stored in a small studio on the Rue Froidevaux, where I went to live after the war.

When we left Paris, we lent the studio to Yves Forget, a Mauritian youth who acted in many of Cocteau's plays. When the war broke out, he was forced to leave. He went back to his native island and started an acting school.

When I returned to France twenty years later, most of the people I had known in this fanciful, unconventional Parisian world were gone. Some were dead, others in exile. Only a few aging specimens were left, living in quiet retirement or grown into pompous, portly gentlemen with ribbons in their lapels. As for me, I had become a quite different person.

During the thirties, automobiles were still beautiful works of art. Some of the more famous brands—Delages, Delahayes, Panhard-Levassors, and Bugatti sports models—were hand-crafted a few dozen at a time. The most wonderful were the English Rolls-Royce, the Italian Isotta-Fraschini, the German Duesenberg, and the Franco-Spanish Hispano-Suiza. These cars were not mass-produced, but fitted up with bodies according to the buyer's whim.

Raymond had a passion for automobiles and was a very good mechanic. In those days all twenty-year-old boys dreamed of owning a Hispano-Suiza, which had a somewhat mythical aura, like Hollywood or Arsène Lupin.* A very popular novel of the time was entitled *L'Homme à l'Hispano.* When Raymond visited the manufacturer, he discovered that not only was his dream possible but also quite affordable. He bought a second-hand rebuilt chassis, and I spent days designing a convertible body that was revolutionary for its time. Though not a very

---

*Arsène Lupin is the elegant "gentleman-burglar" hero of a long series of immensely popular novels by Maurice Leblanc (1864–1941)—*Arsène Lupin, gentleman-cambrioleur* (1907), *Arsène Lupin contre Herlock Sholmès* (1908), etc.—Trans.

practical car, it was quite spectacular—red and white, with red leather walls and upholstery. We called it "Choléra II," later "Télégraphiste."

This car, if anything, enhanced our notoriety, sometimes in rather disagreeable ways. On two occasions we found our tires slashed to ribbons. One day, on the Avenue de l'Opéra, the Hispano brushed against a small delivery van. An enormous bully in blue overalls jumped out of the van and ran towards us with his fists clenched, ready to massacre these filthy capitalists. He was completely taken aback by the sight of two obviously frightened boys, one very fair, the other very dark. He burst out laughing, bowed ceremoniously, and saluted us with the cry "Go ahead, my little cherry blossoms!"

The Hispano did not last very long. Because it was so light, one tended to drive it far too fast. The engine broke down twice. The second time, we were driving in the middle of Hungary; we had to send it back home at great expense and sold it very cheaply. I am told that it is still running.

During Raymond's rather unhappy years in Switzerland, he had made friends with a French boy, Pierre Arnal, who was two years his senior and had a similar Protestant background. He came from a family of aristocratic intellectuals. His mother had made a second marriage and was the wife of a well-known writer, Edouard Estaunié; his aunt was the Princesse de Béarn. Pierre had a nobility of character and a respect for culture typical of a world that no longer exists today. When Raymond was seventeen, he and Pierre had made a trip to Venice that left him with glowing memories. The friendship lasted all their lives. It was Pierre who gave Raymond his first camera, a Leica. Raymond nicknamed Pierre "Encolpius," after the narrator in Petronius' *Satyricon*.

It was fashionable in those days for Parisian bourgeois of a certain type to take up farming and agriculture. Pierre, following the trend, became an enterprising gentleman farmer. He got married, started a farm in the Landes—on the southwest coast of France—and grew produce with which many of his needy friends were well supplied during the war. He then created a plantation of mimosas near Cannes, where I often paid him visits. Later he grew olive trees on an enormous property near Brignoles, which had a charming eighteenth-century house and a Roman pool. Pierre was very interested in the arts and often helped artists, musicians, architects, and theatrical groups when they were in financial straits. He showed exemplary courage and loyalty in his support of Fernand Pouillon, a great architect who was being persecuted by jealous rivals; he also backed his vast construction projects in Algeria after it gained its independence.

I have always felt that in the great symbolic theater of the world Pierre represented the character of the friend, unshakeable in his loyalty, never motivated by the passion and self-interest that so often distort human relationships.

Despite their long separations, Pierre and Raymond remained very close and never ceased to write one another. At first, Pierre's reaction to me was somewhat ambiguous, but he remained wonderfully tactful and polite, never showing his feelings, never interfering in our lives.

Soon after we settled in Benares, Raymond wrote him: "Friendship is unalterable. My first journey, my first moments of freedom, my first Leica, my first lesson in double-clutching, my first betrayals, Venice—all were with you and because of you. Now I am nearly twenty-eight, and I have learned nothing new, absolutely nothing. I think that even today the shade under the chestnut trees, with a faint smell of warm tar floating in the air, would have the same dangerous appeal for us as it did all those years ago." (Benares, 29 April 1940)

After Raymond's death, Pierre helped me in my work and for a short time administered the music institute I had created in Venice.

One summer, Raymond rented an attractive house in the south of France that belonged to a teacher and friend of Sauguet's, the musician Charles Koechlin. The house, built on rocks and surrounded with pine trees, was located near the small village of Canadel. We spent a happy, peaceful summer there, bathed in sunshine. Not far from us lived a Belgian couple called Levêque. The husband wore a grayish beard and spent all his time on his boat, pretending to be a Dutch pirate.

His wife was a languid creature with a horror of germs. Nicole, her daughter by a first marriage, was a pretty girl with a long silky body; she would spend her days alone on a canoe and reminded me of an eel. "Mammy" soon took us under her wing and treated us as if we were her own children; later she invited us to Brussels. Nicole, who was interested in dance, was sent to work with me in Paris and thus became an habituée of la Montsouricière. She completely lacked the drive and energy that are essential to a dancer, so our lessons were somewhat lifeless.

Encolpius had given me a roguish and high-spirited little monkey who constantly pursued Nicole and frightened her with his attentions. Raymond gave him the humiliating name of "Vaseline." The monkey was a liar and, whenever I came home, pretended he had been beaten during my absence. He devoured entire tubes of toothpaste and shaving cream, which made him sick. Fortunately our good Alsatian cleaning woman adored him and would exclaim: "He's so sweet—he makes love to my arm!" This kind of lovemaking was not at all to Nicole's taste.

Nicole was obviously infatuated with Raymond and, a few years later, came to see us one summer when we were staying in the Himalayas. She remained with us for a while, then returned to France, changed her name, tried to start a career in the theater, and married the very famous and handsome actor Gérard Philipe, who died soon afterward. It was thus, in the role of a grieving widow, that she finally fulfilled her destiny.

Raymond kept Pierre informed on all of Vaseline's latest adventures: "Vaseline the monkey spent a very pleasant vacation in Alsace. He came back an alcoholic, but perfectly sweet. He drinks Cologne water and hard cider. Alain spends hours quietly caressing him, which is very good—it gives him a chance to rest. They both send their love." (Montsouricière, 10 November 1933)

When we moved to India we left the monkey with the Alsatian cleaning woman, but he did not survive our absence or the war. We learned of his death much later, after communications with France were restored. "Vaseline the monkey has finally died of 'pulmonia,' a very elegant disease for monkeys before the invention of penicillin. What will elegant monkeys die of next? Here, monkeys are very ordinary and die like everyone else, mostly of stupidity. But Giraudoux's death made me very sad." (Letter from Raymond, Benares, 7 March 1945)

Max d'Ollone was a professor of composition at the Paris Conservatoire and highly respected and appreciated by his pupils. He had seen me dance, admired my very personal style, and wanted to meet me; later, he took an interest in my singing. Between this sensitive old man and the artistic young maverick I was in those days, a strong, deep bond of friendship soon developed. Through him I met Reynaldo Hahn, a musician who had been a friend of Proust's.

Max had been a pupil of Gounod's. He won the Prix de Rome the same year as Debussy, whom he detested. During his stay at the Villa Medici, he had a romantic affair which caused his family a great deal of anxiety, so he was promptly married off to a young lady of his milieu. In spite of this inauspicious beginning, the couple grew very close. At the time I knew them, they had several children in their twenties. The family soon adopted me and Raymond into their midst and used to call us "the flowers." Sunshine and springtime were never as eagerly awaited as the "flowers" who brightened their humdrum lives. Max and I played a lot of music together; he would accompany me on the piano while I sang. He was an excellent pianist but refused to perform in public. It was impossible, he said, to play music as one felt it without being massacred by the critics. He hated the cold, technical perfectionism that was fashionable at the time: music for him was not a series of acrobatic arabesques, but a way to reach the furthest regions of the soul. He disliked Bach and Brahms as much as I did, but loved Italian opera, especially bad productions sung by flamboyant overpassionate singers on small Italian stages. Max liked to say that when music was executed too well, it became just that—an execution. Through him I came to know the works of Bellini, whom he considered one of the greatest of all composers. Max often accompanied me on the piano during my dance performances. He wrote several operas and ballets, which are very rarely played, though *La Samaritaine*, his most important work, has many fine qualities. I learned a great deal from him about composition and orchestration; we made several trips together and I unquestionably played a very important role in his life. As a result of a dream, Raymond nicknamed him "Lyvet" and his wife "Hérésie."

Hérésie was a bit of a magician. She had curious intuitions, lived in an almost psychedelic world, and believed in supernatural powers. Max had never actually been unfaithful to her, but sought refuge in an imaginary and poetic world filled with beautiful adolescent gods. One summer afternoon, while the aging Max was lying alone in his dreary bourgeois apartment on the Rue de Grenelle, the gods took pity on him and sent him an angel. As he trembled with emotion and wonder, trying to make up his mind whether to pay homage to this celestial being, the doorbell suddenly rang. It was a telegram: Hérésie was dead!

Max had a Hungarian pupil, Anton Sztaraï, who came from a noble family. His mother had been lady-in-waiting to the Empress of Hungary and Austria. Anton invited us to visit him in Budapest. We accepted the invitation and left for Vienna, then Budapest, where I gave a dance recital. The painter Bathyani made a large portrait of me in a dancing pose, which my mother later threw away. Life in Vienna and Budapest was very lively and gay. Even the little Austrian Fascists, easily recognizable by their white stockings, were pleasant and friendly, and quite willing to embrace the homosexual lifestyle. Most of them were later massacred in Stalingrad. Nothing remains of that generation.

Young people seem to join political parties or revolutionary movements the same way they become fanatical about sports—just for the fun of it; they do this without any thought for the consequences. They would be just as happy devoting themselves to other activities like ecology, archaeology, or animal photography. Children should be given a civic education very early on, rather than waste years being filled with political and abstract ideas; but there is no such thing in the Western world as a civic education. At twelve, children are perfectly capable of understanding and getting involved in the problems of an adult society; at that age they have a great deal of common sense, but they lose it after years of imprisonment in schools and among families that offer them no ideals in life.

Anton had invited us to his castle in Transylvania. We left in the Hispano which, as mentioned earlier, broke down on the road and had to be sent back to Paris. After a long delay, we finally arrived in Kosice. After the First World War and the Treaty of Trianon, of which my father had been rapporteur, Anton's castle suddenly found itself in Czechoslovakia and his brother's in Rumania, although the population was Hungarian. The castle was surrounded with vast tracts of land, and the peasants, who were all very respectful and devoted, seemed to have stepped out of medieval tapestries. We were magnificently received. It was here that I met a young Viennese doctor who specialized in nutrition; he had just settled in America and was already enormously successful. His name was Gayelord Hauser. He invited us to visit him in Hollywood.

I saw Anton again after the war. His father had refused to leave his country, and Anton did not want to abandon him. Everything they possessed had been taken away from them. Anton had spent several years in a Russian concentration camp in Siberia. He had been considerably weakened by the experience and settled with his father and sister in a small room in the city of Kosice.

Anton did not own a passport and was not allowed to work or leave the city. He and his father only managed to drag out their miserable lives thanks to the peasants who had once worked for them and now secretly provided them with food and supplies. When the authorities tried to put an end to it, hundreds of Anton's and his father's former "serfs" descended upon the city and started a riot; after this they were left in relative peace. Anton survived by giving language lessons. He spoke German, French, English, Italian, and Hungarian without a trace of an accent; he was also fascinated by astrology and quite an expert in this somewhat fantastical science. During the Prague Spring, he was given permission to accept invitations from friends and relatives in Western Europe and spent some time with me in Venice. He never complained and spoke with great simplicity of his hard life—his problems obtaining bread, paper, and stamps—as though it were the most natural thing in the world. He never accepted anything from me, only a few books. He wrote to me from time to time, describing his long walks and the beauties of the forest. He died in 1979.

While travelling between Austria and Hungary, we made several stops in Germany. In the light of the events that followed, it is difficult to conceive the spectacular attraction of Germany at the dawn of Nazism. People who were impressed by the sight of the Moscow Olympics a few years ago were also very much aware of Soviet oppression and imperialism, gulags, and so forth. In the early thirties, Hitler could not really be accused of any wrongdoing except on an ideological and political plane. German anti-Semitism had not yet taken the massive proportions of a genocide, and the French liked to think of it as a phenomenon similar to the Dreyfus Affair. Nazi Germany, with its organized, enthusiastic, uniformed youths and spectacular constructions, was a fantastic and thrilling sight to behold. Though they had no special love for the military, many political moderates in France believed that, in the long run, the rebirth of German power was the only way to avoid the subjection of all of Europe to the Soviet Union. They advocated peaceful coexistence, even collaboration with the Hitler regime, in exactly the same way that people speak of détente with the Soviet Union today. I sometimes wonder if, by pursuing this line of action, we might not have avoided the occupation, the genocides, the Communist control of half of Europe, perhaps even the subjection of the entire continent—a state of regression that would be comparable to the destruction of the Roman Empire in the name of another brand of totalitarian ideology, Christianity. But though we may speculate, we shall never know the answer.

In 1936 we visited one of Hitler's youth camps in Heidelberg. The atmosphere was far from unpleasant, but two boys who had just been expelled—probably for some sexual indiscretion—were terrified, even in tears. Suddenly we felt afraid. Hitler's magnificent political machine seemed ready to crush anything that lay in its path.

Italy was very different. Here, Fascism was beautifully theatrical. Life was easy and agreeable, except for those who opposed the regime and were kept under house arrest. Italians have always been able to adapt to various forms of tyranny without taking them too seriously. Persecution and anti-Semitism only became real threats after the Germans occupied the country, leaving the field open to sadists who, under the guise of patriotism, always seem to surface in times of war.

Hitler's craze for power was exacerbated by the opposition of most of the world to his regime. All the German and Austrian Jews or homosexuals I knew who were unable to escape in time died horribly in extermination camps.

I often wonder at the way people who speak of genocide always seem to forget the Gypsies, the homosexuals, and the German dissidents who died at the hands of the Nazis; by limiting their condemnation, they only weaken their argument. It is not just because the victims were Jewish that extermination camps were so abominable. I never quite trust the sincerity of people who openly condemn anti-Semitism but conveniently forget the many other victims of Nazism.

CHAPTER SEVEN

Travels

HENRY DE MONFREID

Raymond had been quite captivated by Indonesia and dreamed of buying a boat so that he could sail through Oceania. Georges Henry Rivière, curator of the Musée de l'Homme in Paris, suggested the name of a famous navigator who might be able to give him good advice. He arranged a meeting with Henry de Monfreid, who invited us to discuss our sailing trip in Obock, his Somalian domain.

In March 1934 we left for Marseilles and boarded a steamship of the Messageries Maritimes, the only company that stopped in Djibouti. The journey was not very pleasant. Our fellow passengers were minor civil servants leaving for the colonies because of the higher salaries—most of them mediocre, racist, arrogant, and puffed up with self-importance. They knew nothing of the history or culture of the countries they were about to administer, and seemed to have benefited very little from those so-called blessings of civilization they had come to bestow. From the very start their attitude towards us, who neither looked, spoke, nor acted like *petits fonctionnaires*, was hostile. Their wives, however, were more soft-hearted and, fearing that these two naïve young men would do something foolish and come to grief, warned us of a dangerous character who might carry us off and sell us as slaves in Arabia. When we finally dropped anchor in the port of Djibouti, a small Arabian *boutre*, all sails unfurled, came speeding towards us and drew elegantly alongside the ship. Henry de Monfreid leaped aboard crying: "Alain! Raymond! What a pleasure to see you here!" The passengers' faces were convulsed with horror. It was almost as though Mesrine, our most notorious modern-day bandit, had come to greet us.

We sailed to Obock all through the night, feeling somewhat alarmed. Our pirate host sat in the narrow cabin, casually smoking his opium pipe. The tall, silent, and powerful Dankali sailors who made up the crew were obviously capable of anything.

Obock was an abandoned military outpost in the middle of the desert, right across the gulf. There was only one house, a two-story structure that had once been the commanding officer's headquarters; it was surrounded by mud cabins, most of them in ruins. Monfreid occupied the house, which was filled with all kinds of objects, chests, and old cannons fished out of wrecked ships. In the middle of all this stood a tiny piano on which the pirate fumbled through Mozart sonatas each night, just like a little girl.

At the suggestion of Joseph Kessel, the famous French author, Monfreid described his adventurous life as a smuggler and pirate in *Les Secrets de la mer Rouge* and several other works. These confessions are not at all exaggerated—quite the contrary, in fact.

Monfreid came from an old family of landed gentry who lived in the ancient province of Béarn, near the Pyrenees. The elegant language and courtly manners he had learned in childhood were rather startling, considering what he had become.

Aside from his drug trafficking and pearl smuggling operations, he sank ships with his cannons, then looted them. He was also said to be a slave trader, dealing mostly in young boys who were kidnapped in Ethiopia, then castrated and sold to Arabian harems.

The Obock landscape was quite austere, a vast, interminable plain with a few shadeless bushes growing here and there. In the distance a barrier of bluish mountains hid the western horizon, beyond which lay Ethiopia and the Sudan. But the underwater landscape was an enchanted world of coral forests and multicolored marine plants, with myriads of fish swimming through the crystalline waters.

Our visit was both pleasant and interesting. We went shark fishing on tiny vessels. Shark fins are very much prized by the Chinese and therefore quite valuable; no other part of the fish is eaten. We opened the bellies of these voracious predators and often found bracelets, rings, necklaces, and other trinkets. The black sailors stretched large nets between the corals. Enormous sharks swam around the boat, which they could easily have capsized with a swish of the tail.

In the shallow lagoons that formed near the shore, forests of mangroves, like giant spiders, stood on their tentacular roots while enormous crabs swam in the muddy waters.

At night we slept without blankets directly on the sand. One evening Raymond had a severe bout of fever but fortunately brought his temperature down by swimming across the lagoon towards our little boat.

The Dankalis, who made up Monfreid's crew and private guard, were magnificent Negroes with noble profiles and smooth hair. They looked like ancient Egyptians. They seemed to feel boundless admiration and devotion for their valiant and daring captain who flouted danger, laws, and governments, and brought off the most spectacular naval operations.

Raymond dreamed of owning a boat so that he could cruise down to the Southern Islands. But he soon realized that Monfreid had other plans. What he was really looking for was someone willing to finance the building of a ship that would travel further than his *boutres* for his contraband operations. We decided that it would be wiser to leave this project in abeyance; it also occurred to us that spending several days in a narrow boat might not, after all, be so very pleasant. The pirate took us back to Djibouti, which gave us a chance to admire that ridiculous little provincial French city with its zinc palm trees. It had not rained for two years. We sailed back to Marseilles on the first available steamer.

Monfreid was the incarnation of the type of gentleman-privateer one usually only reads about in novels. He was a cultivated and extremely distinguished man, cruel yet capable of great compassion. He truly loved the Eritreans and considered them his own people, but he hated the Ethiopians who had always tried to oppress and destroy them. This is why, at the time of the Italian conquest of Ethiopia, he was willing to serve as guide to the Italian Army, an action that caused him many problems later on. Heroes and traitors are made according to the vagaries of war. Monfreid nevertheless remained a great hero in the hearts of the Eritreans, most of whom were wiped out by the savage Ethiopian Army.

PARIS—CALCUTTA

In 1935, Raymond decided that we should travel to India by car. Since no such thing had ever been done before, we were persuaded to take along a journalist. We finally chose Jacques Duflos, a reporter for *Candide* and the son of the actress Huguette Duflos. He was a pleasant, decent fellow and a girl-chaser, somewhat lacking in energy and purpose and completely unaware of what such a trip entailed. When Raymond realized how little character he had, he nicknamed him "the Widow." We dragged our groaning "Widow" all the way to India, which turned out to be a complete waste of time because "she" never published a word about our adventure.

Since we were not interested in driving through Eastern Europe, we went to Marseilles and, on April 7th, sailed for Beirut with our Ford rumble-seat roadster. The car had been equipped with extra reservoirs for gasoline. When we arrived in Lebanon, we went to visit an uncle of Raymond's who worked for the League of Nations and looked after Assyro-Chaldean refugees who, like the Kurds, had lost their country after the arbitrary division of the Ottoman Empire. We were received with open arms but remained only a short time in Lebanon, the period between the spring thaws and the beginning of the hot season being the only possible time we could travel through certain regions.

So we gaily set forth across the Syrian Desert, which was all covered with spring flowers. First we visited Damascus and its marvelous mosque, where the floors were piled with many thicknesses of rare and precious rugs. Then we saw Palmyra and its famous Hellenistic ruins. The Comtesse d'Andurain, a very curious woman whose extravagant romances and adventures filled the local columns, reigned over the city, where she kept a hotel. People said that she danced naked among the ruins at night. She was still beautiful and always happy to bring comfort to lonesome travellers. It was also rumored that she played a political role.

From here on there were no roads, so we had to follow a vague trail to reach Baghdad, a gloomy, yellowish city built on the banks of a muddy river. Nothing remotely suggested the poetic splendor of the city of the caliphs. From there, in order to reach Kermanshah, in Iran, we had to travel through steep mountain passes, where the snows had just recently melted. In Iran, a rough road led to Hamadan, then Teheran.

Teheran in those days was a small city surrounded by walls, beyond which lay the recently-built palace, several walled-in embassies that looked like fortresses, and a few villas. There was only one hotel in the city, built by Reza Shah, who ruled Iran at the time. The hotel was very pleasant with its large, carpet-covered rooms, its blue-tiled bathrooms and seatless lavatories, and its finely-worked red copper ewers which were used for various hygienic purposes. The enormous modern city that extends all the way to the northern mountains did not yet exist. Iran was a poor country then, rugs being its principal industry; but, as is so often the case in the so-called underdeveloped nations, the people seemed fairly happy. The bazaars were very animated, bursting with hand-crafted objects, rugs, copper, and pottery. After a few days, we left for the sacred city of Meshed. The journey was not particularly interesting. When we arrived in Meshed, a group of Persian inspection officers, who kept watch over the pilgrims, gave us a very warm welcome. They tried, quite unsuccessfully, to entice us with very attractive fifteen or sixteen-year-old girl prostitutes. They also introduced us to a young French official who seemed very nervous and edgy.

On a sight-seeing tour to the border, as our Persian inspector friends gleefully told us, this unfortunate man and his wife had been carried off by a group of Afghans, who had shared the booty according to their tastes. The wretched couple was repeatedly raped, then, bewildered and throbbing with pain, finally set free. They were not yet over the shock and had requested a transfer, though they hardly dared give too many details of their misfortune to the ministry.

From Meshed we drove southward to Zahedan. The road, little more than a rocky path, was so rough that the car broke a spring. Raymond, always ready for any emergency, had brought along an extra spring and spent several hours wallowing in car grease in his attempts to replace it. No mechanic of any kind could be found anywhere in the area. The people stood around and watched us work with great curiosity.

After Zahedan we set off on a real adventure: the crossing of the Baluchistan Desert, which no one had attempted for many years. Fortunately there was an abandoned railroad track which years before had connected Zahedan and Quetta. All we had to do was drive along it. We stocked up on gasoline tanks, drinking water, and water for the car, and set off across the rocky and mountainous desert—five hundred miles of rocks and sand without a path or hint of an oasis. The car got stuck in the sand several times and slid into ravines. We had quite a bit of trouble getting it out. "The Widow" was completely useless and spent "her" time groaning and whimpering.

A few hundred miles or so before reaching Quetta, we finally saw some human beings—a group of Baluchi warriors armed to the teeth. One of them spoke a few words of English: "Where do you come from?" "Persia." "You crossed the desert?" "Yes." "Really?" Had we told them that we came directly from Allah's Paradise, they would hardly have been more surprised. "We're very tired. Is it possible to find something to eat and a place to sleep?" "I shall take you to our chief." They led us to a tiny village hidden among the rocks. A very handsome black-bearded Moslem, surrounded by armed guards, was sitting on a rug. He spoke English quite well: "Where do you come from?" "From Paris." "From France! And you have crossed the desert in that little car?" "Yes." "Well, you are certainly very brave!" "Can we have something to eat and a place to sleep?" "Please be my guests." The chief gave us a very good meal of roast mutton with a sort of pancake, as well as several thick rugs to sleep on.

The next morning we asked to see the chief so that we could thank him. He greeted us with courtesy and told me: "If you are satisfied with our hospitality, I should like to ask you a favor: please write a short note saying that you have been well treated." I was quite surprised: "Of course, it's the least I can do." I carefully wrote out a certificate of good treatment, after which we took our leave. A group of warriors accompanied us a short distance, then turned back. After travelling thirty miles, we were greeted by a detachment of British soldiers spread out across the desert, barring our way. They fired several warning shots. We stopped and I climbed out of the car. A British officer approached us, holding a pistol: "Where do you come from?" "From Paris." "From Paris! Are you mad? You mean to say that you crossed the desert in this little car?" "Yes, we did." "And did you meet anyone?" "No. Only a group of Moslems whose chief was very nice to us and gave us shelter for the night." "Ah! And what did this chief look like?" "He was about thirty-five, with a black beard and lots of soldiers around him." "Very nice indeed! This man is a notorious bandit. Only the day before yesterday he raided two buses and killed eighty-four people. The entire army has been mobilized to capture him."

We were allowed to continue on our way. I never found out what happened to the famous bandit, but have always hoped that he managed to escape the British Army. Soon afterward we reached Quetta, a delightful winter resort for high government officials, and found rooms in one of those wonderful old one-story colonial hotels with large verandahs surrounded by bougainvillea. We had to wear ties for dinner.

"The Widow" and I made up our minds to spend several days in this restful oasis, but it was not to be. Very early the next morning, Raymond, who often had strange premonitions, roused us from our sleep. He had been awakened by a nightmare and felt that we were in serious danger. He insisted that we leave immediately, so, feeling rather ill-humored, we reluctantly left our paradise. The next day, the entire city of Quetta was destroyed by an earthquake so calamitous that it has gone down in history. There were no survivors in the hotel.

It was the month of May. A narrow road wound down the Quetta Plateau, which drops sharply into the Indus Valley. As we descended, the heat grew more and more fierce. We had to find rafts to cross the Indus, then the Chenab. The English had built a vast railway network and took very little care of the roads in order to avoid competition for their trains. The magnificent ancient roadways built by the Moghul Empire had been abandoned, and all the bridges had collapsed. During our trip to Multan, then Delhi, the heat was so fierce that we were half dazed. It was impossible to touch a metal object without burning our hands; we needed to use rags to open the car doors. In Delhi we went to a hotel in the old city where the verandahs were cooled off by sweet-smelling grass hangings sprayed constantly with water; this grass is used to extract a perfume called patchouli, which our grandmothers used to love to wear. "The Widow," grown worn and thin and quite dismayed at having allowed "herself" to be dragged into such adventures, decided to run away, took the train to Bombay, and boarded the first ship headed for France and the adventurous Parisian *bistrot* life. We never saw "her" again.

From Delhi we trotted on to Benares, then Calcutta, and finally reached our paradise in Shantiniketan. This time we remained several months, except for a few sightseeing trips to the great medieval temples of Konarak and Bhuvaneshvar. Christine, who had just arrived, accompanied us.

Finally we went to Bombay, loaded our car on an Italian ship, and returned to France via Genoa.

Around the World

In 1936 we decided to accept Gayelord Hauser's invitation, which gave us a chance to visit America on our way to India. Pierre Gaxotte arranged for me to write a story about our trip for a weekly review that was willing to publish it in installments, along with some of my drawings. We left Cherbourg on a magnificent German ship. Gayelord Hauser and his friend and associate Frey Brown were waiting for us in New York. After we had been there a few days, they asked Raymond, who was an excellent driver, to take their brand-new orange-brown luxury De Soto to California.

So we set off on our long motor trip, making a detour through the Middle West. We visited the Grand Canyon, the prehistoric sites of New Mexico, several Texas nightclubs which seemed lifted out of an American western, and an Indian festival in Flagstaff, Arizona. After arriving in Los Angeles without any problem, we spent some time in Gayelord's house in Beverly Hills and also visited San Francisco. We ordered a trailer at the Hollywood Trailer Company and had it sent to India. Gayelord owned a very good piano which no one had ever played; a plump, very maternal black maid would go into raptures listening to me play. When we finally left, we gave the black servants generous tips, which was apparently not customary, and they covered us with their blessings.

Later, in Italy, I occasionally saw Gayelord, who had bought a property in Taormina. A few years before I first met him, he had been romantically involved with Greta Garbo, but they were both too independent to live together as a couple. Gayelord, the champion of health food and the "natural life," was the favorite doctor of all the Hollywood stars. He gave parties everywhere he went and would appear very elegantly dressed in a white suit against a background of flowers and vegetables, with garlands of onions and orchids strung over borders of carrots and Jerusalem artichokes.

Gayelord and Frey came to see me several times in Zagarolo. One day I received a call from Gayelord: Frey had just died. In spite of all his glory and fortune, the celebrated health food king felt completely alone.

Then we sailed off on an American ship to Honolulu, the Philippines, then Japan. In those days, colored people were not allowed on the upper decks. Chinese businessmen, who had to travel in steerage, would play million-dollar poker games in stifling little cubby-holes, while modest American secretaries walked around in the sunshine with their noses in the air. One easily forgets the degree of racial prejudice that existed in the United States only a few years ago and still exists today.

I wrote an outraged article about Honolulu, its beaches, hotels, and military bases, and the appalling vulgarity and indecency of its invaders, who prance around in their flower garlands doing wahine dances, aping a conquered and annihilated people. This burlesque comedy, played over the graves of their victims, is even more revolting than the genocide itself.

In the Philippines the Spanish have put on a similar show,

modified by the American influence; here, at least, the natives are still visible, though they were deprived of their culture by Christian missionaries long ago. Nevertheless, the Philippines seemed a very cheerful country with its gaily painted carts and its pleasantly corrupted people.

Japan was a revelation. It was still quite isolated at the time and there were very few tourists. If, when travelling at full speed by railroad, one happened to meet the imperial train coming from the opposite direction, all the curtains were carefully drawn lest unworthy eyes should fall upon the sacred figure of the Emperor. Schedules were so rigorously kept that one frequently missed one's train; the train engineer committed suicide if he was two minutes late. We made a number of friends and were invited to Japanese homes. We visited Kyoto, Nara, and Nikko, with its Buddhist monasteries perched on the mountaintops or lost in the woods. We also went cormorant fishing on the lakes of the interior.

I have returned many times to Japan, which still remains a pleasant and welcoming country if one is willing to adapt to the Japanese way of life. The art of travelling consists in abandoning one's habits as well as any feeling of nationalism or superiority. One must carefully observe customs and manners. It is not enough to put on an act, bowing pretentiously in the Japanese or Indian style, ill-humoredly removing one's shoes, or sitting on the floor with obvious discomfort. These things have to be felt so that they immediately become second nature. Many years later, I was invited by a noble Japanese to view his collection of rare objects. I had brought along the mother of a famous Italian publisher, a man who ended rather badly. While the guests were examining the collection, a servant brought out a rare Scythian dagger of chiseled gold on a velvet-lined tray. Giannalisa Feltrinelli, my companion, immediately pounced on the treasure. Unable to stop myself, I rather brutally prevented her from touching it. Our host smiled without saying a word, but when I went back to see him, he offered me a very beautiful object, never mentioning the incident.

During one of my visits, a Japanese friend of mine, who was

a doctor, took me to a very special kind of brothel usually closed to foreigners, where young boys, for a fee, were offered to the guests. The atmosphere was extremely sophisticated: after drinking tea and listening to *samisen* music, one slipped away with a companion for a few moments of subtle pleasure on conveniently secluded *tatamis*. When Pierre Landy, the French chargé d'affaires who had introduced me to the Japanese doctor, heard about it, he was quite indignant. "I have been living here for two years," he said, "and never once did you escort me to one of those charming places. Alain has only been here two weeks, and you have already taken him!" The Japanese doctor raised his eyes heavenward and said: "What can I do? With boys, Pierre does not understand the poetry."

Then we went to China, the wonderful decadent China that existed before the Japanese invasion and all the calamities that followed. Shanghai had the most luxurious hotels in the world, with suites decorated in red and gold lacquer. In the corridors, which smelled pleasantly of opium, one often met Chinamen wearing luxuriously embroidered robes. Vast entertainment palaces offered several Chinese plays at the same time; there were also circuses, theater cafés, restaurants, and dancers. After paying an admission fee, one could go about wherever one wished, just like in Copenhagen's Tivoli Gardens. In Shanghai I saw the famous actor Mei Lanfang, who was already quite old and only played the roles of young girls. Then we went to Peking, the capital of Chinese civilization. The Forbidden City was no longer forbidden. The palaces, made of rare and precious wood, were all crumbling, the pink lotus pools filled with weeds; the marble ship built by the last Empress rose bleakly over murky waters. It was said that the Empress had been asked by the government to create a war flotilla. She agreed and, two years later, called her ministers before her; then, pointing to the marble ship, she announced: "This is the Chinese flotilla."

The Temple of Heaven was now deserted, and no one came to visit its sacred ground. The terraces on which the Emperor had once stood alone with his gods, drawing heavenly inspiration, were covered with bird droppings; patches of grass grew between the paving stones. Raymond took a series of magnificent photographs of Peking, which have never been shown.

For a few dollars, I bought a small bronze Han Dynasty horse, which was obviously stolen, and a teapot belonging to a rickshaw driver who claimed that it came from his ancestors and kept it hidden under the seat.

In Peking the brothels, called "family houses," were not frequented by Europeans, who never moved from their "concessions"; this was a pity, for they were certainly well worth a visit. So-called families received guests in their pretty Chinese houses, where one could choose between father, mother, uncles, sisters-in-law, daughters, and sons of all ages. If one appeared to hesitate, the master of the house, a vigorous Chinaman in his thirties, would ask: "Would you like me to try one of them out in front of you?"

In spite of the beauty of China and the refinement of its culture, I never had any desire to live there. Raymond felt the same way. "China is beautiful," he wrote. "It has everything, and yet I feel bored. Here one can buy first-rate cherubs for anything between ten and thirty dollars, depending on their age—and in inverse proportion, of course."

I have never gone back to China. To all appearances, the fabulous China of the past no longer exists, but I am convinced that it is secretly hidden somewhere and will rise again one day from its ashes.

The bronze horse left us in the same way it had appeared. I showed it to an expert, who said: "It's a fake, of course. You don't really think dealers would allow such a rare object to remain on the market, do you?" So I wrapped the horse rather carelessly, and one of its legs got broken. When I arrived in Paris, I took the broken pieces to an expert, who cried: "But it is absolutely authentic!" The horse finally found a home in Zagarolo, where we placed it in a prettily carved wood niche. When Raymond died, his Italian heir Franco decided to sell it. He found a willing buyer who came to the house, offered a great deal of money for the horse, and took it with him . . . leaving a bad check.

In Peking and Shanghai, carefully decorated Chinese restaurants—the kind one sees all over the world—were only patronized by foreign diplomats. Chinese gourmets went to very different establishments. These restaurants, located on dirty little lanes in densely populated, rather sordid areas, were smoke-filled dens, very rustic and incredibly filthy. Fine cooking does not thrive in an antiseptic atmosphere. Customers sat on small benches and were served at wooden tables, with tubs placed underneath for food scraps. People ate voraciously, disgustingly, as though partaking in some kind of sensual orgy. Only in these gastronomic temples could one find the sort of delicacies that are considered the most refined in Chinese cooking. I saw people eating fried cockroaches and hundred-year-old rotten eggs. Tiny monkeys were brought to the table live, and the top of their skulls chopped off with a small hatchet right in front of the customer, who immediately plunged his spoon into the succulent, still vibrant brains. The most delicious turtle soup was made by securing the animal's head outside the cooking pot and keeping it alive by means of a steady stream of cold water, while the body slowly dissolved in the boiling brew. Not even the French, who certainly love good food, can approach the level of perverse, profoundly sensual delight of the Chinese, for whom the experience of eating is almost sado-masochistic in its intensity. I am told that these temples of gastronomic art no longer exist.

After a brief visit to Singapore we joyfully returned to Shantiniketan, where the poet welcomed us with open arms and offered us a pretty house under the palm trees.

Raymond, always a lover of reptiles, caught and tamed an emerald-green snake, which lived in the Virginia creeper that covered the house. The snake got into the habit of slithering down the roof onto the electric wire of a lamp that hung right above our table, then would drink milk while we had our breakfast. After we left the house, we were replaced by new guests. Our sociable little snake decided to come down as usual and keep them company, but far from appreciating this mark of courtesy, the guests were frightened and ran away.

CHAPTER EIGHT

Life in India

REWA KOTHI

One day in 1937, during an extended visit to Benares just before returning to Europe, we went for a walk on the *ghats*, those gigantic staircases that lead down to the Ganges, with a young Brahman guide called Prianâth. As we were admiring the magnificent marble-balconied palaces that nobly dominate the Ganges, Raymond exclaimed: "Wouldn't it be fantastic to live in one of those palaces?" "You might like to rent this one," suggested Prianâth, as he pointed to one of the more grandiose structures. "It's not very expensive." After making inquiries, Raymond decided to rent the palace, which belonged to the Maharajah of Rewa—a small state in Central India—and only cost one hundred rupees (about $100) a month. "Even if we only come here from time to time," reasoned Raymond, "it will still be better than living at Clark's Hotel." This very mediocre hotel was located in the only "proper" part of Benares, the hideous British military section right outside the city. Little did we know that we would be living in the palace for fifteen years. In March 1939, I registered as a permanent resident of India at the Calcutta consulate.

Rewa Kothi was a huge house. It could be reached by a small lane which was much too narrow for cars, so that we had to leave them in an empty lot not far from our property. The monumental entranceway opened out into a vast cloister whose colonnade supported a circular balcony. In the back was

· 124 ·

a small sanctuary dedicated to the god Shiva. We hired a Brahman friend of Prianâth's to perform the daily ritual ceremony, called *puja*.

Between the cloister and the main part of the building overlooking the Ganges, one had to pass through another large entryway flanked by two small, windowless rooms, one of which Raymond used as a photographic laboratory. A colonnaded passageway led through a dark gallery which became our library. Finally one reached a huge hall, about eighty feet long, with sixteen-foot ceilings; an open-work marble loggia looked out upon the Ganges. In two of the corners within the towers were small round rooms which we used as studies; Raymond took possession of the left tower and I the right. On the second floor was a long hall overlooking the court; we turned it into a dining room. On the third floor were three bedrooms with windows facing in two directions, the Ganges on one side, the cloister on the other. Along the courtyard and across from the main entranceway were two floors of kitchens and outbuildings. Behind the temple, in the back, a zigzagging corridor led to the ancient harem, made up of several darkish rooms overlooking an attractive little courtyard shaped in a square. A large colonnaded hall supported the inner balconies, which could be used as bedrooms. Under the main building were several huge halls facing the Ganges, which were flooded each year after the spring thaws. Under the harem we discovered a secret cave, an ancient treasure vault where jewels had once been kept; it could be reached by sliding a wall panel in the back of a closet and moving a stone slab. We also found a very cool cellar where we sought refuge during the hottest weather.

The terraces dominated the river as well as the entire city; we could also see the countryside, for we lived in the first of the large palaces built above Benares. Large stone staircases led down to the Ganges, whose waters were very clear.

We covered our stone floors with thick woven Indian carpets called *daris* and spread cushions and small rugs over them. After a while, I designed a few pieces of furniture and had them built and carved by a local cabinet maker; this created a problem with Raymond, who hated to burden himself with objects. I also discovered frescoes by removing the whitewash from some of the walls, and had new ones made by local artisans, who copied them from ancient paintings. This experiment proved quite interesting. The painters, who normally decorated houses or large earthenware jars for carrying wedding gifts, always worked in pairs. One of them painted while the other described the picture that was to be copied: "On the left side there is a tree, a young girl is sitting on a branch, a gazelle is nibbling on the grass, there are flowers all around, etc." The result was quite charming. We had to install bathrooms and lavatories; Indians usually bathe in the courtyard, squatting under the water tap. The house was quite huge, with innumerable passageways and staircases; there were eight different ways to go from my room to the main harem, where I often invited musicians to play their instruments.

From the windows one could see vast crowds taking their baths in the river. Priests sitting under rattan parasols would mark the foreheads of the faithful with sandalwood paste and red powder before pronouncing the sacred words that made the pilgrimage official. One could also see yogis in prayer and boatmen who transported pilgrims and other travellers. A saintly man called Hari-Hara-Baba lived on a boat where he received his numerous visitors completely naked. Twice a day his vigorous disciples would row him to the opposite side of the Ganges, for he had made a vow never to soil the sacred river bank with human excrement. During the flood season, with the rain pouring down, the Ganges was an extraordinary sight: the river was then one and a half miles wide, with currents reaching speeds of eight miles an hour. The old saint would sit imperturbably at the stern while his disheveled disciples struggled at the oars against wind, rain, and storm.

Sometimes wandering monks would ask us permission to stay in the lower rooms of the palace, directly facing the Ganges. They usually remained a few days, meditating. One of them, a young man from the south, stayed nearly two months. We used to take flowers to him for his *puja*; he would go out and beg for his food. One day he came to me and said: "I am too attached to wordly goods. I give you all that I possess."

He offered me a colored image representing a god and a copper chandelier shaped like an AUM, the sacred syllable. Then he put his blanket on the floor, dropped the saffron-colored piece of cloth that was his only clothing, and left completely naked towards his spiritual destiny. We never saw him again.

At night, groups of folk musicians would sit on the river bank and spend hours singing those wonderful mystical poems that are the glory of Hindi literature. The atmosphere they created was incredibly poetic.

In maharajahs' palaces, comforts and luxuries were generally somewhat erratic, guest houses were ultramodern, and problems of etiquette made life rather difficult. In Bombay, Delhi, and Calcutta, most people—except the very poor—lived in modern houses with English furnishings. It was almost impossible to visit an ancient palace decorated in pure Indian style yet at the same time sufficiently comfortable. There was no other livable palace near the Ganges besides our own, so it soon became quite famous. Travellers of distinction, foreign ambassadors, and members of the Viceroy's circle all came to stay with us. Later, when Nehru became prime minister, he often asked us to receive his most important visitors, saying that our house was one of the few places that could give foreigners an idea of India's true beauty.

The magnificent palaces of Benares had all been built by maharajahs when they came with their courtiers on religious pilgrimages—sometimes to die, but often for entertainment, Benares being a city of many pleasures, famous for its dancers, musicians, and courtesans. Great feasts were sometimes given on boats. But little by little, as British puritanism grew prevalent and royal families were destroyed, this ancient capital of pleasure and death fell into decay and most of the palaces were abandoned. Nevertheless, a few families noted for their famous musicians and wonderful singers were still living in the city.

Rewa Kothi had not been lived in for many years. It was sometimes rented out for weddings, but no one wanted to live there, for it was known to be haunted. People said that a disciple had killed his master in the palace, then committed suicide. No one warned us about the ghost, but we soon became aware of his presence. When Raymond and I first started hearing sighs and sounds of laughter coming from the galleries, we thought we were playing tricks on each other, but soon realized that there was no one there. Little by little we grew accustomed to the ghost and spoke very politely to him when he manifested his presence. Our servants, however, refused to sleep in the house. The ghost normally lived in the back part of the palace, in the ancient harem where we had arranged a few rooms for our guests. The stories we heard from them were always the same. In the middle of the night, they would hear the sound of a door being opened from the underground gallery beneath them. Someone would then climb up the stairs and wander around the terrace on the second floor, talking to himself the whole time. Finally he would go on to the main building, return, and calmly go back down the stairs. One day at breakfast, Madame Wadia, president of the Indian PEN Club, who was staying with us for a few days, asked us in an embarrassed voice: "Is one of you by any chance a sleepwalker?" "No." "I really don't know what else it can be. The person who walks near my room at night speaks French!" This is how we found out that our sharp-eared ghost had learned to speak our language. I wonder if he ever found this useful in the world of shadows.

The ghost did not remain our sole companion for very long and was soon joined by several animals, to Raymond's great delight: "Our house is perfect. At last I have a new pet, a thirty-inch lizard called Ashoka. He runs freely around the courtyard, in the company of a wild goose. We also have a regular aviary, with a cockatoo called 'Aurore,' a mynah called 'Epoch,' and many other wonderful birds." (Benares, 29 April 1940)

Raymond, who loved reptiles, once owned a python that ended up biting his eye; we had to give him away to a snake charmer. The giant lizard was the kind frequently used by thieves. They tie a light rope around its body and make it climb up a wall. As soon as the lizard finds a crevice, the rope is pulled and the animal locks into position, enabling the thief to climb the wall, his whole weight supported by the lizard.

We also had a pair of martens, which had been brought to us

quite young from the Himalayas and spent all their time running around the palace cloister. These animals are very gay and lively and tend to hunt in pairs; one of them hides while the other chases birds into the corner where his partner lies in wait. At first, the martens were quite wild and did not allow us to approach them, but they were tamed by a fearless little monkey who slapped them, climbed on their backs, pulled their ears, and told them to behave themselves and let me caress them. This monkey was carniverous, which is quite unusual: he would proudly brandish a chicken thigh, looking very much like a miniature caveman. For a while we also had a mongoose living in the house. These animals are very affectionate and amusing, but are in the bad habit of sliding underneath tableclothes so that all the dishes and glasses come crashing to the ground, a little game they find extremely amusing. With the most wonderful display of courage, our mongoose, though quite small, once killed a cobra that had slithered into the house. Our most beautiful pets were two gray cranes with bright red cheeks which Raymond had caught in the Rajputana Desert when they were still chicks—a very dangerous feat, for cranes are very large birds with beaks as sharp as daggers. The cranes grew quite splendid and lived for a long time in the palace's inner garden. They would perform their magnificent dances before us and would come and nibble on my eyebrows to show their affection. They often disappeared for hours to fly around the Ganges, but obediently came home in the evening. Once, however, when Raymond and I stayed away too long, the cranes flew away and never came back. Animals do not like servants.

Alice, who had just abandoned Uday Shankar, lived three hundred yards away from the palace of Rewa. She had adopted a gray langur, a handsome, black-faced monkey. As the monkey grew, it began to smell foul and took up more and more space, so Alice finally decided to get rid of him. She took the langur to the opposite bank of the Ganges and abandoned him there. A few weeks later the monkey, who had probably hidden in a boat at night, reappeared. He never went back to Alice, whose betrayal had wounded him deeply, but often came to see me, for he knew me well. He had struck up a friendship with a male monkey of the same breed. When he came to see me, he would enter the house quite fearlessly, allow me to pet him, and ask for a few bananas. His friend would wait for him outside and, as soon as he came out of the house, would punish him severely for maintaining this shameful relationship with the world of men. The poor, terrified monkey visited the house less and less often and finally ceased coming altogether. From time to time I would see him sitting mournfully on the edge of the terrace, looking from afar at the happy world of his childhood, a world now closed to him forever.

We also had a cow, which was lovingly looked after by Raymond's Brahman friend Murlidhar. Bovines are very intelligent and affectionate animals. When the cow gave birth to a pretty little bull, we had a great feast; we painted her horns gold and covered her with flower garlands, which made her very proud. But when the Maharajah of Vizianagram presented me with a doe, there was a terrible scene. The cow was very jealous and flew into a great rage. She went after the doe in hot pursuit, climbing narrow staircases, crashing through doors, destroying everything on her path, and nearly breaking a leg. It took us a long time to calm her down; we had to send away the doe and offer the cow many gracious apologies before she would deign to forgive us.

Prianâth remained with us for several years, acting as a kind of secretary; because he was a Brahman, however, he was not allowed to perform menial tasks. When we first moved to Benares, a young man, who appeared to be Nepalese, offered us his services as a cook. We hired him, and he became a loyal companion, sharing in all our adventures. He was brave, efficient, and scrupulously honest. His name was Gulab Singh. Singh is the name of a warrior caste whose members are not supposed to be employed as servants. Gulab was a wonderful worker and a miracle of resourcefulness, particularly during our difficult trips in the trailer. Whenever we had to cross a shaky bridge or a dangerous river ford, he always insisted on trying it out first and would simply say: "If I die, you will take care of my children. If you die, what will become of us all?"

One day, the dowager queen of a great family of maharajahs came to our house for tea. Gulab brought out the trays, the teapots, and the cakes; then, just as he was about to serve us, he prostrated himself before the queen and touched her feet. She expressed the greatest astonishment, blessed him, kissed him, and cried: "Gulab! It's you! How happy I am to see you!"

Gulab, in fact, was her grandson. One of her daughters had had an affair with a palace guard. As a result, she was rejected by her caste—not banished, but completely ignored from that time on by her family; she was forced to live in a corner of the palace as a mere soldier's wife. No one paid any attention to her children, who became part of an anonymous crowd of servants and spent their time climbing trees and scrounging around for food. The old queen could not help being charmed by these little savages and, from time to time, would offer them small gifts in secret. She was very happy to know that Gulab was well employed, able to live independently and with dignity, even though he was a servant.

Later, when Gulab became gravely ill, a stupid nurse gave him an injection in the sciatic nerve, which left him with a slight paralysis in his leg. When we moved from Benares, Raymond bought him a little shop.

We had another faithful servant and friend called Ramprasad, known to everyone as Mamma (uncle) because one of his nephews was always running after him and calling him by that name. Mamma belonged to the boatman caste. He was very well built and treated his body like a precious object, keeping it fit through wrestling, exercise, and massages. In the small world that lived on the banks of the Ganges he enjoyed great prestige, which he bore with all the self-confidence of a youth conscious of his strength and beauty.

I originally hired Mamma as an oarsman, having bought a small boat to take me to my daily music lessons. But little by little he began to take charge of the household. He joined us on all our travels and, after I left Benares, followed me to Madras, then Pondicherry.

Mamma was an extremely elegant youth, always wearing a *dhoti** of dazzling whiteness and without the slightest crease,

---

*A *dhoti* is a long strip of white cotton fastened at the waist and beautifully draped around the lower part of the body. Some *dhotis* are spun and woven by hand with threads of gold, and are very expensive.

for he changed it several times a day. He became a member, later the president of the Panchayat of his caste. The Panchyat, or "Council of Five," is a Hindu institution that arbitrates all the internal problems of the group without having to refer to the legal authorities; it settles all questions of adultery, divorce, compensation, inheritance, petty larceny, and property dispute. Everyone is judged by his peers, which is essential, since each caste has a different set of rules and prohibitions. Boatmen belong to one of the lowest castes, the so-called untouchables; yet Mamma was very proud of his caste and would have burst out laughing if anyone had offered to turn him into a trader, a warrior, or a Brahman. The pride of the supposed lower castes is one of the elements of Hindu society that foreigners have never been able to understand.

In India, it is customary for the younger members of a family to help their elders free of charge. As a result, Gulab's young brother Kamal and Mamma's nephew Babunandan soon appeared at Rewa Khoti, made themselves useful in various ways, gradually became indispensable, and were eventually hired as official members of the household. Several other servants worked for us, but never became part of the "family."

The names of these people were quite colorful: Gulab means "Rose," and Kamal, "Lotus"; Ramprasad is "the gift of Rama" and Babunandan, "the delight of his father."

Babunandan was a very beautiful child. One day he was taken ill, and the local doctor insisted on sending him to the hospital. He had smallpox. Smallpox is a horrible disease. The entire body is covered with greenish pustules; they are everywhere—the nose, the mouth, the eyes. Mamma came to us in a state of great distress and begged us to take the child out of the hospital. "If he stays," he said, "he will surely die." We finally decided to see for ourselves what was happening. The wretched boy was locked up in a cabin, lying on the ground on a bit of straw; water and a few *chapattis* were slipped in from the outside. "There is no cure for smallpox," said the doctor. "The important thing is to avoid contagion." Mamma wanted us to take the boy back to his house; we could not let him "die like a dog" in that sordid cabin. With his usual courage and decisiveness, Raymond, disobeying all the rules and exposing himself to a very real danger, broke down the cabin door, took the poor, festering body in his arms, carried the boy to the jeep, and drove him to the tiny mud house where Mamma lived with his wife and children.

Then the healing ritual began. For several long weeks the child's body was rubbed with a vegetable oil extracted from a plant called *shilmogra*; a special kind of incense filled the small room with acrid-smelling smoke, and the women chanted prayers from morning till night. The half-conscious child, intoxicated by the smoke, soothed by the constant sound of chanting, and frequently rubbed with the magic oil, ceased to sigh and moan and seemed no longer to suffer. Little by little the pustules began to form scars. Babunandan was cured. He remained terribly pockmarked but soon recovered his high spirits and his gaiety.

When I decided to leave India, I bought Mamma a shop; later, it passed into the hands of his nephew. With his usual panache, Babunandan has turned it into a lively teashop, well-known to the foreign students and vagabonds who crowd the sacred city today.

Kamal was fond of drawing; I enrolled him in the university's school of art. He is now one of the local painters.

The Discovery of the Hindu World

Benares is the heart of the Hindu world. It is a sacred and mysterious city, a sanctuary for great scholars, and a meeting place for wandering monks who pass on the traditions of a civilization many thousands of years old. Foreign occupation—first by the Moslems, then by the British—has created deep rifts in the society of India. Those who were forced to collaborate with the invaders, learn their language, and attend their schools and universities, still believe themselves to be Hindus, but in fact have only very vague notions of Indian science, philosophy, and cosmology. They have had to accept so many infractions to the rules of their society, so many moral and dietary compromises and absorbed so many points of view foreign to their own culture that they have completely cut themselves off from any real knowledge of their traditions. All the Indians who ever occupied official functions and university and administrative posts were English-speaking and British-educated, not only under British rule, but in the Indian administration that followed. Men like Nehru knew nothing about Hindu culture except through British authors.

Besides this anglicized group—the only one foreigners are likely to meet—there also exists a traditional world of writers, scholars, Brahmans, and monks, who are completely indifferent to modern trends of thought and preserve the traditional ideas, sciences, rites, and philosophic systems of ancient India. These two worlds have practically no contact; they speak different languages.

I soon discovered that I had nothing to learn from English-speaking Indians—not even from such well-known philosophers as Vivekananda, Radhakrishnan, Aurobindo, or Bhagawan Das. Tagore himself had learned Hindu philosophy through British authors and was very much opposed to the rigors of the traditional society.

It soon became clear that I had to learn Hindi and Sanskrit, so, with my usual tenacity, I set to work. For a long time, I read nothing besides these two languages. After I had learned to speak and write Hindi fairly well, Vijayanand Tripathi, one of the great scholars of Benares, was kind enough to answer many of the questions I had been asking myself about Hindu religion, philosophy, and society.

Vijayanand was a very remarkable man. Every evening, he taught on a raised platform in front of his house before a group of followers from many different castes. He had been the disciple of a famous yogi and, aside from his great learning and his knowledge of classical philosophy, rituals, and textual interpretation, he was also initiated into the deepest mysteries of tantric doctrine and yoga. In his public lectures, he explained the themes and hidden meanings of the famous Hindi version of the *Ramayana*, written by the great poet Tulsi Das.

It did not take me long to understand that this austere scholar had a completely open mind and could discuss not only such topics as human sacrifices, omophagia, and erotic rites, but also the origins of language, cosmology, and Indian theories on the nature of the world, the atom, time, and space.

Not being a Brahman, I could not live with a master or attend classes in a school. I was too old, in any case, to benefit from a type of education that devotes the first few years of study to pure memorization. It was possible for me to take private lessons, however. These lessons were given in the master's house, in a room that was separated from the family quarters. While he sat on a *chauki*, a kind of large, low table, the pupil remained seated on the floor and had to be very careful not to touch the master or any object belonging to him. The master also had to make sure that the pupil had taken his ritual bath in the Ganges and performed all the necessary acts of purification; he could then teach him anything he pleased, except the psalmody of the sacred *Veda* texts, which only figure in rituals.

For several years I read nothing but Hindu and Sanskrit, no book, newspaper, or article besides those I had to translate. I found this very difficult at first, but the discipline I imposed on myself allowed me to grow accustomed to another mode of thought, a different conception of life and the world.

In order to study Sanskrit and philosophy under a Hindu scholar and master, it was necessary to live and think exactly like a Hindu. I had to become a strict vegetarian, observe all the customs and taboos, and wear the spotless, elegant, and completely seamless *dhoti* and *chhaddar* (a silk shawl). Raymond never learned to speak Hindi very well, but he was interested in the rites and learned to perform the *puja*, a minutely detailed and very poetic ceremony which all Hindus must perform in their homes before the image of a god.

Vijayanand had two sons. The eldest, Brahmanand, was studying the ritual to become a Brahman priest, whose duties include the performing of sacramental rites, marriage and funeral ceremonies, and services in the temple. The younger son, whom people called Kouttour, was a very charming boy, cheerful and carefree; he was not in the least interested in metaphysical matters and was studying ayurvedic medicine.

Vijayanand assigned Brahmanand the task of teaching me *shastri*, the learned form of Hindi that is spoken by scholars and philosophers; I studied Sanskrit with other teachers. For several years, I was in daily contact with Brahmanand, a very strange and ugly young man who was mostly interested in the magical forms of tantrism. Sometimes he would appear wearing bracelets, necklace, and belt which were all made of iron, for it is considered a sacred metal by adepts of the malefic rites of the Goddess. Through him I became acquainted with some very arcane details of tantric rites, particularly those relating to the significance of the labyrinth and the predictions that can be read in the bowels of sacrificial victims; all of this I have mentioned in my book *Shiva and Dionysus*. I have always avoided anything having to do with magic practices, which frighten me, but, thanks to Brahmanand, I was able to learn certain secrets usually known only to initiates. Sometimes Brahmanand was quite frightening and seemed on the verge of some kind of ecstatic frenzy, but he was an excellent teacher and extremely well-versed in the esoteric and mystical language that sheds light on the hidden meaning of texts.

Little by little I entered into a mode of thinking so subtle, so complex, and so difficult that I sometimes felt myself reaching the limits of my mental faculties and capacity for understanding. I found myself immersed in a society whose conceptions of the nature of man and the divine, of morality, love, and wisdom were so different from those I had learned in childhood that I had to make a clean sweep of everything I believed I knew, all my habits, all my patterns of thought. This system of values could not have been more unfamiliar to me if I had suddenly found myself transported into Egypt during the reign of Ramses II.

Brahmanand taught me Hindu rites, customs, and proprieties: the ritual baths in the Ganges at sunrise, the dietary restrictions, the *puja* ceremonies, the acts of purification, the days of fasting. I had to grow a sacred lock of hair on the top of my head and gird my loins with the black sash of my lowly caste.

A man born outside of India is considered a *mleccha*, a barbarian who is assimilated with the lowest castes of artisans; he can never touch a Brahman or enter his house, nor can he recite the *Veda*. If he observes the proprieties and taboos, however, he is allowed to be instructed in the highest teachings of traditional philosophy and science. Many of the great Indian mystics, poets, painters, musicians, and sculptors who were honored by kings belonged to the castes of artisans that, as a result of some very stupid propaganda, people sometimes call "the untouchables."

"The untouchable" is in fact the Brahman who, being a priest, must observe the strictest rules of ritual purity; he cannot accept food from anyone outside his own family, nor can he touch anyone. One of the most typical characteristics of the European mentality is its ability to present everything backwards.

Swami Karpâtrî was a wandering monk—*a sannyasi*—and a man of astounding knowledge. He came to Benares from time to time and stayed there during the rainy season. He could only live in a temple or, if necessary, in the house of an unmarried Brahman who strictly observed the rules of everyday life, the acts of purification, and all the other rites of his caste.

Ganga Shankar Mishra, the librarian of the Hindu university, fitted these various requirements. He had built a house outside the city where *sannyasis* could accept his hospitality, and it was here that Swami Karpâtrî lived when he came to Benares. The learned swami was small and thin and wore nothing but a bit of saffron-colored cloth. He seemed frail and sensitive to the cold, travelled only on foot, yet covered great distances. He was considered the spiritual leader of a large part of northern India. Although he refused all honors, he selected the *shankarâchâryas*, the four monks who are the spiritual leaders of Hinduism. These monks can sometimes be seen at important ceremonies being carried about on magnificent golden palanquins with all the royal appurtenances, wearing nothing but a piece of rough, orange-colored cloth around their loins.

Vijayanand had spoken about me to Swami Karpâtrî, and I was allowed to attend his *darshana*. The *darshana* (vision) is a kind of reception where saints, yogis, or kings permit their followers to contemplate them in silence. Sometimes they remain quite still and motionless; at other times they converse with a small, chosen group on various topics relating to philosophy, dogma, or even current events.

I was allowed to go up to the terrace of the house. The swami was sitting on one of those low, wooden tables, covered with an immaculate sheet, that also serve as beds. A hundred of his followers were seated on the floor in four groups, depending on their rank.

According to form, I prostrated myself flat on the floor with my hands crossed at the proper distance away from the monk, then went to sit among my lowly peers. The master did not appear to see me. He said nothing to me, but that was not necessary, for he could read people's minds. He began to speak of things that were of very special interest to me. I found it extremely difficult to adjust to this phenomenon: being in the presence of someone who *knew* everything I thought, everything I was. With such a man one could not lie, there was not need for apologies or excuses. I went several times to the master's *darshana*. Later, when he created the Dharma Sangh, a movement for the defense of Hinduism against modern trends, we had many long conversations together.

The first effort of this new movement was a monthly journal called *Siddhanta* (Principles), which dealt with questions of traditional philosophy, theology, and rites. When I was introduced to Hindu mythology, it seemed like an incomprehensible jungle. I tried to grasp the significance of the different gods, their relationship to cosmological theories on the nature of the world. I asked the swami many questions, which he answered in writing in a series of articles published by *Siddhanta*. It was on the basis of these questions and articles that I later wrote my book *Hindu Polytheism*.

The enemy of the Dharma Sangh was not the British Empire, whose representatives never interfered with the rites and religion of the Hindus. What seemed far more dangerous to the traditionalists was the false Hinduism of anglicized Indians, who claimed to adapt traditional Hindu doctrines to Christian conceptions, considered more relevant to the realities of the modern age. The true war had to be waged against the so-called ashrams, which exploited people's gullibility, against theosophism, Aurobindo, Ramakrishna followers, but

especially against politicians. Gandhi seemed the very type of
the modern reformer, more Christian than Hindu, fighting
like Don Quixote against nonexistent problems such as the
caste system and the so-called "untouchables," which gener-
ated considerable publicity in his favor among British socialists
but did not really interest the Indian people.

After India became independent, Swami Karpâtrî created a
political movement, the Jana Sangh (people's assembly). Many
people belonging to what is called the lower castes joined this
movement, including my faithful boatman who, along with a
group of his fellowmen, was thrown into prison by Nehru's
government.

Swami Karpâtrî himself was sent to prison by Nehru. When
he arrived, the warden and the prison guards threw themselves flat on the ground to allow him to pass, then kissed the
marks of his footsteps.

When the political war waged by the Jana Sangh grew more
intense, Swami Karpâtrî advised me to return to Europe and
try to educate people on the basic principles of Hinduism;
being a foreigner, I could not take part in the political struggle
of India.

Following the tradition of non-information established by
the British, the Indian press—which was controlled by the
Congress—carefully avoided mention of the Jana Sangh. The
diplomats and foreign correspondents who lived in Delhi only
heard about it the day the party suddenly gained a majority in
the coalition that overthrew Indira Gandhi.

I wrote several articles for *Siddhanta* and translated into
Hindi a number of Western texts touching upon certain details
of history and doctrine that could be of interest to Hindu
traditionalists. I also translated into English a number of
Swami Karpâtrî's works on iconography, the symbolism of
temples, erotic sculpture, etc., which were published in Calcutta in the *Journal of the Indian Society of Oriental Art*.

Swami Karpâtrî ordered Brahmanand to perform my initiation rites as well as Raymond's. He and I, it seems, are the only
foreigners who were ever initiated and incorporated into orthodox Hinduism; no other foreign names besides ours appear

in the register of the Linga Râja (the great temple of Bhuvanesvar) which lists all the families that are permitted to worship the image of the god in this most holy of places.

The period preceding the initiation ritual is quite long, since it involves all kinds of preparations: fasting, acts of purification, and ritual baths. First, all one's hair is shaved off, except the eyelashes and eyebrows. A skillful barber begins by shaving the head, then all other hairy areas, even in the most hidden corners. After taking a bath in the sacred waters of the Ganges, the future initiate must perform certain *puja* rites (veneration of a god) and yoga exercises.

On the day favored by the stars, Brahmanand took me to an isolated spot in the forest near the Ganges, carrying flowers, fruit, holy water, offerings, as well as the ritual fire. It was here that the ceremony took place.

Shiva is the god of the universe, the ruler of all living things, trees and animals as well as men. In temples devoted to his worship he is represented as an erect phallus, source of all life, but also symbol of pleasure and sensuous delight, the earthly image of the state of godliness. Shiva is *Sat-Chit-Ananda*—Existence, Consciousness, and Bliss. Men build sanctuaries to honor him, but his true temple is nature, especially the forest, where he sometimes appears in the form of a naked, priapic adolescent. Shivaist initiation rites always take place in the forest, never in a temple. Here at last was the god I had vaguely sensed in my childhood and had secretly been searching for all my life.

Brahmanand made me sit on the ground, facing westward, while he sat across from me facing east. I then had to perform a *puja* for my initiator, worshipping him like a god with flowers, holy water, and an oil lamp lit by a flame we had brought with us, all the while pronouncing ritual formulas. Then Brahmanand, holding his hands over my head, spoke the words of initiation. He whispered into my ear the *mantra*, the sacred and secret formula I was to repeat all through my life, and revealed my secret name and the new name I was to be known by in the society of men. After this he performed a *puja* for the new initiate. From then on my new name would be Shiva Sharan (He who is protected by Shiva).

All this was very simple, like a kind of game, with no drama or apparent mystery. I passed from one state to another almost without knowing it; but little by little I realized that I was no longer quite the same, that life had a new basis, new purposes, goals, and duties—that I had finally become what I had been meant to be all along.

We walked back to the holy city and I went on living as before—outwardly, at any rate—studying, performing rites, making love, and going on long journeys in search of forgotten temples in the forests of central India and the deserts of the west.

The high priest of one of the principal temples of Benares was a very curious man. His position was hereditary and not the result of any real aptitude; he had been born a religious leader, a *mahant*.

He was a robust and athletic young man with no special interest in things of the intellect. His house was on the banks of the Ganges, quite close to ours, and he had built an open pavilion in the empty lot that separated our properties. Here, on a floor covered with fine sand, he practiced Indian wrestling, a rather brutal sport. In spite of his low caste, Mamma, my boatman, was part of his team.

Every day we would come to see these contests and watch the wrestlers' magnificent brown bodies, gleaming with oil. The vigorous masseurs on the Ganges' river bank also participated in the sport.

Like Brahmanand, the *mahant* was attracted by magic, but his aims were purely materialistic; although he was a pleasant, obliging man, his main goal was to acquire power, money, and dominance over men. Often, at night, we would assemble in the courtyard of the temple dedicated to the goddess Kâlî, after it was closed. The *mahant* and his companions would prepare and drink large quantities of *bhang*, a sacred potion made with Indian hemp. Some weakness in my constitution made it impossible for me to enjoy this drink, which made me quite ill. Otherwise, I found the atmosphere among these athletes quite entertaining. In one of the tales I wrote about India, I described the tragic end of the *mahant*, whose ventures into black magic finally turned against him, transforming him into a wild beast.

Bhang is made with fresh Indian hemp leaves, which are crushed against a rock and carefully washed to eliminate certain toxic elements that remain when hemp is used for smoking. A modest amount of this spinach-like substance, the size of a small hazelnut, is mixed with almond milk and sweetened water. The result is a drink that not only tastes very pleasant but is apparently quite harmless. *Bhang* can also be mixed with cakes and sweets. Proper Hindus never smoke hashish—only cab drivers and other people belonging to the most discredited classes. When it is drunk, *bhang* has no immediate effect. This is why, after enjoying it with a small group of friends—just like tea—one can usually go home, take a bath, dress up for the evening, and sit down to dinner. Only then does the drug begin to take effect: a strange sensation in the spine, a complete loss of the sense of time, a sharp intensification of all the perceptions, and heightened powers of analysis. If one is listening to music, for instance, it becomes possible to hear the separate parts played by each of the instruments, the double bass, the flute, the oboe, which normally cannot be distinguished from the ensemble.

These heightened perceptions are such that people begin to notice all the absurd and ridiculous peculiarities of their companions—the shapes of their noses or ears, their way of speaking—and are seized with an irresistible need to giggle; those who tend to be depressed, however, must be very careful with *bhang*, for it will probably make them dissolve into tears. Yogis often use it to facilitate meditation, mental concentration, and extra-sensory perception.

Sometimes Raymond would organize *bhang* parties for his foreign visitors, and they were always highly successful; Ramprasad, our boatman, prepared the potion very well. Cecil Beaton, the famous photographer, often spoke of his *bhang* party at Rewa Khoti as the most amusing evening in his life.

I have never been able to take drugs. A pipeful of opium makes me feel ill for several days. For this reason I was always very careful to take the smallest possible amount of *bhang*. One day Ramprasad decided to play a trick on me and gave me a larger dose than usual. I soon fell into a half faint, a peculiar hallucinatory state. I went off into a wonderful world filled with strange and sublime forms and was encircled with multi-colored streamers of light different from anything I had ever seen. I was carried to my bed. Raymond grew quite worried and sent for a woman doctor who lived in the neighborhood. I heard her say: "If you wish, I can give him an injection for his heart." It was impossible for me to move. I could hear and feel everything, and yet I was elsewhere. I thought: "I am dead, I have almost reached Paradise, and those idiots want to give me an injection."

In fact, no one has ever died of an overdose of *bhang*: it is a perfectly harmless and non-addictive drug. After taking it, one usually feels in a wonderful mood for the rest of the week, with a very optimistic outlook on the world. It is quite absurd to say that *bhang* leads to other drugs; apart from being illegal, they have nothing else in common. It is said that *bhang*-induced visions are similar to those experienced at the moment of death, in that intermediate state where one is already in the other world yet still connected to earth. This "small death" gives us a foretaste of the splendors and joys of the afterlife. This is why *bhang* is considered the sacred potion of Shiva, the god of sensuous delight and death.

THE TRADITIONAL EDUCATION

On the outskirts of Benares, the British administration had founded a school of Sanskrit where Indian civilization was taught according to Western methods. This school was never very successful because great Hindu scholars are not allowed to "sell" their knowledge, therefore cannot receive a fixed salary or teach just anyone.

The powerful Indian industrialists who supported Gandhi's nationalist movement raised large sums of money to create a university. It was not, as people claimed, a genuine Hindu university but a national school, neither British nor Moslem, modeled on its Western counterparts. This university met with the same problem as the British school of Sanskrit. The only successful departments were in the traditional sciences such as ayurvedic medicine and music; the people who taught these subjects did not have to be Brahmans—did not, at any rate, have to lecture on the sacred texts—so they were not restricted by any taboos.

In reality, the cultural importance of Benares has nothing to do with the university. It depends on the great traditional scholars who teach a few chosen disciples in their homes. When I was living in Benares, there were two thousand students in the university. At the same time, six thousand Brahman children who, at the age of ten or twelve, had travelled from distant villages in search of a master, were living in the city. They would present themselves before the great scholars and were eventually accepted as students. The scholars, who considered it their duty to impart knowledge, each took on five or six disciples. Once adopted, a disciple became a member of the family. He lived with his master, helped with the housework and, if the master was poor, would go to the homes of wealthy and respected Brahman families, begging for food. The student paid nothing to his master. Each year, however, on the day of the *guru puja*, when the master is worshipped like a temple god, he was allowed to bring him whatever offering he could afford. On that day, I would carry a silver tray bearing flowers, fruit, a piece of clothing, and a few gold coins, and lay it at Vijayanand's feet.

Traditional Hindu studies are quite arduous. The students must memorize the entire Sanskrit grammar, written in verse, as well as the dictionary and all the ritual texts and ceremonial practices required by the priesthood. If they have the ability, they can then study cosmology, astrology, the philosophic systems, and the traditional sciences.

This training has nothing to do with the education that is offered in India's modern universities. The two civilizations live side by side but are totally unaware of one another, which creates a strange contrast. Their views on life, society, culture, morality, rituals, and the destiny of man are quite distinct.

In an effort to solve the economic problems of traditional education—no help being forthcoming from the wealthier classes of Indian society—a number of scholars had grouped together to create such schools as the Dharma Sangh Mahāvidyalaya, where Brahman children who wished to become officiating priests were offered free lodging and exposed to the teachings of several different masters.

When I first became interested in the religion and philosophy of India, the only works I found useful were those of René
Guénon. I had carefully read all his books and subscribed to *Le
Voile d'Isis*, a review published under his patronage, later called
Etudes traditionelles. L'Introduction aux doctrines hindoues remains one
of the few works of scholarship that give a true picture of the
philosophic and cosmological foundations of Indian civilization. Guénon had studied under an authentic Hindu mystic
whose teachings he summarized with wonderful clarity. Unfortunately this great scholar was refused a visa to travel to
India. There were several possible reasons for this. British
policy, at the time, frowned on any kind of glorification of
Hinduism lest it encourage nationalism. Another reason may
have been Guénon's strong opposition to the Theosophical
Society, whose aberrations he had revealed in a famous book;
in those days, Annie Besant, president of the Society, played a
very important role in the British politics of India.

Guénon then settled in Egypt and became interested in the
surviving elements of what he called "the primordial tradition"
in Christianity and especially Islam. He published superb articles on Moslem Sufism and esoterism. The sources of these
traditions were unfortunately beyond his reach, and he was
unable to come in contact with the pre-Aryan religions of
India, particularly Shivaism, whose texts and rites are not
easily accessible. Guénon's efforts, moreover, were severely
hindered by Moslem puritanism.

At the time, Guénon's influence on certain Western intellectual circles was very great, and it has remained so. Thanks to
him, specialists in Indian philosophy and art—Ananda Coo-
maswamy in the United States for instance—changed their
views and interpretations of Indian civilization, in spite of
strong opposition from conventional university circles and
Indianist groups. Guénon undoubtedly had a great influence
on the thinking of Mircea Eliade.

Guénon found himself surrounded by a loyal group of disciples who collaborated on his review *Etudes traditionelles*. As time
passed, however, they began to live in a kind of ivory tower.
They considered themselves "initiates" and hinted that Guénon was the messenger of a mysterious "King of the world" on
whom he had written a book based on a romanticized story by

Ossendowski. They created a kind of chapel that reeked of dogmatism. Whether one is talking of Euclidian geometry, Pythagorean theories of music, or even historic or symbolic interpretations, all systems of thought are false when carried to extremes. One should never forget that no explanation of the world's creation and man's destiny can ever be more than relative; the ultimate reality can never be known. There is always a thin line between a cosmological conception of creation and evolution and its actual application. The moment of truth is taken as dogma, it becomes false.

Guénon's work was completely unknown in India, but some of the broader lines of his philosophy were consistent with the general principles of Hindu tradition. Although in form and expression his thinking gradually took on a different direction, it remains the best starting point for a real understanding of Hindu conceptions of the world. Guénon's ideas were of great interest to Hindu scholars, and my ability to communicate these ideas to them was a positive contribution; it also made our relations easier. I translated a great many passages from Guénon's work into Hindi, and published them in *Siddhanta*. This led to some interesting discussions and learned commentaries, regarding which I corresponded at length with Guénon himself. Guénon sent me several of his disciples who were interested in Hindu theories on sound, language, and music, and invited me to visit him in Cairo. For various reasons, unfortunately, the trip had to be postponed several times, and René Guénon died before I could meet him. It is very unfortunate that, with his exceptional gifts and superb initial training, this fine scholar was never able to come in contact with the esoteric tradition of India, which is unattainable without a perfect knowledge of Indian languages; this, however, in no way diminishes the importance of his work and the new direction he gave to the study of the evolution and sources of human thought.

INDIAN MUSIC

When I went to Algeria in my youth, I was surprised and interested by Arab music. Later I went to China, Japan, and Indonesia. On my many visits to Rabindranath Tagore, I loved to listen to his musical poems and their delicate melodies, which were sung by his disciples with beautiful and intense emotion; they were not unlike the songs of a Jacques Brel. Although the venerable poet wanted me to direct his school of music, I was not sufficiently interested in songs to accept the post. In Benares, however, when I came in contact with the great tradition of classical Indian music, I finally discovered a deep, complex, refined, and subtle art that fully satisfied me and to which I felt I could devote myself wholeheartedly.

Shivendranath Basu, known to his familiars as Shantu Babu, lived in the middle of Benares in a sort of manor that took up over an acre and included courtyards, uninhabited buildings, and passageways; the monumental entranceway could only be reached by narrow lanes. Shantu Babu lived here all year round with his older brother, his sons, nephews, and cousins. The women's quarters were separate; the wives, nieces, widows, and women cousins were never seen.

After performing his ablutions, Shantu Babu would sit in his large, sunlit living room, which was of relatively recent construction and looked out onto terraces through arched French windows with panes of colored glass, a style reminiscent of the French eighteenth century that became enormously popular in the nineteenth century in southern Russia, central Africa, the Middle East, even westernized India.

Shantu Babu was a rich man, a *zamindhar*, that is, a kind of semi-aristocrat of the landed gentry. He came from East Bengal. He had a passion for music, had studied with the greatest musicians, and was considered one of the finest—if not the very finest—*vînâ* player in northern India. Because of his rank, however, he could not play professionally, so he only gave occasional private concerts for his friends. He spent all the rest of his time playing for himself. When I was introduced to him by friends, he was about sixty. He reluctantly agreed to teach me music. In the beginning, all I was supposed to do was listen to the *râgâs* and recognize them. After a while, he allowed me to take notes on the different modes and the emotional qualities of the intervals. With wonderful patience he explained and demonstrated the subtleties of the ornaments and the exact pitch of the notes, which differs according to the *râgâs*.

He gave me a small *vînâ* so that I could practice the music and verify my notations, but forbade me to play in front of him. "You would ruin my ears," he said. "I could not bear it."

I would go to his house each day for two or three hours to listen and take notes. I was also supposed to perform some of the small services to which a master is entitled: light his opium pipe, bring flowers and incense to honor his instruments.

Working with Shantu Babu was very demanding, for he only played *râgâs* at certain fixed hours. I had to be there at six in the morning for the sunrise *râgâs* and at ten in the evening for *râgâs* of the night; morning, noontime, and afternoon *râgâs* were much easier to attend. It would have been impossible to walk the long distance to his house each day through the maze of small city streets, so I found a boat and a boatman. Later I even bought an outboard motorboat so that I could travel against the current when the river was flooding. Each day I would go down the Ganges by boat to the *ghat* closest to Shantu Babu's house; when I got home, I practiced for several hours a day. After two years, I was allowed to play for a few moments in front of my master. He gave me some advice, said that I played abominably, but apparently told his son that he was very pleased with my work. After I had studied for four years, Shantu Babu was still criticizing me for my terrible playing and telling me that I was good for nothing; but to anyone who would listen to him, he would say: "He's my best pupil, a true musician, the only one capable of continuing my tradition." Finally we gave me a beautiful old instrument which had belonged to a famous musician of the last century. I was also granted the great honor—an honor only bestowed on a favorite disciple—of carrying his instrument when he had to go somewhere to give a concert, a duty I performed with reverence.

I studied with him for six years. Then, one day, I lost patience. I no longer had enough energy to bear the caprices of the venerable man, always having to beg him to play, always listening to the same absurd stories about musicians who could evoke spring or night and burn entire cities to ashes by the force of the fire *râgâ*, which he prudently refused to play himself, only showing me the outline.

At the time, I was very much involved with the Hindu

cultural movement and trying to create a school of music within the university.

I stopped going to my lessons quite suddenly, which caused Shantu Babu much distress; he bitterly complained, with good reason, of my ingratitude. This has always been one of my greatest faults. My patience seems without limit until one day I suddenly feel that I have had enough and make a clean break, with no possibility of ever turning back. My excessive patience leaves me no strength for negotiation, and I see no other way but escape.

I had gradually gained a certain reputation in India as a musician and musicologist. My interest in the great classical tradition of music and my vigorous opposition to all its hybrid, so-called modern forms, which were encouraged by pressure groups and radio, had earned me strong sympathies and created a certain impact. I was the first European to proclaim that not only was this trend towards an "international" conception of music avoidable, but that such a development, in India, would be a cultural disaster. In 1950 I was named president of Calcutta's All India Music Conference, an important festival that gathers the most famous musicians in India before an audience of several thousands. I was asked, along with the famous singer Omkarnath Thakur, to organize a music school in the Benares Hindu University. Omkarnath became its director and I the assistant director; I was also made a "professor." Here, with the help of a dozen scholars, I created a research center for musical documents written in Sanskrit. I had already collected several hundred manuscripts on musical theory written between 500 B.C. and the sixteenth century. We compared texts and prepared a card index on terminology. During that period I published several articles on music and musical scholarship written in Sanskrit.

The search for texts involved a great deal of work. First I had to find the manuscripts in public or private libraries, then have them recopied, and finally transcribe them into *devanagari*, the classical Sanskrit alphabet—for even in Sanskrit, each province uses a different writing system. In fact, I was far too ambitious. Instead of working on a few texts and preparing an

imperfect edition, which even then would have made my reputation shine, we assembled documents on more than eight
hundred works. We prepared over three hundred thousand
index cards, and though this vast project was later abandoned,
it still remains accessible to scholars in the Oriental section of
the Cini Foundation in Venice, to which I have donated my
library.

When I was in Paris in 1953, I met a young Frenchman who
had been unable to pursue regular studies but longed for a
university education. His name was Georges Guette. I managed to enroll him in the Benares Hindu University, which at
the time did not normally accept foreign students. Georges,
who was a lively and inquisitive young man, adapted very well
to Indian life. When he returned to France, he wrote a very
amusing book called *Un Gaulois chez les Hindous*; he spent some
time working for a publisher, then became a jack-of-all-trades
at the TNP (Jean Vilar's Théâtre National Populaire) in its
greatest period of glory. When I saw him again a few years
later, I was not surprised to learn that he had become the
secretary-general of the Comédie Française. He was as amusing, clever, and unpolished as ever and wonderfully efficient.

SACRED PLACES, RITES, AND MAGIC

Certain sacred places "breathe of the spirit." Pilgrims go to
them in search of miracles. Temples are built. Sometimes they
have been abandoned for many centuries; the sanctuaries are in
ruins or have completely disappeared. And yet, when the
moon enters one of its "houses" on the zodiac, enormous
crowds gather on these sacred sites; merchants selling various
wares and entertainers go there as well. Some of these feasts
take place once a year, others every four years or twice a
century. They are called *melas*. There are similar feasts in Britanny, called *pardons*. The famous *Kumbha mela* (the feast of
Aquarius) takes place every twelve years.

In the days when Raymond and I would camp out for long
periods in order to photograph temple sculptures, the dead
city of Khajuraho was normally quite deserted. Then, during
the annual *mela*, the entire area was suddenly invaded by

thousands of carts, tents, peddlers' stalls, clowns, sleight-of-hand performers, and small fires where people cooked *chapattis*. Pilgrims came on foot from all the neighboring region. There were no priests. No rites or ceremonies were performed, yet, responding to some kind of ancestral reflex, throngs of humble people would periodically return for a visit to this most sacred and propitious place.

The same thing happens during the great *mela* of Amarkantak, in central India, near the headwaters of the Sône and Narmada rivers. The site, with its magnificent ruins of abandoned temples, is almost inaccessible. For the *Kumbha mela* of Prayag (Allahabad), millions of pilgrims come to bathe in the place where the Jumna and Ganges rivers meet; many are drowned or trampled to death. Claude Renoir, the famous cameraman, nephew of Jean Renoir, wanted to film the *Kumbha mela*; he was caught in the crowd, fell into the river with all his equipment, and was rescued with great difficulty. In Benares, during solar and lunar eclipses, hundreds of thousands of pilgrims would spread all over the sacred river bank in order to bathe and cleanse their bodies of the baneful influence of Rahu, the god who devours stars.

The most remarkable feasts of all take place in eastern India and are dedicated to the Goddess. On an ancient sacred site that once boasted a miraculous sanctuary but is now only a large field, male goats are sacrificed by the thousands, each family bringing its own animal. At dusk their heads are cut off with a single blow of an axe or scimitar. The earth and the participants are all covered with blood. People move about in a bloodstained swamp. The ponds and rice paddies turn completely red.

In the Himalayas, the sacrificial victims are buffaloes and bulls. These sacrifices are performed by experts, for the animal's head has to be severed in one blow.

Foreigners speak indignantly of the barbarity of such sacrifices, conveniently forgetting the unseen horrors of the slaughterhouse. The purpose of the sacrifices is to make the gods bear witness to the terrible cruelty of a world where living creatures cannot survive without killing and devouring one another. Man too must be made aware of the seriousness of the act of killing so that he will avoid doing so needlessly. Hindus are not supposed to eat the flesh of an animal which they have not killed themselves; this is why many of them prefer to become vegetarians. Buddhists do exactly the contrary. Killing is not allowed, yet they eat meat. Buddhism is a hypocritical religion.

The bloodbaths resulting from these sacrifices seem to produce a state of collective intoxication that reminds one of Dionysian rites, or Euripides' Bacchae. Sacrifices satisfy one of man's deepest needs and definitely play an important role in the psychology of the masses. This orgy of blood is a kind of revenge against the gods, against the world and all the frustrations it imposes on the less favored members of society. Having satisfied their vendetta, Hindus immediately revert to their wonderfully gentle selves, always kind towards animals and their fellowmen. Brahmans cannot participate in these popular feasts, for any form of violence is forbidden to them. Warriors and princes may witness but cannot take part in them; their violence must be expressed through the art of hunting—a prelude to the art of war, another form of murderous frenzy.

In 1942, when the Indian National Congress headed by Gandhi revealed its socialistic and progressive goals, Swami Karpâtrî decided that Hindu civilization was becoming seriously threatened: it was time for the Brahmans and *sannyasis*, who are not supposed to take part in politics, to "descend upon the battlefield" according to the predictions of the sacred texts. Before Swami Karpâtrî created the Jana Sangh political movement for the defense of traditional values, he ordered the preparation of one of those astonishing rituals called *yajñas*, on which kings have sometimes spent their entire fortunes. This particular feast was financed by the very rich caste of tradesmen, who are always conservative in matters of religion.

In a vast field on the banks of the Ganges River, a gigantic pavilion was built, covering several acres. It was supported by bamboo pillars twenty feet high and covered with palm leaves and straw thatch. Underneath this shelter, a thousand fireplaces were dug and carefully lined with clay. Five Brahmans took turns sitting by each fire and kept it going without interruption for ten whole days, murmuring ritual formulas and making offerings of grain, oil, and butter to Agni the firegod. As I watched, the immense column of prayers and smoke rising heavenward in the sky seemed like a link between the world of men and the world of gods.

Neither the Congress nor the British press ever mentioned this extraordinary event which had attracted over ten thousand Brahmans and nearly a million pilgrims to the sacred city.

Certain yoga practices can develop "magic" powers: hypnosis, mindreading, long-distance vision, levitation, and the temporary suspension of heartbeat and breathing. The power of hypnosis can be so great that it is often difficult to tell whether what one sees is really happening. Yogis who truly seek spiritual fulfillment never use these tools, which are considered temptations put in their way to prevent further progress in their conquest of Heaven.

Often, while witnessing *melas*, I saw yogis fall into a cataleptic state and become as stiff as boards. They were laid upon two sharp-bladed swords, one under the neck, the other under the ankles. Rocks were placed on their stomachs and broken to pieces with enormous hammers, but their bodies did not even bend. Then they were buried and left underground for several hours. They would reemerge somewhat flushed, but apparently unhurt.

Sometimes, when we had visitors, we would put on magic shows. When Cecil Beaton, who loved this kind of thing, came to stay with us, we organized a particularly successful evening. The magician threw a rope in the air, where it remained suspended, though nothing held it from above, and sent an acolyte shinnying up it; the child disappeared into the sky. Then he placed a gold paper crown on the head of a little girl and lit a fire that seemed to come out of the child's head. He cooked fritters on a frying pan on the flames, and we ate them. After this, he made a mango tree grow before our eyes. It was wonderful to watch the plant growing little by little, the leaves opening up, finally the fruit budding and ripening. In less than fifteen minutes, the magician was able to pick the fruit off his miniature tree and offer it to the audience.

A yogi who spent some time in the house next to ours could

execute the "inner washings" of yoga, drawing water through his rectum or, more surprisingly, through his penis. On several occasions I saw him "drink" his morning glass of water with his sex, which must have required the most astounding muscular control. This yogi used to draw very beautiful *yantras*, or magic diagrams. I offered him some canvases, which he needed. A small *yantra* he gave me still hangs over my bed.

The practice of levitation is rare and difficult. I saw this feat performed a few times, but always in dark and smoky places; it was impossible to tell whether or not it was a trick.

Yogi magicians are sometimes very frightening people. When they look at you, you can feel all our willpower gradually disintegrating. They can seize the will of any person they choose and make him do what they want. They absorb one's psychic substance and feed on it. Like vampires, they grow to be very old but never lose their adolescent bodies, even when their faces have become ravaged and wrinkled.

I have always been afraid of yogi magicians; as soon as I began to feel the effect of their hypnotic power, I would move away. I have never taken part in experiments in spiritism and magic. Unfortunately, I have seen many people fall victim to these practices. Many of the young people who go off to India nowadays in search of "spiritual adventures" become the easy prey of these yogi magicians. Some of them remain unbalanced for the rest of their lives.

THE TRAILER

During the winter of 1934–35, we spent a holiday near the sea in Puri, in the province of Orissa. We saw some marvelous carved-wood chariots in which the images of the gods are driven about, and also visited the Sun Temple of Konarak. In those days, it was a difficult expedition. We had to rent elephants from the Rajah of Puri so that we could go across the estuaries of the rivers along the coast. Konarak, which the British call the "Black Pagoda," is a huge, abandoned temple on a sandy peninsula. Very few foreign visitors had ever seen this temple whose erotic sculptures seemed just another example of Hindu barbarity; it was unthinkable to take along "the ladies." There was a small shed belonging to the Indian Department of Archaeology where one could spread blankets and spend the night. The high tower of the temple had collapsed. The nave, or *mandapa*, was built in the shape of a chariot and decorated with a profusion of sculptures in a style quite different from that of the other temples of India. Raymond took a great many pictures of the sculptures; it was his first attempt at photography, a craft that later earned him an important reputation. In Paris, at the end of 1935, he published his first book of photographs, *Konarak*, accompanied by a text written in flowery poetic prose by a novelist of the time, André Doderet.

These photographs are now of considerable interest. A few years after they were taken, the Department of Archaeology decided to clean the temple and remove the black coating that covered it. They used pressurized water sprays and damaged all the sculptures, destroying the delicate cement that covered the small holes in the porous rock, and leaving the faces so pockmarked it looked as though the temple had been visited by the goddess of smallpox. The difficulties and discomforts of this kind of expedition were very great. We decided that the only way to visit Indian monuments, which are usually quite distant from inhabited areas, was to travel by trailer. In those days, these peculiar objects were only made in America. In 1936, when we stopped in Los Angeles on our trip around the world, Raymond went to the Hollywood Trailer Corporation and ordered the magnificent four-bed trailer that would allow us not only to travel over the roughest terrains and jungle paths, but to sleep comfortably in the most isolated places, near temples lost in the forests of central India, the southern and Rajputana Deserts, Kashmir, and the Himalayas.

The trailer reached Calcutta the following year, packed in an enormous crate. For several years we dragged it behind our Ford rumble-seat roadster, later behind our jeep. It was the first trailer anyone had ever seen in India. When Tagore first saw it, he insisted on trying it out. He sat majestically on the cushions, surrounded by several young girls, and was driven on the dirt road between the school and the agricultural institute. But a trailer is not meant to be sat in while it is being driven; the venerable poet was tossed about as if he were in a salad basket and sent flying through the air while the girls tumbled pell-mell in all directions. He never repeated the experience.

For ten years, we spent several months a year in the trailer and travelled to every corner of India. Much later, after the war, when we left Benares and moved south, we sold the trailer—still in very good condition—to a rich merchant. Even then it was still the only trailer in India.

CHAPTER NINE

Away from the Turmoil

THE YEARS OF WAR

A year after we moved permanently to Benares, England declared war on Germany, and like all the rest of the British Empire, India was involved in the conflict. In those days, there were no civilian airplanes. Sea travel and postal services came to a halt. All communications with Europe suddenly ceased. When France was invaded, consuls and other French citizens considered dependent on the Vichy government were sent to camps in the Himalayas, where they were apparently quite comfortable. Raymond, being Swiss, was untouchable. There was no reason to leave him free and arrest me, but because of our links with the pro-Japanese Hindu world, we were considered suspicious characters. Fortunately we had friends in the Viceroy's circle, in particular Jack Hughes, an intelligent and cultivated young man in his thirties who, as we later found out, ran the Intelligence Bureau in India and became head of the famous British Intelligence Service after he returned to London. As a result, no one caused us any real problems. Thanks to the protection of Mortimer Wheeler, who ran the Department of Archaeology, we were even allowed to continue travelling in India.

Wheeler became famous for his extraordinary discoveries in India, notably in the Indus Valley, now part of Pakistan. He was an amazing character. This elegant and well-bred Englishman, who liked to appear as an amateur, had all the qualities of a water witch. He would stroll casually through potential sites, talking about anything that came into his head; then suddenly he would stop, touch the earth with his cane, and say: "Dig here." Whatever monument or important object he was searching for was always lying underneath. After the war, the British could no longer afford to support archaeological research. Wheeler was not interested in bureaucracy or in honorary posts, so, after his return to England, he began to create television programs, which he found very amusing. It was a great loss to archaeology.

An English spinster who lived in an annex of the Theosophical Society at the other end of town became interested in my musical studies and research. Her name was Juliette Merston. Each year, as a joke, Raymond would remove a letter from her name: first she was Uliette, then Liette, Iette, etc. I put her seriously to work, typewriting, editing texts, and making endless calculations of musical intervals. She was extraordinarily devoted, and we were quite fond of her. It was obvious, however, that she had to make weekly reports on everything that was said or done at Rewa Kothi.

Because she was genuinely attached to Raymond and me and seriously interested in my work, her reports were probably very useful to us and counteracted many of the efforts of some local officials who detested these Europeans "turned native" and denounced us several times for subversive activities.

The day of Juliette's sixtieth birthday, we organized a very beautiful party in her honor. The house was decorated with oil lamps, flowers, and garlands; we had prepared a feast and wrapped presents. It was obvious that no one had celebrated this lonely old spinster's birthday since her childhood. Juliette broke down and burst into tears: "But you don't know who I am or what I do!" "Of course we know; but it doesn't really matter, because we love you." Juliette left Benares shortly after the end of the war. She retired to an ashram in southern India, for reasons probably connected with her work. She continued to write me from time to time. In her last letter, she wrote: "I am suffering from a hemmorhage, and no one can stop it. In a few days, I shall be dead. I just want to tell how much I have loved you both and thank you for all the happiness you have given me." After that I received nothing more. Juliette had lost the last letter of her name.

Before she came to work for us, she was a disciple of Gurdjieff's and spied on him as well. She often spoke of her years with him.

In spite of Juliette, the denunciations continued. Their source was the British Resident, who had never set foot in the Indian part of the city: he claimed that it was far too dangerous to enter. Wishing to help me in my work, Raymond was working on a large harmonium tuned to produce fifty-two intervals per octave. In Calcutta, we had bought the frames of two church harmoniums with bellows and identical sets of reeds, two rows each. In order to build a mechanism that would allow for the individual control of each reed, Raymond bought several hundred bicycle spokes. For some reason this was considered highly suspicious. One day, when the instrument was nearly finished, a young Englishman burst into the house. He showed great interest in the instrument and spent three entire days talking to us. He was a highly cultivated man and very pleasant company. Before he left he apologized for having intruded on us and confessed: "You have no idea what problems you have caused us! You have been accused of building a radio transmitter to communicate with the Japanese, and throwing it into the Ganges. We spent an entire week scraping the bottom of the river. We even found a broken-down receiver. I was summoned from Delhi to make absolutely sure that you weren't engaged in any scandalous or subversive activities. I am delighted to have had the chance to meet you. I congratulate you on your instrument—a splendid piece of work!"

The Indians were not interested in Europe's wars; no matter who they were, Europeans were the enemy. In British colonial circles, people spoke vaguely of resistance movements in Greece, Yugoslavia, and France. France was the Vichy government. It was only at the very end of the war that I first heard the name of General de Gaulle. French people who worshipped the general always seem to imagine that his coming made a tremendous impact on British circles, in the same way that Christians believe Jesus revolutionized Judaea during his lifetime.

I had become a Hindu, living in a different world and completely detached from the dramas of Europe. The only war that seemed real was the Anglo-Japanese conflict, and, in the world I lived in, England was considered the enemy. All the sympathies and hopes were turned, rightly or wrongly, towards Japan, a heroic Eastern land struggling against European imperialism.

Shubhas Chandra Bose, one of the most important leaders of the Indian National Congress, had sided with Japan and commanded an Indian division in the Japanese army in Burma. I had met him several times. He was a very affable man, as well as brilliant and daring. Later, he was killed in an airplane accident.

On the banks of the Ganges River, no one knew very much about the war. No English language newspapers ever reached the city, and the Hindi press was pro-Japanese. The only thing we could hear on the wireless was the powerful German station. Its brilliant announcer was William Joyce, an Englishman who had gone over to the enemy; people called him Lord Haw-Haw, and he was executed at the end of the war. It was on this station that we learned that the war was over—a last, dramatic broadcast, punctuated by the funeral march from *Siegfried* and *Deutsche Volk, dein Führer ist tot*. India was supposedly free of censorship, but from time to time an anxious young man would discreetly come to the house carrying some letters I had written and ask me to explain certain sentences that he did not understand; he needed to know what they meant in order to prepare his report.

A minor movement called "la France Libre" was created in Delhi at the end of the war. The English were tolerant but distrusted its organizers; they had little respect for General de Gaulle. The Indians, who considered me one of their own, would never have understood my joining a group allied with England. There was nothing, in any case, that I could do. The partisans of the movement were rather disagreeable people, the false Résistance type, ambitious and insincere. It was better to remain as I was.

There was no possible communication with France, no letters or news. My mother had written to the King of Afghanistan to find out if I was still alive. The king received the information from his embassy in Delhi and sent the reassuring news on to my mother.

Raymond had hired an assistant called Murlidhar, a young Brahman student of Mahrattan origin with whom he was quite smitten. The youth suddenly left without warning, announcing in a note his intention to become a monk. Raymond stopped eating and said that he would perish unless the boy returned. I went to a great deal of trouble getting information from all the religious authorities of the city, who were quite sympathetic. Vijayanand told me that unconditional friendship was the highest of virtues. Finally we managed to bring Murlidhar back for three days. Raymond spent an entire day with him on a boat on the opposite bank of the Ganges, while I waited anxiously and made little drawings of the boat from afar. After Murlidhar left, Raymond remained edgy and difficult. The fact that we were considered suspicious, he said, had tarnished our image in the eyes of the youth and probably caused him to leave us. Raymond wished he could have fought in the war and joined the Air Force; it was only to protect me from danger, he claimed, that he had subjected himself to this lonely, unadventurous life. He became unpleasant and irritable. In the end, I fell into a deep depression and caught typhoid fever.

I was taken to a hospital in Calcutta. The cycle of the fever normally lasts twenty-one days, but I went through a second cycle, then a third. I could not eat or drink and was kept alive by intravenous feeding. I weighed only seventy pounds. The doctors told Raymond that he was spending a fortune on nothing, for there was no hope that I could ever be saved.

During all this time Raymond had remained attentive, though nervous and irritable. Suddenly he realized that I was going to die. He came to my bedside and spoke to me with infinite gentleness, evoking all those wonderfully happy years that we had spent together. While he was talking, I could feel his words entering my body like a miraculous remedy. Finally he asked me if I wanted him to try to reach Martha Voegeli, the Swiss lady doctor who had nursed us a few years before in Calcutta; she had just retired in southern India. Raymond's words had given me back some of my courage and energy, and I answered yes. Why had he not thought of it sooner? He must have known that I would never have dared suggest such an expense. I was already in the hands of the best doctors in India, who also happened to be friends; the hospital was supposed to be the best in the country, and Martha Voegeli was considered a charlatan by the entire medical profession. Three days later, after several exchanges of telegrams and the promise of a small fortune, Martha arrived brandishing her needles like a wasp. Antibiotics did not exist in those days; she treated typhoid fever like a blood disease, which was considered absurd by all the profession. It was essential that we find a drug called scepticemin, unfortunately quite hard to come by because it was also an aphrodisiac, therefore highly prized by maharajahs. A helpful pharmacist, who was a friend of ours, sent messengers to all the small cities of Bengal, Bihar, and Orissa. Little by little, they gathered the necessary supply.

It was also necessary to fortify my heart and my failing lungs. Martha gave me all sorts of injections. After three days, she made me take some liquids, to the astonishment of all the nurses.

The doctors felt very differently, however. Raymond was told that the hospital could no longer tolerate the presence of an outside doctor who used such unorthodox methods. They had given up on me; the prestige of science was at stake; no one had the right to keep me alive. I had to be taken to another hospital—less luxurious but far more welcoming. For several days I heard the groans of a wretched girl whose abortion had been bungled; little by little her groans grew fainter until they finally died down altogether. It took me a long time to recover. I was a good patient and left myself entirely in the hands of the Eurasian nurses, who told me incredible stories about the vanity and stubbornness of the doctors. Martha finally went back south, and Raymond left on a holiday by the sea, in Orissa. Two months with a dying man is not an easy thing! He had found a replacement for Murlidhar—Gulab's younger brother Kamal—and took him along. For several years Kamal remained Raymond's companion and consolation. After the war, Raymond even took him to Europe and America. When Kamal went to New York, he was both confounded and horrified by the city, and exclaimed: "Here, one is always above, in the sky, or below, in Hell—but never on earth where life is so sweet!"

Many of my friends have expressed surprise that Raymond and I should both have had so many serious or fleeting love affairs, yet never ceased to feel affection for one another. The success of our relationship was a result of our conceptions of life and love. Love is a wonderful experience, a total gift of oneself, the merging of two beings into one; but physical attraction is a temporary thing and at best lasts only three or four years. One must learn to make the most of those blessed years, establishing a true friendship, an unalterable feeling of mutual trust, which can then last to the end of one's life. Prolonging a sexual relationship, which soon becomes dulled by routine, jealousy, and practical considerations, is the best way to destroy friendship and true love. If one really loves someone, it is wrong to prevent him for enjoying sexual experiences and love affairs that keep him happy and well-balanced. Even when this freedom creates temporary problems, it never destroys a real bond or diminishes true loyalty. During the thirty-eight years we lived together—years punctuated by many affairs and tender relationships, various crises, even a marriage—nothing ever spoiled or weakened the absolute friendship that had drawn us together in our youth and lasted until we were parted by death.

Martha had made me promise two things: to change my vegetarian habits and to spend several months in the mountains, for my heart was not strong. It was a long time before I was able to resume any kind of physical activity. And that was how we discovered Binsar and Almora.

Almora

West of Nepal, in the Himalayas, there is a series of valleys and foothills separated from one of the most barren regions of Tibet by a wall of very high, nearly impassable mountain peaks. This may explain why the area was never influenced by

Tibetan Buddhism and why its population is not racially mixed like Nepal's.

About sixty (impassable) miles away from the Nepalese border lies the ancient capital of the Rajahs of Almora. The descendants of these deposed kings still live in a modest house in a secluded spot deep in the mountains. The population, with its brown skin and harmonious features, is a perfect specimen of the ancient pre-Aryan Shivaist race called "Gangetic" that fled into the mountains centuries ago to escape Aryan domination.

Almora is a small city built entirely of dry stones and wood and perched on a mountain spur. All the houses have lovely carved balconies. It is a bazaar, a commercial center for mountain people who come down to buy supplies and sell rustic woven fabrics, sheepskins, and produce.

We reached Almora by a long, narrow road, ninety-five miles long, that wound dangerously along the brinks of deep ravines. From time to time, when we looked down, we could see the remains of buses that had missed a turning. Halfway to Almora was a wooden cabin where tea and *chapattis* were served. After stopping in a primitive "hotel" in town, I was driven in a rickety old car to the very end of the road; from there I was carried in a sedan chair by four vigorous mountainmen up a steep and rocky goat path, six miles long, to Devi Lodge, the house Raymond had rented in Binsar.

Binsar is quite an extraordinary place. At the beginning of the nineteenth century, the governor of the region, an eccentric Englishman who detested the natives, had decided to build several villas for himself and his aides on a mountaintop covered with oak forests and rhododendrons, which in the Himalayas develop into very tall trees. The houses were built in pure British style, with English furniture, curtains made of English materials, even a few harpsichords. In order to build this aerie, where everything had to be carried up on men's backs, the governor had rounded up the men in their villages and organized a system of forced labor. People said that many of these men had died at the task. Twice a week, the governor would ride down on horseback to Almora so that he could dispense justice and administer the village. Every day, runners were sent down to Almora for supplies; the round trip was forty-seven miles. Water had to be brought in buckets from springs three hundred yards down a steep slope.

In 1920 or thereabouts began the great movement of non-cooperation that was to lead to the Indian struggle for independence. It became impossible to find porters or servants. The occupants of the Binsar houses could no longer obtain supplies so they were forced to leave, abandoning all their possessions. The houses were bought at very low prices by Hindu merchants from Almora; since then they had remained abandoned. Nothing had been moved: there were still books on the tables, and mouldy curtains hung dismally from the windows; some of the furniture crumbled at a mere touch.

Gulab and Ramprasad, our two Benares servants, cleaned up a few of the rooms. We hired a water carrier and two runners, who made daily trips to the village for supplies. Without apparent difficulty—in the daytime at least—they would make the arduous trip to Almora and back, carrying very heavy loads. All the walls of the house were covered with engravings of various breeds of dogs. I asked Gulab to take the pictures down. After a secret conference with the local staff, Gulab told me with some embarrassment: "I cannot take down these engravings: they represent the gods of the English people." It had never occurred to them that anything but divine images could be hung on the walls. No matter how much we repeated that the images were profane, Gulab and his friends were never quite convinced. Everyone knew that Europeans were bizarre and unpredictable, but such an aberration was unthinkable: why hang a picture on a wall unless one intended to worship it?

Almora is about 5,800 feet high and Binsar 7,200 feet, but these altitudes do not correspond with those of Europe: the mountains, being near the tropics, are still covered with thick woods. The view from Binsar was spectacular. The hill stood three thousand feet above a deep valley; beyond it, like a wall, rose the ice-covered 25,000-foot mountain range of the Nanda Devi, the Nanda Kot, and the Trishul, which glistened so brightly they appeared luminous even at night.

For several years afterwards, during the hot season, we

always spent three months in Almora; but instead of climbing all the way to Binsar, we decided that it would be more practical, though less poetic, to rent one of the houses that had been built many years before by missionaries on the hills just above the town, quite near the road.

Because these houses were inhabited by very strange characters, the people in the area had nicknamed the hills "Cranks' Corner." A former Danish gardener called Sorensen, who liked to dress up as a shabby monk, had built himself a hermitage surrounded by a maze of plants. Further up, a German Buddhist monk had adopted the name Anagarika Govinda. He became quite famous and wrote rather questionable books about Buddhist philosophy. On the pretext that an obscure Tibetan sect authorized the marriage of monks, he took to wife a rich Parsee widow from Bombay whom I had met at Shantiniketan. This peculiar couple later created a kind of ashram in California, and the Parsee lady became its goddess.

In another house lived a white-haired Englishman, a former member of the Secret Service, whom Raymond liked to call "Agathon." He was a very gentle and cultivated man. His adopted son, a sturdy Tibetan called Ram Jor, was a defrocked monk who had been placed as a child in a monastery from which he later escaped. Ram Jor painted naïve and rather curious pictures of magical-looking landscapes, in a style not unlike Nicolas de Roerich's. I still have some of his paintings. Agathon put together a few exhibitions of his protégé's work in Calcutta. The Tibetan tried to commit suicide and finally ran away to Darjeeling, where he opened a teashop.

Some distance away lived a Bengali scientist, Boshi Sen, a former student of the famous physicist Jagadish Chandra Bose. With the help of his wife Gertrude, who was an American, Boshi Sen carried on his master's research on plant sensitivity. He would drug the plants, keep the light on at night to prevent them from sleeping, frighten them, and film them in slow motion. These experiments, which have remained quite famous, reveal almost human behavior in plants: pleasure, fear, excitement, horror, sometimes even affection.

It was also in Cranks' Corner that Uday Shankar created his dance center a few years later.

The most interesting people in the area were an American couple called Earl and Achsah Brewster, both painters, whose story I described in one of my tales in *Le Bétail des dieux*.

Earl Brewster had lived for many years in Italy and was a great friend of D. H. Lawrence; he had stayed with him in Capri. After travelling to Ceylon with Lawrence, the Brewsters became very enthusiastic about "the Orient." They went to India and settled permanently in the most beautiful house in the Almora Hills. Achsah was an intelligent and languid creature who reminded me of some of the famous women of the early 1900s. She liked to tell highly implausible stories, and Earl was always saying that she had "a creative memory." They entertained with elegant simplicity and a great deal of style. We were good neighbors at first and soon became excellent friends. Earl knew many people and often had interesting visitors in his home. When Nehru, after a long stretch in Almora's prison, was finally released, he went directly to the Brewsters' house and joined us for his first cup of tea "as a free man." He spoke at great length about his projects, India's problems, and the future of his country.

Earl did not know very much about India. His ideas about the East were typically Western. For him, Almora was an eternal holiday spot in an imaginary Orient. He felt nostalgic about the West and longed to go back someday, but he never did. He was the prisoner of a dream and at times seemed hardly alive.

On the other side of a deep valley that could only be reached by a steep path was a large property called Mirtola. Here, an old Bengali visionary called Mrs. Chakravarty had created an ashram with the help of her disciple, an Englishman who had once been a professor of literature but now considered himself a Brahman; he had adopted the name Krishna Prem and practiced so-called Vedic rites. Another Englishman, a doctor called Alexander, had come to live with them. The old lady also had a parrot, which completed the family. Some time later they took in a sailor, who was more or less a deserter and did not remain very long. After this came an extremely good-looking young man who called himself Aschich and had given up an important post in a Calcutta oil company to join the ashram. His departure had caused great turmoil in the hearts of both sexes, but nothing they could do ever brought him back. Krishna Prem published several well-known works on Indian mysticism and philosophy. The old lady had a daughter who suffered from tuberculosis and died. She had expressed the desire to be cremated in Calcutta. The transfer of the body on mules, then in rented cars that kept breaking down, gave rise to a series of fantastic adventures.

Between Almora and Binsar was a beautiful property owned by Nehru's sister, Vijayalakshmi Pandit, where she used to spend her summers. We often went to see her. I deeply admired this intelligent, moderate, and courageous woman who tried in vain to temper her brother's high-flown socialist ideas, for Nehru knew absolutely nothing about the Hindu mentality. Later she was cast aside by the government and sent to London as India's High Commissioner. She had two unmarried daughters, and I sometimes wondered whether her gracious attentions to Raymond and me did not, perhaps, conceal an ulterior motive.

During the most critical phase of the independence movement, Mme. Pandit managed to escape British surveillance and went to the United States. Her long speech before the United Nations General Assembly in New York undoubtedly had an effect on the ensuing events.

Some distance away lived a Catholic priest who had built himself a small chapel where he celebrated mass for the few Christians of the area. He lived alone and when he died, the nuns of a neighboring convent rushed over hoping not only to retrieve sacred objects, but to verify a rumor of some significance. As it turned out, the rumor was accurate: the priest was a woman. We had already learned this through the Danish gardener, who was a good friend of hers. He was in her house when she died and stole everything he could carry along with him before the nuns arrived.

Some years, a Dutch couple would come to spend the summer. The man, whose name was Arnold Blake, was a musician of sorts and sang the melodies of Fauré with great delicacy. He suffered from tuberculosis and was not very active. He had received grants from various Anglo-Dutch foundations to write a book on Indian music, but it never saw the light of day. His only defense was to declare in all the musicology circles that my studies and writings were lacking in "scientific value"; he was quite vicious about it. Apart from that, he was a friendly and pleasant man. He spent his last years teaching Oriental musicology in England.

The climate in Almora was wonderful during the hot months, but the rainy season was interminable and rather depressing. We spent several summers there. I studied Sanskrit with a Brahman who taught in the village school.

In Almora I had several charming pets. Apart from the martens which we later took back to Benares, I had a very beautiful, very affectionate white parrot. He was also quite useful: whenever there was an earthquake—and they are not infrequent in Almora—he would begin to shriek long before the first tremor. I also rescued a little doe and had to feed her with a bottle. Very early one morning, I heard a wild commotion in the garden, rushed outside, and saw a wolf chasing my doe. I went after him in hot pursuit, with Gulab behind me. At the very moment the ferocious beast caught the poor, innocent creature, I grabbed his tail. The wolf was so offended by this blow to his pride that he immediately let go of his prey and huffily walked away. The doe had fainted. It took us a long time to revive her and get her over her terrible fright.

Our servants, who lived in a small house near the kitchens, would spend hours in serious conference with the local shepherds. I was curious to know what kind of stories they were telling each other. I finally listened to them one day and was astonished to find them deeply involved in a theological discussion. The question was: Rama is a god, therefore he is omnipotent. Sita, his wife, was carried off by the demon Ravana—how could Rama allow him to do this? I used to be quite amazed at the cultural level of low-caste Indians, most of whom were illiterate. The reason for this, I believe, is that they listened very attentively to the monks and Brahmans who taught in the public squares; also, street plays and spectacles always seemed to revolve around mythological characters. All this must be very different now, with radio and television filling people's minds with foolish drivel.

After the war ended and we were able to leave India, we decided that it would be more interesting to spend the hot months (April, May, June) in Europe, and abandoned the house in Almora. Achsah had died and Earl Brewster only survived her by a few months.

In India, well-brought-up people never eat mushrooms, which grew very abundantly in Almora, especially chanterelles. Mushrooms are considered impure, and are called *kukkuta mutha* (dog piss). The most interesting were the truffles, which were sniffed out by Tibetan women, their bodies bent double, their noses on the ground. We feasted on these delicacies, though our more "proper" friends disapproved. It has always seemed to me that someone with good business sense could make a fortune exporting these truffles, which are extremely rare in other parts of the world but seem to grow in abundance on the mountaintops of Almora.

During my summers in Almora I would divert myself with the local shepherds while Raymond, besides the loyal Kamal, had fairly lengthy affairs with several women who came to visit us. I have already mentioned Nicole, a girl we had met in the south of France, who was so infatuated with Raymond that she came all the way to Almora to see him. One day, Berko, the Hungarian photographer who had been our neighbor on the Rue Montsouris, appeared out of the blue and rented a house quite near ours. His wife Mirka, a tall, thin German redhead, was Raymond's mistress for several months. After the war, she and her husband went to America, where Berko did extremely well. I doubt he gave much thought to his wife's infidelities.

Another of our regular visitors was Usha. Usha was the daughter of an Indian general called Chatterjee, who was rumored to have gone over to the Japanese. Usha and her sister Mira were very pretty and outrageously elegant young girls who led a very gay life in Calcutta and spent their time drinking and dancing in nightclubs with British officers. Usha probably hoped that Raymond would marry her, which explains why this sophisticated city girl so often came to see us and stayed so long. Raymond found it great fun to take her out for long walks in the mountains. She would twist her ankles in her high heels and tear her delicate saris, then rush home in an angry fit of tears. She finally married a very rich Frenchman who took her to Paris, but soon discovered that, in spite of her great beauty, cocktail parties and rock 'n' roll would never lead her to glory. From one day to the next Usha, who had always scoffed at Hinduism, suddenly began to put on mystical airs, gave up whiskey and took up vegetarianism, wrote a book on yoga, and became the center of a small pseudo-Hindu circle.

At the time, I was translating some very beautiful poems by Tagore from Bengali into English and transcribing his melodies. I was also studying difficult Sanskrit texts with a remarkable old Brahman who lived in seclusion in a tiny house perched on tall posts, overlooking a deep valley. I have written about this curious man in one of my tales.

With all this work, I had no trouble occupying my time during our long months in Almora. For Raymond, however, things were very different. When he had nothing to do, he very quickly became depressed and would spend entire days lying in his bed reading and daydreaming. He would grow very difficult, and I seemed unable to help him. If I proposed a walk or a visit, he would immediately fly into a rage.

For many years Raymond's character remained a mystery to me, until one day I realized that he was two different people. All of us, to some degree, have a split personality; certain people believe that it has something to do with our two brain hemispheres. In Raymond, however, the separation was absolute. His two personalities were in perpetual conflict, embodying the eternal struggle between gods and Titans. Raymond I was a luminous being, a model of rectitude, intelligence, and loyalty. He was extraordinarily well-organized and capable, could take anything apart—a camera, a watch, an automobile engine—fix it, then put it back together again. He had the courage, the wit, the sense of duty, as well as the physical appearance of a true knight. Raymond II was destructive, egotistical, domineering, and deceitful. Raymond I knew his double very well and often spoke of him in the third person: "He will never accept this! I shan't be able to control him!" Sometimes a clumsy turn of phrase, a seemingly insignificant action

would suddenly bring out "the other," who then took possession of him and seemed almost perversely determined to destroy everything, including himself. Several years later, when
Raymond decided to marry Radha, a young Indian girl he was
in love with, he told me that he had already estimated the cost
of a divorce, just to appease his double. During the nearly
forty years we lived together, we never spoke of money, our
financial security, or the future. I never found out the extent
of his fortune and never asked him. He would gladly have told
me, but "the other" would have borne me a grudge for this
intrusion on his privacy.

The presence of this unpredictable other being was the
reason why Raymond, who was a man of exceptional talent,
never really fulfilled his destiny as an artist. His superb photographic work was produced by fits and starts, as well as by
various ruses on his part and mine to outsmart his double.
Many times I was forced to finish work that Raymond had
abandoned, and save the negatives he wanted to destroy in
moments of depression when "the other" was dominant.
When Raymond was bored—which often happened in Almora— he had fits of melancholy and would spend days lying
on his bed. It then became necessary to confront his double,
and I had to insist on our leaving, knowing that for several
days Raymond would be cruel, obnoxious, deceitful. After that
everything returned to normal, and the true Raymond—intelligent, sensitive, and delicate—would reappear.

Although Raymond was always ready to help me in all my
undertakings, "the other" would create difficulties whenever I
threatened his supremacy by achieving success on my own.
This is one of the reasons why I was forced to give up the all
too vulnerable arts and find refuge in abstract studies, which
allowed me to develop my ideas quietly and in secret.

Raymond's character helped me to understand people, who
all, to some extent, possess an "other." The mean and ugly
sides of their personalities are often quite unimportant. One
must learn to overlook that negative side and have faith in the
true, the good, the essential being who is being mistreated by
his double. In life we must always deal with people's doubles as
well as our own. True friendship can only be achieved with

those who know or feel that we can close our eyes to their treacherous other self, that we shall always be ready to help them fight against that mysterious demon who lives within us all.

DISCOVERY OF THE TEMPLES

Raymond had always been interested in photography and soon acquired a professional technique. He developed his own films and made enlargements with meticulous care, dosing his chemicals for the particular effects he desired. I still have the negatives of some remarkable photographs he took in 1933, when we first went to Japan, China, and Shantiniketan: they are superb, of unequalled quality. As soon as we moved to Benares, Raymond set up a laboratory and a dark room. Soon afterward, we became interested in the type of sculpture that is called medieval, which goes from the ninth to the twelfth century, a time when Indian artists achieved a unique balance between stylization and realism and discovered a kind of geometry of life. It was during this period that the greatest numbers of temples were built in northern India. This particular period of Indian art was not at all popular with specialists. It was fashionable in those days to admire the more realistic earlier eras, Graeco-Buddhist sculpture or sixth-century art from the Gupta period, which is not unlike the baroque. The beautifully sober, stylized erotic and symbolic tradition of the Middle Ages was considered decadent and unworthy of attention. Although we were advised against it, we decided to explore medieval temples almost exclusively. Raymond ordered a ten-foot teakwood extension ladder that could be dismantled; he also bought large mirrors to reflect sunlight on the sculptures.

Each year, we would take our trailer and go off on one or two expeditions, accompanied by our two servants, Gulab and Ramprasad, and sometimes even an assistant. Our first discovery was Khajuraho, whose temples were practically abandoned at the time. During the long months we spent there we never saw a visitor or any member of the Department of Archaeology, only the crowds of peasants who came for the annual feast. There were no bungalows, no places to sleep or eat, no shops.

We took baths in lotus-filled ponds and bought vegetables, rice, and flour in small villages some distance away.

The work was very difficult. We had to clean the sculptures, remove wasp nests, and carefully scrape off the remains of lime that coated the temples. Then we had to build scaffoldings, wait under the burning sun for the perfect light, and adjust the mirrors to enhance it.

Raymond worked with passion, striving to reanimate the stone gods that had been abandoned for centuries in secluded forests. The moment he got home, he would lock himself in his laboratory and remain there for several days. When the marvelous images would begin to appear, one after the other, he was so elated he could neither eat nor sleep. Some of the statues became so real to him that he would fall passionately in love with them. In a letter to Pierre Arnal, he wrote: "These thousand-year-old statues have finally been released from their stone bodies and found another form, more volatile, more subtle, more alive. They will find their way to you. They will travel around the world." (Benares, 17 November, 1946)

Raymond's photographs were a revelation. It was thanks to him that Khajuraho became famous. When Nehru came to power, he decorated his office with very large prints we had made for him. Raymond was a superb technician and the thirty-two-inch-high enlargements he printed from his negatives were of exceptional quality; I was in charge of the touching up. In 1949, the Metropolitan Museum of New York, which had never shown photographs before, presented a large exhibition of Raymond's work; they said that at this level photography was truly a great art. A similar exhibition had already been shown in Paris, under the auspices of Pierre Bérès.

But Khajuraho is not the only center of medieval art. There are nearly a hundred of these temple groupings lost in jungles, mountains, and deserts. Those which happened to be near urban centers were systematically destroyed by Moslem invaders. Later, when British engineers built the large railway network, they used the temples as quarries; in some roadbeds of central India I found small stone hands, mutilated faces of statues, and fragments of all kinds. The last enemy of the temples was Gandhi who, in one of his mad, puritanical frenzies, sent armies of young people to destroy all the erotic sculptures. This massacre was fortunately brought to an end by the vehement protests of the great Bengali painter, Nandalal Bose, who was director of the school of art at Shantiniketan.

As a rule, all the important temples were indicated on maps put out by the Department of Archaeology, but they were not always easy to reach. Roads and paths were everywhere, joining all the villages; from time to time, we saw ox-drawn carts driving along them. But many of these roads had been abandoned for years. Often we had to ford rivers, build rafts, or creep along gutted forest paths. By nightfall we were so covered with dust that we looked like statues just pulled out of a mudbath; our hands and faces could not be distinguished from our clothes.

We would stop near rivers and waterfalls, take baths, and wash our clothes. At night, while the heat was slowly subsiding, we would look at the stars and listen to the sounds of the forest. The trailer protected us from tigers, wolves, snakes, and mosquitoes. We often met tigers and leopards; in the morning, we could see their footprints around the trailer. But we strictly observed the law of the forest tribes, which forbids the carrying of any kind of weapon, even a concealed knife, on the grounds that tigers will never attack an unarmed man. When we were in Ramgarh, in the Rajputana, I was calling Raymond to show him a particularly fine sculpture when I suddenly found myself face to face with a tiger, who was just stepping out of the ruined temple. We politely saluted each other, and the tiger continued on his way.

The information we got from the Department of Archaeology was always very vague. Sometimes, after a long and difficult journey, we would finally reach the site we were looking for and find nothing but fragments. Other times we would suddenly discover, half hidden under the *banyans* and *pippals*— the sacred fig trees that always seem to take root in the stones—the most beautiful and sublime monuments. Even today many of these temples are almost inaccessible and practically unknown. In recent years, some of them were discovered by sculpture dealers and taken apart. Raymond's photographs, which I still have in my possession, are the only evidence of their former splendor.

Once, in the mountains of central India, we were slowly travelling between Amarkantak and Chilpi on a narrow and winding forest path full of bumps and hollows, when our trailer, which was going down one slope, and the car, which was creeping up the next, suddenly got caught together, and the coupler snapped. We were quite dismayed. We were a hundred and twenty-five miles away from the nearest city: now we would have to abandon the trailer and travel for several days on unknown, perhaps dangerous paths. The situation was rather serious. We were just about to camp for the night when several young Munda warriors, armed with bows and arrows, cautiously stepped out of the jungle. These people speak a language of prehistoric origin which nobody can understand, but several of the youths knew a few words of a dialect called *budelkhandi*, which closely resembles Hindi. We explained our situation, hoping they would give us a few supplies. They carefully examined the broken piece and said: "We shall call our chief." The chief turned out to be a wrinkled old woman. She carefully studied the problem, took measurements, and told us that she would repair the coupler. We were rather skeptical. We were taken to a small village of huts hidden in the forest. In the middle of village was a forge used to manufacture arrowheads. It consisted of a small clay tower, ten feet high, in which various pieces of scrap iron were thrown, with an open furnace at the bottom and bellows made of whole cowhides. Small boys, stepping from one foot to the other, activated the bellows which fanned the flames; a system of ropes and counterweights allowed the cowhides to fill and refill with air. The old woman gave orders with great authority. A thick iron plate from some abandoned truck was cut to size, then pierced with holes to fit the bolts. After the piece of iron had cooled off and was fastened to the car, the bolt holes were in exactly the right place, to a millimeter. We had no problem reassembling the car and trailer. Raymond thought that by being very careful he might manage to haul the trailer to the next city; but the new piece was a perfect fit and we never had to replace it.

The old woman refused any kind of payment or gift and gave our small group her blessing. We continued on our way and, in the heart of the forest, discovered the magnificent ruins of the temple of Chilpi overlooking an abandoned lake. It has probably not been visited since.

The trailer also made it possible for us to travel in comfort to the abandoned temples of the Rajputana Desert—Osian, Janjgir, Rampur, Kekind, Kiradu. In central India, we visited Madanpur, Dudahi, Deogarh, Chandpur, Bilva, Pali, etc. We also saw temples in Kashmir and other Himalayan regions.

Sir Mortimer Wheeler made Raymond an honorary officer of the Department of Archaeology, which allowed him to continue his work without too many problems.

Stella Kramrisch, professor of Indian art at the University of Calcutta, used Raymond's photographs to illustrate her great work, *The Hindu Temple*.

Stella was a very interesting woman. She had studied art history in Vienna, then gone to India, first to Shantiniketan then to Calcutta, where she founded the Indian Society of Oriental Art as well as a journal by the same name. Raymond became an associate editor; I contributed translations of Hindi and Sanskrit texts. Stella owned a large collection of sculptures and paintings which she later donated to the Philadelphia Museum of Art. She was then named curator of the museum and professor of Oriental art.

Stella was an intelligent and likeable woman, but in her classes and written works she always insisted on using the convoluted scientific language that had been fashionable in Vienna when she was a student; translated into English, this jargon was not only incomprehensible but also quite comical, with its interminable sentences filled with reflections on mythology, philosophy, and esthetics.

She was a very active woman and constantly travelled from one end of India to another so that she could enrich her collections. She was married to a businessman who was inter-

ested neither in culture nor in art. They adored each other but
never lived together. From time to time they would arrange a
meeting in one of those private rooms for government officials that can be found in all the Indian railroad stations. They
were a very united couple.

We also made many trips to the south of India; the distances
are incredibly long there, so our trips were slow and difficult.
We visited all the great southern temples, which are still quite
active. They are vast, enclosed spaces with immense "thousand-
columned" halls (there are only five or six hundred, in fact),
ritual bathing ponds, and innumerable sanctuaries, where
priests carry visitors' offerings to the idols and the sanctuary
lamp is presented for worship to the faithful. The fact that I
spoke Hindi without an accent and dressed like a northern
Hindu made it easier for me to enter the sanctuaries and
worship the images of the gods. Raymond took very few
pictures. He was not interested in the sculptures of southern
India and found them far less refined, warm, and human than
those of the north.

We made several long visits to the Kalamandalam, the Kathakali dance school Alice had told us about; it had recently
been founded by the poet Vallathol in the province of Kerala.
This center, created to preserve India's ancient theatrical art,
had very little funding at the time and could afford only a few
masters: the old dancers had almost no pupils and were practically destitute. Raymond organized and financed a small
school for one of the great masters of Kathakali, who did not
get along with Vallathol and has since died. This school did a
great deal to maintain the tradition, and the Kathakali dancing
that can be seen today is partly derived from it. The old
masters taught in small huts made of woven branches and
tortured their very young pupils with massages and muscle-
stretching exercises, for the technique is very difficult. Children must begin training before the age of ten and are given
up by their parents to the masters, who from then on are
responsible for their support. During the war it became impossible to finance the school, but fortunately it was incorporated
by the Kalamandalam.

CHAPTER TEN

Political India

GANDHI—NEHRU

I had often met Gandhi and Nehru at Shantiniketan and saw them many times afterwards. I found Gandhi quite repulsive and did all I could to avoid him and his entourage. This skinny, puritanical, and neurotic little man seemed the embodiment of the type of revolutionary who creates an ideology to fire up the crowds, but really identifies it with himself and his secret desire for absolute power. People of this kind have no concrete or practical ideas when it comes to replacing an old government with a new one; for them, such things matter very little. Gandhi was married to a humble and horribly frustrated creature whom he reproached himself for having sexually known in his younger days; now he considered this a mortal sin. Every day he had his legs massaged by young girls and insisted on sleeping beside one of them in order to test his chastity. He lived in a luxurious state of abstinence and took his young she-goat everywhere he went so that he could drink her fresh milk. He travelled in a large third-class carriage that had been specially fitted up for his comfort and was closed to everyone except members of his retinue. He constantly chewed garlic—someone having told him that this would prolong his life—and smelled so foul that, according to the poetess Sarojini Naidu, even his most faithful followers kept their distance. His retinue was thoroughly infiltrated and controlled by the British Secret Service, represented by English ladies who wore saris and flattered him outrageously.

Born of a family of tradesmen in the Gujerat, Gandhi, throughout his life, was supported by the Indian industrial and commercial class, whose members conceal their fraudulent dealings beneath a veil of sentimental religiosity and hypocritical puritanism. When he was very young, he was sent to study law in England and became a member of the London Bar. Eager to play a political role, he went to South Africa and organized a movement for Indian tradesmen who demanded special privileges and refused to be assimilated with the blacks. He spent some time in prison; the obligatory white cap sported by his followers was similar to those worn by the prisoners of Pretoria.

When he returned to India, he organized a movement of rebellion against British rule, cleverly based on the principle of nonviolence and noncooperation. Noncooperation, a kind of permanent strike that paralyzed the economy and ruined the country, made British "repression" appear like a hateful tyranny. His followers were not allowed to use any kind of industrial fabrics and spent their time spinning cotton. Everyone had to wear a rustic material woven by hand and called *khaddar*. As a result, all the textile factories were forced to close down.

It was apparently Jinnah, the Moslem leader, who explained to Gandhi that he would never gain the support of the Hindu masses unless he took on the guise of a holy man bearing a pilgrim's staff.

Like Nehru, Gandhi had been formed in the British mold of romantic socialism and knew very little about the class structure of the Hindus, which he loathed and did all he could to destroy. He quoted constantly from the *Bhagavat-Gîtâ,* a short text taken from the *Mahâbhârata*, but apparently knew nothing else about the great body of religious, philosophic, and political literature of India. Tagore considered him a very dangerous character and withdrew from the nationalist movement when Gandhi became its leader.

Gandhi was one of three lawyers for the London Bar chosen as mediators to impose the division of India; the other two were Nehru and Jinnah, the Moslem leader. When, in cooperation with Lord Mountbatten, they engineered the partition of

India and created Pakistan, I called them "the prince and the three bandits."

Gandhi signed India's Partition Act, leaving the power in the hands of the National Congress of which he was the leader, but also creating a theocratic Moslem state in the east and west of India. The new state was ruled by Islamic law, which does not consider the murder of non-Moslems a crime. This led to a tremendous massacre of Hindus, who in many places formed half the population. There were millions of dead and an influx of refugees so great that it was almost impossible to integrate them; many of them died of hunger and various epidemics. More than half the Moslems continued to live in India, which proved that the division of the country had been quite unnecessary in the first place.

Gandhi continued to preach nonviolence and love of his Moslem brothers while Pakistani warriors sang, "We got Pakistan for a song, we shall have Delhi for a battle." It was then that a young Brahman decided to sacrifice himself and assassinated Gandhi. Any publication or mention of the moving words spoken by the assassin before his judges is strictly forbidden in India. I read the speech at the time of his trial in a Hindi newspaper before it was suppressed, but was never able to find another copy.

When the news of Gandhi's death became public, there was a huge celebration in the city of Benares. Food and gifts were distributed among the poor, and thanksgiving services were offered to the gods.

The leaders of the Congress made a show of deep grief but were quite satisfied to be rid of this cumbersome and authoritarian idealist.

Gandhi had expressed a wish that part of his ashes be scattered over the Indian Ocean. A great ceremony was organized in Bombay, and all the government officials and foreign diplomats were invited. They went aboard the finest ship of the Indian Navy, which sailed a few miles out into the open sea. At one point, the fleet's band began to play a tune that was part of their repertoire and, not being a British military air, seemed more fitting to the occasion. The ambassadors, standing to attention, were startled, then seized with an irresistible fit of giggles. The tune was: "Mont' la d'sus, tu verras Montmartre," a popular Parisian song.

Like Gandhi, Nehru had been trained as a London barrister. Although he came from a rich Kashmir family of Brahmans, he had chosen the West—in other words, had rejected all the prohibitions of his social group and adopted the customs and prejudices of Westerners. His own mother could no longer share a meal with him. He suffered a great deal from British ostracism, which is fairly polite in London but very unpleasant in India, and also from the barely concealed scorn of orthodox Hindus. This is probably why he chose to associate with Moslem groups, whose racism is concealed so long as they are not in power. People said that his greatest ambition was to be treated as a friend and equal by Lady Mountbatten and be received in her home. He succeeded quite well; it was later suggested that he had been her lover. Great English ladies were apparently willing to make certain sacrifices for the glory of the Empire.

Nehru knew nothing about India and its civilization, of which he spoke as scornfully as any Englishman. Later he published a book about Indian culture that was entirely based on texts written in English, mainly by Aurobindo. So great was his Anglo-Saxon snobbery that he even spoke condescendingly about the French and Germans as "continental people," in the same tone of voice the French somtimes use when they mention Italians.

He spoke impeccable English but could not read Hindi. He understood popular Urdu, the language of Moslems and servants, and made as many crude mistakes as a British sergeant. For this distinguished, refined, elegant man who did not belong to any group, there could only be one role, one goal: to be absolute master of the entire continent. He found ways to use Gandhi, whose vulgarity and unsavory religiosity he secretly scorned.

I met him many times, first at Shantiniketan, then quite often in Delhi, Benares, and Almora. Nehru had two sisters. One of them, married to a Bombay industrialist called Huthee

Singh, was quite detached from politics; the other, Vijayalakshmi Pandit, was a remarkable and energetic woman, far
more moderate than her brother, and a good friend of ours.
She treated us like members of the family, whereas our relationship with Nehru and his daughter Indira was cordial but
somewhat distant. Indira worshipped her father and accompanied him everywhere he went. She had married a Parsee by
the name of Gandhi, who was no relation of the Mahatma's
and was treated by the family as a complete nonentity. She
had been partly educated in Switzerland and spoke quite good
French, with a slight Swiss Vaudois accent.

Once Nehru came to power, he grew haughty, inaccessible,
and self-important, though he remained elegantly casual with
the English, and with them only.

Another member of the group was the famous poetess Sarojini Naidu, a very witty and generous woman, though somewhat fat and sickly. Her two daughters, Padmaja and Lilamani,
were also great friends of ours. When the government passed
into Indian hands, Sarojini and Padmaja were the only ones of
the group whose attitude towards us did not change. I was
welcomed with open arms by Sarojini, now governor of Luck-
now, and Padmaja, Governor of Bengal. They received me
simply, "just like before."

When it became obvious that India would gain its independence, the British authorities decided to divide the country,
hoping in this way to maintain the two newly established
states in the Commonwealth. This political strategy had been
carefully prepared for several years. The Indian National Congress, to which all powers were to be transferred, had been
created by an Englishman and was directed for many years by
a woman, Annie Besant, who was also president of the Theosophical Society. In due time Mohamed Ali Jinnah, an elegant
Moslem who was a member of the London Bar and had never
set foot in a mosque, was asked to create the Moslem League,
which later withdrew from the National Congress. A number
of conflicts between Hindus and Moslems were cleverly organized, creating a state of tension so great that the partition
of India would appear to be the only answer. Many conscien-

tious and honorable English civil servants were shocked by this political strategy which could only end in massacre. They were quickly replaced.

I witnessed some of this organized rioting in Benares. One night two Moslems were assassinated, the following night two Hindus. The authorities predicted trouble. The local British Commissioner ordered stores closed, then had them reopened, which made people uneasy. They formed groups in their neighborhoods. Finally a few skirmishes broke out between Hindus and Moslems. But Benares was a small city and people soon realized that the men who were causing trouble were not from the area. The fighting stopped. Things were very different in Calcutta, where trainloads of Moslems imported from the Punjab created riots that degenerated into a civil war with thousands of victims.

Although a number of important and far more moderate movements had been created by Hindus and Moslems, the English refused to have anything to do with them and dealt strictly with the Congress and the Moslem League; the importance they gave these groups was completely arbitrary, the price being the partition of India. The Soviets have often used this method: creating a minority party, then refusing to deal with any other.

All the Indian moderates, the scholars and the rajahs' chief ministers, were very worried by the Congress's attitude. They knew that, whatever happened, the English would have to leave, and were opposed to any concessions—namely the division of India. It was important, they felt, to maintain the country's religious and social structures to ensure its unity and stability. They found it difficult, however, to oppose a party that was fighting for independence and whose leaders were bravely marching off to prison.

The Hindu party was organized too late to oppose the Congress. As was later the case in Iran with Khomeini, they thought an agreement could be reached after independence was won. Even I believed that once the struggle was over, the Congress would show some interest in the traditional values of India; but I was wrong. Nehru eliminated all the princes' chief ministers and all the experienced administrators, then assigned his former "resistance workers" to various posts all over the country, which led to disastrous results, for these men were corrupt and totally lacking in experience. Nehru's iconoclasm was deep-rooted and irrational. The English had destroyed sacred treaties between the British Crown and the princely states, which covered about half of India and were by far the most modern and prosperous parts of the country. Using force when necessary, Nehru made these states accede to National India, then went back on his word and dethroned the princes. He also ruined all the important landowners, distributed the land to the peasants—a typically romantic gesture—but was unable to find new ways to finance agriculture and the distribution of produce. Within a few years the peasants, ruined by moneylenders, were completely destitute, and the entire agriculture was in a state of collapse. The peasants begged their former feudal lords to help them. Nehru had to create a special law preventing the peasants from electing their former landlords or princes as their representatives.

As often happens, the "socialist" government was supported by industrialists and rich bourgeois who knew how to capitalize on governmental corruption. But except for the industrial centers, where the working class was manipulated by leaders—most of them Westernized bourgeois "intellectuals"—all the people of India supported the traditionalist Hindu party, which respected the privileges of castes and corporations as well as all the ethnic, religious, and racial groups.

Today the Jana Sangh, the traditionalist political party founded by Swami Karpâtrî, which I had a small part in helping to create, probably represents the majority of the population. No one can foresee what will happen in the future, however. In countries with Communist tendencies, those who have seized power have never had the majority of the people behind them. By allying themselves with the Socialists to topple the government of Indira Gandhi, the Jana Sangh committed a very grave error. A government based on such contradictory social ideals cannot work.

A number of magnificent ceremonies were organized to celebrate India's independence. Sarojini Naidu and Indira

Gandhi asked us to help them welcome delegations whose members did not speak English. Very few of the delegates were really interesting—mostly typical politicians and diplomats in jackets and ties; but some of them were quite picturesque.

The envoys from Tibet, which was still an independent country at the time, were a wonderful sight. This was the only time I ever met Tibetan "noblemen," who have nothing in common with the seedy Tibetans or the monks one ordinarily sees.

Tibetan princes are of an entirely different race from their subjects and form a very small and special caste, which is probably endogamous. They are very tall and pale, with eyes so slanted they can hardly see anything unless they lift their chins. They reminded me of beautiful highbred animals of very pure race. For the event they wore long, shimmering silk gowns of midnight blue and sky-blue leather boots with gold embroidery; their fingers were covered with rings, and their long black hair was very carefully groomed. They looked like precious objects and seemed to have just stepped out of a jewel case. They offered Nehru handfuls of gold powder and various other gifts.

I was asked to look after the Turks, who spoke French and German, and especially the Indochinese delegation, whose country was then at war with France. The Turks were very decent people, unaffected, sensible, and somewhat vulgar, but the Indochinese were very disturbing characters. I had never met this type of revolutionary—sour, aggressive, thin-skinned, and completely blocked by their political system. A revolutionary ideal easily leads to the imposition of a mode of thinking and acting and ends by creating an army of robots. Like fanatical Catholics, Communist leaders are absolute tyrants who not only seek to dominate human beings but to depersonalize them as well; in reality they are the greatest enemies of the people, whom they claim to represent without ever having been asked.

I met various heads of state, princes, and ministers at the receptions. Of all of these, the princes were the most courteous. During one of the great dinners I found myself seated beside the Maharajah of Bhutan. Looking for a topic of conversation, I asked him if he often went to Delhi. "Very rarely," answered His Highness. "We prefer to go to Lhasa, where the shops are more modern and better stocked." For one who has dreamed of "The King of the World," the Potala, the magic center of the Earth, this kind of return to everyday reality can be quite a shock.

CHAPTER ELEVEN

Encounters

Nicolas de Roerich was a well-known painter who had fled
Russia during the revolution, escaping through Mongolia and
Tibet, where he had lived for some time. His brilliantly colored
paintings represented dramatic landscapes with monasteries
perched on inaccessible rocks. His conception of art was romantic, melodramatic, and modern. There is a museum of his
works in New York that would make an excellent background
for a Tibetan tourist agency, if such a thing were possible. In
the Himalayan town of Nagar he had bought the ancient
palace of the Rajahs of Kulu, a superb construction made
entirely of carved wood. Mrs. de Roerich was a kind of seer
who published short pamphlets in which she described her
dreams and visions.

One day I mysteriously received one of this lady's works
entitled *Agni-Yoga* with a letter from her saying that she had
read some of my articles, had seen me in a dream, wished to
meet me, and hoped that I would pay her a visit in Nagar. I
accepted the invitation. Raymond promptly distorted the title
of the book and irreverently called the lady "Yoni-gaga." It was
a perfect opportunity for us to visit the valley of Kangra,
which is not far from the Kulu Valley and is famous for its
school of miniatures. At the beginning of the century, unfortunately, an English Resident had burned thousands of miniatures he considered obscene from the Rajah's collection. The
few paintings that survived the massacre are considered the
finest in India. Beyond Kangra, a narrow road winds up the

valley towards Kulu, known for its fine apple orchards, then on to Nagar and Manali, from which a tiny mulepath climbs through the glaciers towards Ladakh. The road does not go through Nagar, which is perched on a hill across the river. On the day we had agreed upon, we parked our car and our trailer on the side of the road. Two Tibetan horses with splendid harnesses, finely worked blue leather saddles, and silver stirrups were awaiting us with their grooms, who were hired locally. We had to go down the plunging river bank, ford the river, and climb the equally steep opposite bank. As we entered the palace grounds, two young Tibetan guards wearing monks' robes sounded their horns to announce our arrival.

Mrs. de Roerich was a stout, matronly lady who sported a wimple and a corset and wore her hair in a crown; she seemed to step right out of a novel of the early 1900s about the Russian Court. She received us with elegant graciousness, as though she were still in Saint Petersburg. Some time later, the painter made his entrance, wearing a Tibetan robe and the air of a prophet. His two sons, both in their late twenties, lived with them. The youngest, Svetoslav, a handsome and elegant youth, married a very wealthy Indian movie star a few years later and went to live with her in Bangalore, in southern India. The eldest son, Peter, with his pointed beard shaped like the Czar's and his old-fashioned round spectacles, looked exactly like a Russian intellectual of the beginning of the century. He was working on a Tibetan-English dictionary. He died a few years later.

The luncheon took place in a dark candlelit room. The fine lace tablecloth was covered with rare crystal and antique silverware. The meal, with its obligatory caviar, was strictly Russian. Two young Russian girls helped the local servants wait on the table. Mrs. de Roerich explained to me that she had hired them to satisfy the sexual appetites of her sons until fitting wives could be found for them. In that house, everything, it seemed, was done in the grand tradition.

We refused a pressing invitation to spend the night; we did not feel comfortable leaving our trailer and servants beside the road for so long.

We parted on very cordial terms. Mrs. de Roerich wrote to

me several times, but I was not very interested in that vague mixture of Rasputinian shamanism, Tibetan tantrism, spiritism, and theosophism that so many Westerners love to drown in, taking from each tradition whatever least disturbs their own habits. This very widespread attitude is only a dream and never leads to anything.

Rewa Kothi had become a legendary place where foreigners, as had been the case at Shantiniketan, could feel close to the Hindu world, try to understand its basic principles, and admire its outward display, which was impossible to do in the anglicized world of New Delhi.

This was one of the reasons why so many ambassadors, high officials, and visitors from various European countries wanted to visit us. Some of them became friends, others simply passed through.

Count Stanislas Ostrorog, who was the French Ambassador to India for many years, became a close friend of ours and stayed with us many times, first in Benares, then in Madras and Pondicherry. When I went to Delhi I always stayed in his elegant house whose magnificent gardens he had restored to their former splendor.

Stas, as he was called by his friends, was a remarkable man. He came from a great Polish family. His grandfather had been a high-ranking official in the Ottoman Empire, and Stas still owned a magnificent house on the Bosphorus. His mother was French and he had chosen French citizenship. His brother, who was married to a Princess of Bourbon-Parma, lived in Paris.

Stas was a man of vast culture. Because of his links with the Ottoman Court, he easily understood the nuances and susceptibilities of the Asian mentality. In spite of his sympathies for Islam, it was easy for me to speak to him of the unrest that was fermenting in the Hindu world, and which English language newspapers never mentioned. Stas was very much respected by Nehru, in fact he was a very good influence on him, especially in his attitude towards France, which his English upbringing had taught him to scorn; as a result the relations between India and France were much improved.

Stas persuaded me to seek contact with French Indianists,

whom I had practically never heard of. That was how we came to meet the great Sanskrit specialist Louis Renou, who was surprised to discover the high level of Sanskrit scholarship in the traditional world. Like many Western Indianists, he had always believed that Sanskrit was as dead a language as Latin, and only survived in the works of European scholars. He was astounded to discover that it was the common language spoken by Indian scholars and that some journals were even written in Sanskrit. Louis Renou remained a faithful and devoted friend.

When I began to feel uncomfortable working in the Sanskrit studies center of Adyar, which I was directing at the time, Stas found me a post at the French Institute of Indology that had just been created in Pondicherry.

Stas died quite tragically. Towards the end of his career he had become the most popular, competent, and efficient French Ambassador India had ever known. One day he was summoned to Paris by the Minister of Foreign Affairs who bluntly announced to him that, for reasons quite unrelated to his professional qualities, he was to be pensioned off. Stas left the office and dropped dead in the corridor. Nehru was very angry when he found this out. As a result, France lost much of the prestige and good feeling Ostrorog and many of his collaborators had worked so hard to establish in Delhi and Calcutta. I heard about the tragedy from a deeply indignant Venetian nobleman who was the Swiss Ambassador to Delhi at the time.

The Maharajahs of Benares were descended from royal Brahmans and also had a religious function. They had been exiled to the opposite bank of the River Ganges and were not allowed to enter the city of their ancestors. When they were ill, however, they would secretly go to Benares. According to legend, people who die on the left bank of the river go directly to Paradise, whereas those who die on the opposite bank are reincarnated as donkeys.

The "host" of Benares was the Prince of Vizianagram, a very rich man whose brother reigned over vast states in southern India. The prince—Maharaj-Kumar—lived in a huge palace outside the actual city. He was a polo player and a great hunter, very much esteemed by the British, who nicknamed him Vizi.

Vizi gave grand dinners, organized tiger hunts, and lavishly entertained governors, ambassadors, chiefs of state, even the Viceroy.

His palace was a large, relatively modern construction surrounded by vast gardens. Here, the most opulent bad taste was carried to astonishing extremes: solid gold tableware, huge gilded furniture, gigantic elephant tusks, tiger skins by the hundreds, butterfly-shaped Venetian chandeliers. The Maharani wore stupendous jewelry. She once showed me an emerald pendant the size of a large fig, marked with the seal of the Emperor Shah Jahan. She had found it in a strongroom beneath the palace where all the jewels of dead kings, which the living do not like to use, had been thrown for many generations.

I was introduced to the palace by a friend of Alice's, a lawyer named Montu Mitra, who was very close to the Maharaj-Kumar. The prince had a pleasant and easy manner and we got along very well, but the queen mother took a great liking to me. This was how I was introduced into the family.

Behind the huge formal drawing rooms, a small door led into the actual living area. Here there was no sign of the exotic splendors of the official palace. The old queen would sit on a mat in a tiled courtyard, surrounded by children and servants. There were no furnishings in the living quarters, aside from rugs and chests; laundry was strung across the courtyard. Here there was no pretense, and one could feel quite at home. Conversations were peaceful and relaxed, and we spoke Hindu rather than English.

The queen mother did not usually attend the elegant dinners where foreign dishes and alcoholic drinks, which she loathed, were commonly served. When her son was away and she had to entertain important people, she would ask Raymond and me to help her. In this way we did the honors of the palace and city for many important personalities. We were lords-in-waiting to the Queen.

Jean Renoir was far too original and unorthodox a creative artist to be able to work in cooperation with the great movie factories; he always operated under difficult conditions and never took advantage of any of filmdom's vast publicity organizations. He used to say with some bitterness: "My films have always been failures but they all became classics." In 1950 he came to India to make a movie about English colonists based on a novel written by Rumer Godden, an Englishwoman who had been raised in India. It was called *The River*. The film was financed by a rich Hollywood florist with a passion for culture, who later caused Renoir many problems. Christine, who was director of the Alliance Française in Calcutta, advised him to come and see me, so Renoir arrived in Benares. He was looking for an Indian actress.

Raymond, at the time, was having an intermittent affair with Radha, the daughter of the vice-president of the Theosophical Society. She had studied Bharata Natyam and was quite a good dancer. When I introduced Radha to Renoir, he was quite taken with her. He changed the movie script, transformed the part of an insignificant Eurasian girl into that of a Hindu, developed her character so that her role would be more important, and made her dance. It then became necessary to add a background of Indian music that had not been planned on originally, and I was asked to provide it.

Renoir made long visits to Rewa Kothi between shooting scenes, which were being done near Calcutta. Christine did a great deal to help him create the proper tone for the film. The film manager distributed mustard oil among the coolies who were hired as extras: they were supposed to rub their skins with it but always seemed quite dry. It turned out that they were drinking it, for they considered the oil a priceless treat. Another kind of oil had to be found—more expensive but much less palatable.

Once the shooting was over, Renoir left for America. When the film was ready, he insisted on Radha's coming to Hollywood for the presentation, for she was one of the stars. It was obvious that Renoir was quite attracted to her. In a fit of jealousy, Raymond flew to Los Angeles, and within a few days married Radha. He thought he had done this very discreetly, but the following week the couple appeared in full color on the front page of *The Illustrated Weekly of India*. All the important American newspapers and weeklies had articles about the wedding of this graceful Oriental actress, which the film publicists duly exploited. One of the Los Angeles papers even mentioned the diamond Radha wore, Indian style, in one of her nostrils, and entitled the article "Every Time She Sneezes, She Loses a Fortune."

Jean Renoir always remained a faithful friend. In later years I often saw him in Paris or Hollywood. It was through him that I met Charles Laughton and Charlie Chaplin, who asked us to lunch several times in his home. Jean Renoir remained in correspondence with me and especially with Christine until he died in 1978.

Raymond's marriage caused me some very serious problems, not only in our life together, but also because we had sworn at the time of our initiation into Hinduism never to marry outside our caste. If either of us chose to marry, it could only be to a European; that was the only condition. Raymond's marriage was not considered valid by Hindu law, but it was a great embarrassment to our masters and all the more scandalous because Radha, though a theosophist, came from a family of Brahmans. Suddenly we were strangers again, men without faith or law who should normally have become outcasts, rejected by the two communities the couple belonged to. The fact that Raymond had mistresses or homosexual affairs had never been a problem; this was the domain of the *Kama-sutra*, the fulfillment of self on the erotic plane. But marriage is a social contract, and a union between two different races is strictly forbidden.

My mistake had been to draw Raymond, who was always bisexual, into a society that could not accept the violation of certain taboos. His marriage did in fact put an end to a certain way of life, but also made it possible for the traditional world to find another role for me and send me back to the West, where I was able to accomplish what was perhaps my true mission.

Sometimes, visitors of too great importance caused us serious problems. Eleanor Roosevelt, who had met Radha and Raymond when *The River* came out in America, had expressed a desire to spend a few days with them in Benares. Known for her feminine attachments, she was clearly attracted to Radha.

She had also read some of my books and seemed quite eager to meet me.

When Mrs. Roosevelt decided to go to India in 1952, she was treated, of course, like an official visitor. All the local functionaries entertained and persecuted her, forcing her to visit river dams, schools, hospitals, model farms, and industrial plants. All this exhausted Mrs. Roosevelt. She had written Raymond the date and hour of her arrival in Benares. At the appointed time, he and Radha duly went to fetch her at the airport, where he found the entire gamut of officialdom: commissioner, collector, chief of police, presiding judge, and notables of all kinds. They had prepared a program of banquets, speeches, and visits, carefully avoiding the inner city, the Ganges river bank, etc. India was now a modern country, and they had every intention of showing it off. When the famous visitor stepped off the airplane, she was greeted by a cacophonic military band playing English tunes.

Mrs. Roosevelt pushed her way through this official crowd. "I am here to see my friends," she said. She kissed Radha, crying, "How very happy I am to see you!" and drove off in Raymond's car, leaving all the officials of Benares dismayed, angry, and humiliated.

Mrs. Roosevelt's visit to Rewa Khoti went very well. She was an intelligent woman with pleasant and simple manners. We took her boating on the Ganges River and visited some temples. She was particularly interested in the marvelous silk and gold fabrics Benares was famous for and wished to see the weavers at work. Another drama! She was horrified to see a group of pale, thin ten to twelve-year-old boys working in dark subbasements. I did all I could to convince her that the boys were on vacation from school and just learning the trade in their spare time. After she left, we were considerably harassed. It was a long time before we were forgiven for interfering in state matters, and especially for depriving the high officials of the Province of such an illustrious victim, on whom they had hoped to inflict their endless speeches and the so-called glories of their industry and agriculture. After Mrs. Roosevelt returned to America, she published an amusing article about her visit to Benares.

Prince Peter, brother of the heir to the Greek throne, made several visits to Benares, accompanied by his morganatic wife. They were a very pleasant and likeable couple. I had to accompany them on visits to various temples and bazaars. I hated having to perform this kind of duty because innocent foreigners never failed to indulge in unseemly behavior, causing great embarrassment to everyone. As they say in the *Purana*, "What had to happen, happened." The prince suddenly decided to jump on top of a sacred bull that was ambling peacefully through the city streets. The startled animal went galloping into the bazaar, knocking down market stalls and creating a panic. When the princess saw the magnificent flower stalls near the temple, she stuck her nose into the jasmine garlands, sighing, "How beautiful they smell!" But one cannot offer gods flowers that have been smelled, or cakes that have been bitten into. Gods have the right of first choice and must always be served before anyone else. As discreetly as possible, I paid for the entire display, which cost me a great deal of money, and the flowers were thrown in the gutter.

In 1939, the painter Ju Péon (Xu Beihong according to the new writing system) came to stay with us for several weeks. He was the most famous contemporary painter in China, and had spent some time in Paris. He was a very gay and amusing man who thought of nothing but his art. He gave me two of his wonderful drawings of animals, a horse and a rooster. In those days we were strict vegetarians, which Ju Péon found very annoying. When he left, he thanked us for our hospitality, adding: "In China, we eat anything that has four legs, except the table." After he returned to China, he helped create an institute of Fine Arts and refused to leave at the time of Mao's revolution. He died in 1953, long before the cultural revolution.

Another painter who visited Rewa Khoti was Felix Topolski, a Pole who was living in London. He had been commissioned by the Indian government to paint the huge portrait of Gandhi that now hangs in the government palace in Delhi. Nehru had sent him to us so that he could see something of "the real India" without too much discomfort. He remained with us for some time and made several drawings of the Ganges river bank. His style of painting was too modern for my taste: though partly figurative, it did great violence to landscapes and to the human form. I have kept a drawing by him of Rewa Khoti that I find rather charming.

Ashwin zur Lippe, older brother of the Prince Consort of Holland, is one of the greatest experts on Asian art in the world. For many years he directed the Oriental section of New York's Metropolitan Museum of Art. He is an affable, intelligent, amusing man who, with his wife Simone, travels in the most incredibly difficult and uncomfortable conditions in search of unknown monuments as though it were the most natural thing in the world. Then, like those rough seventeenth-century warriors who would appear at Versailles wearing frills and lacy jabots, he turns up in royal courts looking like an elegant man-of-the-world who has never done a thing in his life.

Ashwin first came to see me when I lived in Pondicherry. We soon became good friends. The princess was looking for antique jewelry, and I organized a search, with excellent results. It is difficult to conceive what striking effects the Indian imagination has been able to produce with ill-cut precious stones: jewels for the forehead, the hair, the ankles; nose rings, earrings, necklaces, pendants, glittering belts. In those days, many of the jewels were melted down, for the elegant ladies of Delhi preferred to buy them at Cartier's. Dealers would buy old jewels for their weight in gold without paying any attention to the precious stones. The princess brought home a collection in which she still takes great pride.

Later, I often saw Ashwin in Paris. Since then, he has published a remarkable book about Indian temples.

CHAPTER TWELVE

Southern India

MADRAS

Radha's father, a strange character whom I always suspected of dealing in some kind of black magic, had become president of the Theosophical Society, which was held in great contempt by orthodox Hindus. Raymond settled in Adyar, near Madras, in a vast property that was considered the world center for theosophists.

It was not long, however, before he grew bored with the strange, hushed, cloistered, and puritanical atmosphere of the Society, where nature itself was so controlled that it had a funereal quality. Radha soon became aware of the problem and did all she could to draw me to Madras. She wrote me that Raymond was far too accustomed to living with me to find his bearings in an atmosphere so different from the one he knew. Her father offered me the directorship of the library of Adyar, which included a large collection of ancient manuscripts and Sanskrit texts. The offer was quite tempting and I was feeling rather alone and lost in the vast palace of Rewa. I finally accepted and in 1953 I left Benares forever.

I was firmly settled in Benares and had grown accustomed to a way of life I thought would never end. For some time, however, I had been noticing that the water that bathed the lower part of the house was receding, leaving a sandbar, and this had caused me some anxiety. It seemed like a sign: the sacred river was moving away from me. I could only obey. But as I embarked on my new life I felt a deep nostalgia and preferred not to turn back or maintain any links with the past. When one makes a break of this sort, there is no possible return.

I had to organize the move and dispose of various objects— furniture, rugs, books—before I could start off on my journey to a new and intimidating world. I took along Ramprasad, the boatman, and a young servant called Lallan. Gulab and Kamal remained in Benares, where we had secured their futures.

Rewa Kothi was left abandoned for some time, then was taken up by an American cultural association; later it was given to the university. The inner garden fell into decay, the great rooms were divided by partitions, and the frescoes covered up with whitewash. The house was dead, and never again regained its style and beauty.

In Adyar, south of Madras, the Theosophical Society owns a great park beside the sea, covered with magnificent trees, so that the temperature is always nine degrees lower than in the surrounding countryside, which is quite barren. Pavilions of various sizes and styles are scattered all over the park. There are also a number of small temples, one for each religion: a church, a Buddhist temple, a mosque, and various other buildings; also "a site for a synagogue," the Jews having refused to pay. The property is surrounded by walls, and guards prevent visitors from approaching the beautiful private beach which is covered with fine, white sand and is over a mile long.

The Theosophical Society was created in the nineteenth century by Mrs. Blavatsky, an imposing lady of German origin who had been married to a Russian general and looked rather like Queen Victoria. She was an aunt by marriage to Nicolas and Vladimir Nabokov. This was the first of the "ashrams," organizations that are created to gather together (and exploit) dropouts from society, people vaguely interested in spiritism, magic, "the Orient," vegetarianism, ghosts, and other such nonsense. The Society has branches in every country in the world, and is very, very rich. Its "spiritual center" is in Adyar.

In the beginning, the Society suffered a few setbacks. It was proved that some of Mrs. Blavatsky's "miracles" were frauds. One of the founders, an Englishman called Leadbeater, had carried off a Tamil youth and declared him a reincarnation of the god Krishna, which did not prevent him from enjoying the boy's physical charms. The family took the matter to court, which led, in 1920, to a famous trial. After this the boy, called Krishnamurthy, left the Society, renounced his title of "god incarnate," and created his own sect in California.

These details, however, had been carefully forgotten, and the Society was ruled with the strictest puritanism: no tobacco allowed, obligatory vegetarianism; only unfertilized eggs could be eaten. Mrs. Blavatsky's masterwork, *The Secret Doctrine*, served as a kind of bible. She claimed to have acquired special powers from the mysterious sages of Tibet. The Society was also the center of a new order of freemasonry, open to both men and women; only initiates could enter its temple.

In 1907, the Englishwoman called Annie Besant became president of the Society. She was very active and an excellent organizer. She founded the Central Hindu College in Benares, created the India Home Rule League, and became president of the Indian National Congress in 1917, thereby preparing the ground for a movement of liberation and a transfer of power that England was considering even then.

After Mrs. Besant's death in 1933, the Society had several presidents. One of them, George Arundale, had married a fairly well-known dancer, Rukmini Devi, who created an art center, the Kalâkshetra, and a school of Indian dance within the Society. The art center included weaving workshops which produced very beautiful saris in the ancient fashion. The school of dance was a mixture of different styles. Rukmini was mainly interested in her own glory. She thought of herself as a goddess, a revealer of sacred dance; she was also an extremely domineering woman. After Arundale's death, Shri Ram, who was Rukmini's brother and Radha's father, became world president of the Society. Rukmini, who always hated Radha, had sent her away to one of the Society's branches, in Benares. Later, Radha made a triumphant return to Madras. After her father's death in 1978, she herself became president. According to the terms of her divorce, she was allowed to keep the name of her ex-husband. Today the president of the Society goes by the very Swiss surname of Burnier.

Mrs. Blavatasky's strong personality had made a deep impression on certain late nineteenth-century Indian cliques in search of their identities. She played an important role in creating the vague eclectic religion that later served to justify certain political actions and was the basis of Gandhi's philosophy. In his youth, Jahawarlal Nehru was deeply influenced by his private tutor, Ferdinand Brooks, a theosophist, and later became a member of the Society himself.

One of the Society's founders, an American called Colonel Olcott, was interested in creating a collection of manuscripts. He was offered gifts of private libraries belonging to princes and Brahmans who leaned towards the more modern Anglo-Indian style of life and did not know what to do with their cumbersome patrimony. When I went to Adyar, the library was the only one of its kind searching for manuscripts and now owned a very large collection.

Many of these texts were rituals and philosophic treatises for ordinary use, all very much the same. A large number of them were of considerable interest, however, and some were unique. The Society hired scholars to prepare some of these works for publication, especially rare texts of the *Upanishads* that were almost unknown. During the time I was in charge, we published the *Sangita Ratnakara*, a great twelfth-century Sanskrit work on musical theory. The library also issued a bulletin of Sanskrit studies whose contents and presentation I did much to improve, which earned me many congratulatory letters from Sanskrit scholars from all over the world.

When I took charge of the library, the manuscripts were in deplorable condition, worm-eaten and very badly catalogued. I made a number of trips abroad to study various methods of preservation and restoration of manuscripts, particularly in England and Italy, but also in France, the Bibliothèque Nationale in Paris being equipped with excellent laboratories.

The main problem was that Indian manuscripts were written on palm leaves, so I had to invent a system combining traditional and modern methods. The results were quite satisfactory. Disregarding certain theosophical regulations, I built a sort of gas chamber to eliminate insects and worms.

I created and published a new decimal system for classifying Sanskrit texts that was later adopted by other libraries.

While living in Madras I decided to study Tamil, an important and highly difficult pre-Aryan language of India. With the help of local specialists, I translated from ancient Tamil the great third-century epic romance, the *Shilappadikaram*, which was brought out by Gallimard under the title *Le Roman de l'anneau*. The English version was published in America by New Directions and entitled *The Ankle Bracelet*.

I was very interested in library work, but felt quite alone in this world of false values and intrigues which I found rather sinister and evil.

Raymond himself grew quite exasperated with this group of mediocrities who considered themselves chosen people. He wrote: "We are surrounded with so much stupidity that soon we shall be babbling ourselves." (Theosophical Society, 23 September 1953)

I found the puritanical atmosphere and the various taboos in Adyar extremely difficult to bear. On this occasion, unfortunately, my independent-mindedness played me a very nasty trick. I have always felt that accepting an arbitrary rule was a blow to my integrity, and that by allowing myself to remain passive I risked being caught up in events and circumstances that might lead to undesirable results. Apart from Simon Artz's famous, expensive, ambergris-perfumed Egyptian cigarettes, considered so very elegant at the time of Mata Hari and the Orient Express, and which I pretended to enjoy in my youth, I had never had a taste for tobacco. I began to smoke —an unfortunate habit that I have never since been able to give up.

Radha, who had insisted so much on my coming to Adyar and later expressed a desire to become my assistant, was not happy with her subordinate position. She wanted to manage the library on her own. She then began to create difficulties so that, in 1956, I finally had to resign my post and went to Pondicherry.

Radha had too easily forgotten why she had tried so hard to draw me to Madras. Many women, like spiders, weave a delicate web around the man they possess, as a person but also as a source of material security: a subtle prison of feigned understanding, charming caprices, manifestations of affection, and jealousy. Once caught in this trap, he gradually wastes away. There are exceptions, of course—magnificent, emancipated, generous, and devoted women who are often treated very badly by society. Yet even in the most reasonable and intelligent woman one sometimes feels those surges of effluvia enveloping the man she wishes to possess, like a warm suffocating cloud, something like the mesmerizing power of a magician and totally devoid of sensuality.

During my stay in Madras, I lived for a short time in one of the pavilions of the Society, then found a charming house away from that oppressive atmosphere I loathed. There I entertained some very interesting guests.

When the famous English musician Benjamin Britten visited Madras with his friend, the singer Peter Pears, they often came to see me. One day, when I was expecting them for lunch, I received a message informing me that Lord and Lady Harwood also wished to be invited. Without taking the time to think, I answered that this was impossible. It was a terrible gaffe: one does not refuse the honor of a visit from the Queen's cousin. Britten found himself in an awkward position, and the noble lord openly avoided me from that time on.

One of my most charming visitors was Queen Marie-José of Italy, who was very interested in Indian philosophy and remained in correspondence with me for several years afterwards. She came several times to my house for lunch. For dietary reasons imposed by my religion I could not eat meals in British hotels, but she insisted on inviting me for a cocktail. The barman at the Hotel Conneemara very rudely refused to serve the former queen and her guests. Gandhi and his followers had instituted a peculiar system of prohibition, and if one wished to buy liquor one needed a special "drug addict" permit. I hardly ever drank alcohol, but in order to buy whiskey for my guests I had to swear that I had been drinking since childhood and that my blessed mother was a hopeless alcoholic—after which I obtained all the liquor I wanted. It was I who had to buy the whiskey for the queen and her guests. Having so much insisted on my coming, she was quite embarrassed and felt very humiliated by this incredible lack of courtesy. Puritans are implacable.

PONDICHERRY

Pondicherry is a strange, sleepy little seaside town. A boulevard several hundred yards wide runs along a narrow beach that mostly serves as a dump. It is here, in this isolated spot, that the French chose to build their miniature *sous-préfecture*, which is quite charming with its Place d'Arme, the Residence, the City Hall, the hospital, the bank, a tiny church, and a few houses for civil servants; it looks rather like a toy town. Beyond this section, which is always deserted, is the crowded little Indian city, with its pretty wooden houses built around inner courts just like in Pompeii. Pondicherry has no port. French ships on their way to Indochina used to anchor two miles out in the open sea. They probably only did this so that Pondicherry could be mentioned in their itinerary as part of that prodigious list of Indian trading posts French children used to learn by heart at school. A few crates were then laboriously carried on smaller local boats that could be dragged up on the beach. This did not prevent French legislators from declaring before the Lower House: "We will never give up these naval bases on the route to Indochina." This is the kind of nonsense that influences politics.

Compared to the other trading posts of French India, Pondicherry seemed like a capital city. In Karikal, a Tamil village south of Pondicherry, the French presence was confirmed by three nuns. Yanaon, further north, had nothing but a few straw huts: France was represented here by an Indian sergeant holding a flag. Mahé, on the other side of India, was much the same. As for Chandernagor, a small village far up the river, north of Calcutta, it was practically abandoned.

The Institute of Indology, which had been recently created in Pondicherry, was established in a pretty house with a garden. I brought my library as well as one of my assistants, a distinguished scholar called Ramachandra Bhatt. Thanks to him, the Institute produced several important editions of texts and formed young scholars who were far more open to Indian culture than were students with a European education. Jean Filliozat, director of the Institute, fully appreciated Bhatt's qualities and made excellent use of his remarkable knowledge.

For myself, I found a charming house with a garden by the

sea and moved in with the faithful Mamma, who wasted no time in hiring some friendly local help.

At the Institute, I was asked to prepare a number of Sanskrit texts in the form commonly known as "critical edition," a very stupid and unimaginative system. This means that once the text has been edited according to the manuscripts, one has to prepare notes of all the transcriber's errors, all the possible false interpretations—in fact everything that should be eliminated to produce something readable. For every three lines of text one often has to prepare two pages of notes. I wanted to illustrate some of the texts with beautiful photographs, but this was considered unacceptable. "Artistic photographs are not scientific!" Professor Filliozat told me. We had to use dull, gray, lifeless pictures on which it was impossible to see anything at all. All my life the word "scientific" has loomed over me, denying all that is artistic, everything of the mind and spirit that has any real value; it is a word used by mediocrities to hide their ignorance. A translation must always be incomprehensibly literal, never the transcription of an idea or an image. It has been said of me: "He plays Indian music, therefore he is an artist; what he says about music cannot be scientific." Fortunately, preparing "scientific" editions is mechanical work and very easy to do, which left me plenty of time to concentrate on more serious things.

In every domain I have always met with the hostility of "scientists." On one occasion, when I was being criticized as an "amateur," Louis Renou was so exasperated that he publicly protested: "Daniélou may not be familiar with our methods, but when I don't understand a text, he is the man that I turn to." After that, French Indianists left me in peace.

Life in Pondicherry could be quite pleasant if one avoided its small, narrow-minded colony of civil servants and teachers. The first time I was invited for lunch by the headmaster of the French school, I heard his wife addressing the handsome servant who waited on the table with the familiar "tu." I naïvely assumed that he was her lover, which was probably untrue. In Indian languages, the familiar second person singular is only used between married people when they are alone together; otherwise one always speaks in the third person. In English, "thee" and "thou" are not used. I had forgotten French customs, which allow one to say "tu" to a native as one would to an animal, with the very amusing result that North Africans, among others, only know and use that form of address.

Mamma's elegance and my other servants' smart appearance created a scandal. When people found out that I had installed a bathroom and lavatories for my staff, I became a suspicious character. Most of the teachers and civil servants were left-wingers, but their egalitarian and antiracist principles did not include any thought for their servants' comfort, even though they had a great number of them and would have found exile unendurable without their help.

The preservation of the former colonial outposts, those so-called centers of French civilization, is absurd as well as expensive. The institutions kept up by France only employ civil servants from the home country, who live in comfortable idleness, and never the natives, except in domestic posts. The educational level of this "island of French culture overseas" was quite apparent in some of the touching requests that I sometimes used to receive.

"Dere boss. I undersind Ramou—yore frend. rite a litle wurd for yore gude hart. My father and my mother be ded. Nobody of one singul persun in Pondichéry. My litle Mother theris in Madras. Yu are the onliwun in Pondichéry you argun to. What kunnido nao. If yu givme sumething I go to Madras. No forgit yore Thankyu. I wate fur gud Ansore. Yore verree devotee
M. Ramou"

"My dere boss and my FRIENDS. I undersind Latchoumanin. Rite a litle wurd for yore gude harte, lastnite my mother be ded. theris no munnee. If yu giv Something I mek feoonrul fur my mother. thank yu inadvans. No forgit Our Thankyu. If yu giv helphand fur nao. I wate fur yur gud Ansore Pleze aksept expreshun uf my most dip rispict. Yore verree devotid
Latchoumanin

The local middle class speaks Tamil or English. The few French-speaking settlers have long since returned to France.

Raymond, who had remained in Madras, felt like a prisoner in the atmosphere of the Theosophical Society. He came to see me every week in Pondicherry and his visits grew longer each time.

Rémy Sorel was the head of an institution which France, after abandoning its territorial rights, had continued to maintain in Pondicherry in cooperation with the Indian government. He was an interesting character, far too intelligent and cultivated to easily endure the atmosphere of mediocrity that pervaded this small provincial pseudo-French village. He was delighted to discover someone more open-minded to talk to, and I was quite happy in the company of this learned and very amiable man. When I went to his house, however, I was disturbed by his bizarre behavior. Though not at all inclined towards the fair sex, he had married a woman older than himself whom he treated with embarrassing harshness. He had also adopted three children from the state orphanage and treated them with venomous cruelty. This created a harrowing atmosphere in his home. Behind his extreme courtesy and intellectual refinement lay evidence of inhuman authoritarianism and latent sadism that I found very difficult to bear. His wife, a broken creature who had gone slightly mad, shared his delusions. In her drawling little voice she would say to me, right in front of the children: "Alain, I want a little Chinese boy. Can't you buy one for me?" The children would listen silently, with tragic expressions on their faces. One of them, Marc, had a wonderful talent for drawing. After Rémy was transferred back to France, his adopted children tried to get away from him. I wanted to help Marc. Christine, my sister Catherine, and various friends of mine did all they could to help him find work, earn his living, and sell his drawings, but he remained ill-adjusted and slipped into a world of drugs, alcohol, and madness. Another son ran away and was never heard from again. My relationship with Rémy became quite tense after I tried to help his son in his artistic career. He needed his victims.

Once, Rémy accompanied me on a short trip to Calcutta. He was very eager to be received at the government palace. I sent a word to Padmaja. The Governor of Bengal's palace had been the Viceroy's residence before the capital was transferred to Delhi, and had lost none of its style. As visitors entered the palace they were saluted by a double row of guards wearing red, white, and gold uniforms. Then they were welcomed by a chamberlain who passed them on to an aide who led them to the governor's chambers. Padmaja was sitting on the floor of her sumptuous study, stroking a magnificent angora cat. She kissed me: "Alain, did you see my cat? He was just given to me by the King of Siam. Isn't he beautiful?" We remained talking on the floor for quite some time. Rémy felt very uncomfortable, his sense of grandeur somewhat crushed by this simple and unostentatious reception.

Another time, when Ashwin zur Lippe and his wife came to see me in Pondicherry, Rémy, whom I felt obliged to invite, lost himself in so many bows, "Sirs" and "Your Highnesses" that Simone de Lippe and I nearly burst out laughing.

Rémy always reminded me of those rigid and puritanical pastors of the last century, the kind I had read about in children's storybooks, who would savagely and regularly beat their children though they had done nothing wrong, just for the good of their souls. Nowadays one does not often meet this kind of character, worthy of the Comtesse de Ségur*. I was never able to understand the peculiar nature of this man who always behaved in a set and rigid way, like certain sadists who in ordinary life can seem quite pleasant, intelligent, and normal. In the end I stopped seeing Rémy but felt somewhat guilty, for he had done me many favors and always treated me with great friendliness. His family life, after all, was not my affair, but I could not remain indifferent.

The Institute of Indology was administered by a woman who was also studying Hindu mysticism. She had all the characteristics of a nun. An incurable Catholic, she had once been guided by my brother, the cardinal; later she became a disciple

---

*La Comtesse de Ségur (1799–1874) was a writer of popular children's books famous for their spanking and whipping scenes, cf., Les Malheurs de Sophie, Les Petites filles modèles, Le Général Dourakine, etc.—Trans.

of Père Montchanin and was part of a devoted group of women who surrounded him with sugary piety. She was extremely obliging and invariably sweet and gentle, though tenacious. She was obviously shocked by my pagan ways, but felt hopeful that my soul would some day be saved. "Outside the Church, there is no salvation, and the grace of God can perform miracles."

This virtuous woman had lived through an extraordinary experience. Her father, a doctor, had been stricken with an inoperable cancer of the nasal cavities. According to him, the only way to control the spread of this very painful disease was to take strong doses of morphine. The other doctors refused to use this form of treatment. For many years, Suzanne and her sister had gone to all possible lengths to procure the drug, contacting illegal suppliers and crossing borders with their dangerous goods. It was a magnificent example of filial devotion.

Suzanne skillfully edited and translated some of those pious and insipid works of late Hinduism with which Christians feel so easily at home. When Ramachandra Bhatt decided to visit Europe to attend some conferences on Oriental studies, she accompanied him. In 1976 they came to see me in Zagarolo. Bhatt stayed in the small hermitage I have in my garden. Every morning, at daybreak, he would pick some flowers whose purity had not yet been defiled and use them for his *puja* rites, which lasted all through the morning. I could hear him intoning Vedic hymns as he swung the oil lamp before an image he always carried with him and made offerings of flowers, water, and grains of rice to the gods.

His meals were specially prepared for him with milk we fetched from a neighboring farm and butter that was dutifully churned in his honor by Brian, a young Rhodesian who had come for a few weeks' holiday. While we were visiting Palestrina, a woman, seeing this strange Indian character all dressed in white linen, ran to fetch her son, a boy of seven or eight; and with that instinctive knowledge of true spirituality one so often finds in simple people, she took the boy up to him and humbly said: "My lord, bless this child!"

When Bhatt left he told me: "This is the first time since I

arrived in Europe that I have felt at ease. I feel as though I were still in India, on sacred ground."

Suzanne Siauve died the following year of the same disease that had killed her father; but there was no charitable soul beside her to soften her last moments, as she had done for him.

THE ASHRAMS

Aurobindo Ghosh, the son of a high Bengali official, had been educated in England, first in the house of a Manchester family, then in a London school. When he returned to India to occupy a post with the Maharajah of Baroda, he knew nothing about his own land. He became interested in the revolutionary movements and helped organize terrorist groups in Calcutta. Condemned to death by a British court, he managed to escape into French territory—first Chandernagor, then Pondicherry.

Since he could no longer be actively involved in politics, he devoted himself to the study of Hindu philosophy and created a kind of ashram for himself and a few followers. He wrote a number of books in English that mostly expressed his personal philosophy, a mixture of pseudo-Hinduism, Protestantism, and British socialism. A Lebanese Jewess, married to a man named Paul Richard, had come to India to see Alexandra David-Neel, who suggested a visit to Aurobindo. It was love at first sight. According to Alexandra, Mrs. Richard told her husband: "You can go home. I am staying." She became Aurobindo's Egeria and, being a good business woman, took charge of the ashram, which gradually developed into a vast enterprise, a sort of autonomous city called Auroville. Members gave all their wordly goods to the ashram, life was communal, and money was forbidden. They had to do everything themselves: there were workshops for carpenters, mechanics, masons, as well as bakeries and schools, etc. The devout, back-to-nature atmosphere was very attractive to middle-aged couples who came to live there and, having given everything away, had little choice but to remain. The problem, unfortunately, was that they sometimes brought their children. The latter were educated in the ashram's model schools—which were quite good—but the discipline was very strict, almost jail-like, and they were forced to work in the shops without pay, money being strictly forbidden. As a result, the ashram had a staff of young slaves, which made it possible to build the famous village of Auroville at very little cost. The children earned nothing but the ashram's diploma, which of course had no equivalencies with any other school. They might have run away, but with no money, no clothes, no diplomas, in a country where manual trades were severely restricted to specific castes, where could they possibly go? I often received secret visits from desperate young people who were trying to run away, hoping and begging for any kind of job—anything that would allow them to escape that model prison, that hellish paradise.

When Aurobindo died, his followers declared that his body, like those of the great yogis, was incorruptible, but were soon forced to change their minds. A discreet funeral was quickly and quietly arranged.

After his death, Mrs. Richard ruled this little empire with a firm hand. She was "the Mother," the supreme goddess and earth mother. Everyone had to bow down before her. Once a week she appeared before her adoring followers, sitting on a throne with her feet in a lotus-filled basin. She lived to a very old age.

Aurobindo's ashram was one of the principal commercial enterprises used to distort the message of India and exploit the good will of many sincere people in search of a "different truth." The ashram was all the more pernicious because it had originally been created by people of remarkable intelligence and probably of good faith, but with that irresponsible brand of fanaticism that characterizes many anarchists and gives them their strength.

A great many efforts were made to draw me into the ashram's circle. After a few visits, I was horrified by its sanctimonious atmosphere and from then on avoided any kind of contact with the organization during the years I remained in Pondicherry.

When I was travelling in the central part of southern India, I visited the ashram of Shri Ramana, known as the *maharishi*, "the Great Sage." He was an insignificant man, extremely fat, and allowed himself to be worshipped like a Buddha. His brothers had created a vast enterprise around him, a kind of residential place of retreat where Indians and foreigners could come to stay. The *maharishi* allowed his devotees to contemplate him during certain hours of the day. He would remain silent, though sometimes he managed to utter a few words of sickening banality. His brothers, however, published and sold short pamphlets filled with his so-called words of wisdom.

It was in this strange atmosphere that Juliette, my devoted musical assistant, spent her last years. This kind of ashram, after all, is preferable by far to an old people's home. All the members feel useful and play a role in the life of the community. For young people, however, closed circles of this kind prevent any contact with the real India. The devotees are kept in a sectarian atmosphere of false spiritual values that cannot lead them anywhere.

In Rishikesh, lost in the high valley that lies above the Ganges, was the ashram of Shivananda. This completely uneducated former police officer had chosen the contemplative life and managed to surround himself with a number of very odd characters, most of whom were Westerners.

Far more serious was the ashram of Ananda Maï (Mother Joy), who had been a school teacher in Bengal until one day she left her school, her husband, and her children and went wandering off on the roads of India, begging for her food. She had finally come to live in an abandoned house in Benares, on the banks of the Ganges. Little by little, a group of admirers and devotees formed around her. She bore with these people without really accepting them, and made their lives very difficult. All she wanted them to do was offer food to anyone who was hungry. This was not always easy, for many people in Benares live on ritual begging, not to mention the idlers who take advantage of it. When Ananda Maï was displeased about something, she would wander away on foot without saying a word to anyone or even thinking about them. Her panic-stricken disciples would set off after her. Sometimes she would climb up the Himalayan hills near Almora, where the ashram was being reestablished. Even in her fifties, she was still a very beautiful woman, and sometimes would allow her female worshippers to stroke her long graying hair for hours on end. She did not teach, but patiently listened to the problems of those who came to her, then gave them very simple advice. Her radiance was such that agitated and unhappy people were soon pacified, their anguish dissolving like the morning mists of the river Ganges; all their religious, metaphysical, existential problems would suddenly cease to be. Once their troubles were gone, these people would melt away into a beatific state far removed from life and earthly considerations.

Then there was the curious little ashram of Père Montchanin. This priest, who was either a Dominican or a Jesuit, had been deeply influenced by Hinduism and wanted to combine the two religions. He wore the draped orange cloth of Hindu monks, but obviously did not perform the ritual ablutions or observe the rules of strict cleanliness practiced by Hindus. He lived in a hermitage with a few followers and exerted a great influence on that special brand of foreigner who, while acknowledging the spiritual, philosophical, and moral superiority of Hinduism, still insists on Christian supremacy. This attitude has something to do with the Western sense of superiority and produces a form of religion that simply substitutes Jesus for Krishna and his legend for the Hindu god-hero's. This transposition does not disturb Hindus in the least. In Christians, however, it leads to a very odd mixture, for religion is more than a theology: it is a way of life, a code of ethics. Instead of mellowing through Hinduism, Montchanin and his devotees remained frustrated, neurotic, ill at ease, and, on the whole, rather disagreeable people.

Today the number of ashrams in India has multiplied, and spiritual tourism has become a very lucrative industry. One thing should be made clear, however: there is no link whatsoever between traditional Hinduism and what people today call an ashram. The word *ashram*, which is literally "a place of rest," has come to mean "a pseudo-spiritual gathering place for maladjusted Westerners with a craving for exoticism." In these ashrams the teaching is usually done in English, a language quite ill-suited to Hindu conceptions.

I had many opportunities to meet the victims of these ashrams. On one occasion I was asked to try to find an Argentinian woman whose family was quite worried, for she had long since ceased to write and was gradually giving away her fortune to a "Krishna Mission." After I had made several attempts to see her, she finally came to my house, accompanied by a hideous monk in an orange robe, who refused to let her speak outside his presence. She was obviously in a dangerous state of exhaustion and completely terrorized. The only way to save her would have been to tear her away by force from those ferocious watchdogs who starved, threatened, and probably drugged her. There was nothing I could do for her. She was a human wreck, completely dominated by pious charlatans.

One cannot be too careful in dealing with mystical tourism and ashrams created for foreigners, for these strictly commercial enterprises use very subtle and dangerous methods of brainwashing.

4. I had
acquired quite
a good technique

5. Raymond,
Christine,
and I in
Switzerland

6. Raymond

7. Tagore standing in front of his hermitage

8. Swami Karpatri, founder of the Dharma Sangh

9. The palace by the Ganges where I lived for fifteen years

10. Pilgrims gathered near the abandoned temples of Amarkantak

11. The trailer in front of
one of the temples of Khajuraho

12. Murlidhar and I using
mirrors to light up the sculptures

13. *Nabokov and Jacques Cloarec
after Stravinsky's funeral*

14. *I play the* vînâ

15. *San Zaccaria, where Casanova and d'Annunzio once lived*

16. *Watercolor of Zagarello
by Alain Daniélou*

17. *A young Afghan,
drawing by Alain Daniélou*

18. *Ravi Shankar and I receiving medals from Maurice Fleuret*

19. *Catherine, Zaher, Christine, and me on my seventieth birthday*

20. *The house in Zagarolo, a sacred Etruscan site*

CHAPTER THIRTEEN

Return to the West

"What is the use of conquering the universe if man loses
his soul in the process?"

—Blaise Pascal

When the shifting course of conquests and migrations causes a
people to lose its independence and a nation sees its beliefs, its
institutions, its arts, and its technology scorned, ridiculed, and
reviled, those who wish to maintain a mere semblance of
power and status are forced to collaborate with the occupying
forces and at least pretend to adopt their customs, prejudices,
language, culture, and code of ethics. They must learn to speak
disparagingly of their own institutions and treat them as relics
of a bygone age. If they wish to occupy even a second-rate
position in the administration of their own country, they must
first go off to the Empire's distant capital and imbue themselves with its language and culture. Little by little this culture
becomes theirs also, while the reality of their own, the culture
of their motherland, fades away into a vague and nostalgic
memory.

Some of these people may later wish to explore the culture
of their ancestors as students of religion and ethnology, and
try to present its positive aspects in such a way that it not only
conforms to the standards of their conqueror but is written in
his language.

When movements of independence rise against the occupying forces, these adaptations will then serve as a basis and

philosophy for the new nationalism, for a war of this kind can only be successfully waged in the opponent's territory. The strange result is that when these liberation movements succeed, the men who take over the power are nearly always those who have most profoundly assimilated the culture of their colonizers. They know too little about their ancestral culture, which they have learned to scorn and consider archaic and outmoded, to ever go back to it. The worst colonizers are the native leaders of the post-colonial era. They will do everything they can to suppress those who have remained faithful to their ancient culture.

It is impossible to understand the history of modern India without being aware of the strong feelings of ambiguity of the characters—many of them very distinguished—who played a prominent role in its destiny.

When the British came to India, the land had already suffered five centuries of Moslem occupation and an endless series of conflicts. In these conditions, Hindu institutions were unable to develop and became paralyzed and rigid. The pessimistic and blackened picture of traditional Indian society that was so skillfully drawn by the British was accepted and adopted without question by Indians who were being educated in London, Cambridge, or Manchester.

As far back as the early nineteenth century, a number of important movements were founded that adapted Hindu conceptions to the religious, moral, and social ideas of Anglican Protestantism. Their goal was to create a brand of Hinduism that would appear acceptable, perhaps even respectable to Westerners. It is important to keep this in mind when we consider Swami Dayananda Saraswati's Arya-Samaj, Devendranath Tagore (father of the poet) and Raja Ram Mohan Roy's Brahmosamaj, Mrs. Blavatsky and Annie Besant's Theosophical Society, not to mention Vivekananda and the Rama-Krishna Mission, Sarvapalli Radhakrishna, Aurobindo, and finally Gandhi. These British-style, English-language versions of Hinduism served as religious pretexts for the Indian National Movement and the Congress.

During the Moslem period, a similar movement had given birth to the Hindu-Islamic religion of the Sikhs, created by a disciple of the mystical Moslem poet Kabir, who was imbued with Hinduism.

A knowledge of these facts makes it easier to understand the personalities, ambiguities, and choices of the principal actors of modern political India. All of them had two countries and two allegiances, and were faced with the constant dilemma of betraying the one for the other. This explains the strange mixture of love and hate, admiration and hostility towards England that characterized the Nationalist Movement and the politics of India after independence was won.

The profound influence of British education on the Indian intelligentsia created men who literally had two countries: the land of their birth, with its vast heritage, first imposed on them then disowned, and that faraway ideal, England, where all of them dreamed of going, although it always kept them at a distance and treated them like second-class citizens, neither quite accepted nor rejected.

Even today, Indians of good family still study in England and attach more importance to speaking flawless English than knowing their own language, learning to choose the proper tie than observing the rules of Indian etiquette.

When the government began to promote changes in Indian society, its main goal was more often to appear modern in the eyes of foreigners than to improve the lives of the Indian people.

People may argue that the change was inevitable, that the ancient structures were outmoded and impracticable. This is only partly true. The fundamental changes imposed on India have resulted in such chaos that it will someday become necessary to return to the original structures of the traditional Indian society.

The Indian system is in fact an extension of the family into a social group. India is not a land of arrogant Brahmans and wretched "untouchables," but of hundreds of ethno-social-religious-cultural groups who live alongside each other and are protected by the system.

By denying the reality of castes and abolishing these social divisions, the government has only succeeded in depriving the weaker groups of their autonomy, destroying their means of defense, then dispossessing and annihilating them.

Only recently, Rajiv Gandhi has begun to consider ways of saving the tribal populations from total extinction.

Since earliest recorded times, India has been a land of freedom and a refuge for the persecuted, for its inhabitants were always divided into tribes and ethnic, racial, cultural and religious groups that strived to maintain their autonomy. An egalitarian society that is only interested in individuals can only lead to their depersonalization, for it destroys the framework without which they cannot develop. Independence gained at the expense of the social, religious, and cultural heritage that has made a country great cannot be worth very much.

EXILE

Like the modern Indians I criticize so severely, I too am a product of conflicting civilizations. I had chosen Hindu culture, and Hindi had become my language; yet the first books I published about India were written in English. I was now wholly integrated in the traditional world and avoided making any kind of concession to the synthetic society of anglicized Indians or the small-minded and insignificant colonial civil servants who considered me a European "turned native," a kind of hippie before his time.

I also remained on good terms with foreign personalities, writers, artists, and politicians, and made friends within the Viceroy's circle who found me amusing and original. We had our caste in common; we belonged to the same world by virtue of our heritage.

My unwillingness to benefit from British apartheid, to enter grand hotels, clubs, restaurants where Indians were not admitted, had made me quite popular with the leaders of the Nationalist Movement who suffered from their exclusion. For me, it was a matter of choice. My association with conservative Hindu circles was not a problem for Indian politicians: all of them had relatives among these groups.

Everything changed after India became independent and Congress took power; Nehru's politics tended towards pro-

Soviet socialism, which brought him into conflict with the traditional world.

The Hindu parties had fought as hard as they could against the partition of India, and celebrated Gandhi's death. Their leaders were still violently opposed to the ideas and politics of Nehru and the Congress. Soon the leaders of the Jana Sangh and the Rashtriya Svayam Sevak Sangh (right-wing militarists) began to fill the old British prisons that had only recently been vacated by the Congress leaders who were now in power.

I had been warned long before by friends in orthodox circles that it would soon become too difficult for me to remain in India, that I would eventually have to leave. I was told that I would be more useful spreading the message of India, telling the world of the dangers that threatened its culture and heritage. I had never considered leaving India which was now my home, but I had to face the facts; little by little, I quietly prepared my exile. The Indian ambassador in Paris, a very courteous Moslem, recently asked me: "How is it possible that such a great lover of India can speak so harshly of those whom we consider the fathers of our country?" The reason is simple: I am not "a lover of India," I am a Hindu, a follower of the ancient culture, living in exile.

I do not complain of my lot, for life has been kind to me in my exile; and I have the strange feeling that those who helped to initiate me into the secrets of their ancient knowledge are still watching over me from afar.

A Trip to Europe

In May 1948 I returned to Europe for a short visit. I had spent most of the last sixteen years in India and had not left it for a decade. This journey presented a certain number of difficulties. I had not dressed in European clothes for many years and still wore a sacred lock of hair wound over my head. The new habits I had acquired, my diet, and my ritual bathing created further complications.

I was still living in Benares at the time and the contrast between these two entirely different worlds was very great. I had forgotten some of my French, and it took me some time to learn it again; even now, when I am not careful, I still use anglicisms.

Not knowing where to go, I asked my sister Catherine if I could stay with her for a time, and she welcomed me in her home with a great deal of kindness and understanding. She and her husband were living in a very beautiful apartment in Paris on the Boulevard Saint-Germain, in a large town house—a former *hôtel particulier*—built by Garnier, who also created the Opéra. The house had been incorporated into a modern building but still had beautiful frescoed ceilings and large windowed doors overlooking a garden. I stayed with Catherine for several weeks, then moved to the Hôtel Pont-Royal.

I visited my parents from time to time. My father had heart problems and had long since retired from political life. My mother seemed to have grown more gentle and was far more patient and understanding with her grandchildren than she had ever been with us. My relations with her, however, remained unchanged, affectionate but distant; I had no desire to draw closer to my family.

For someone who had experienced almost nothing of the war, the occupation, or the genocides, Europe made a very strange impression. France seemed to have emerged not just from a war but from a civil war. The country had gone from one form of relatively moderate military dictatorship to another. There were no real battles, only settlings of scores; no armies, but guerrilla warfare. Those who had been favored by one regime were considered traitors by the other. Calculating and ambitious men seeking official, political, and cultural posts seemed to be taking no chances and made up stories about the heroic roles they had played in the Resistance. In some ways nothing seemed to have changed; one heard the same stock phrases, the same slogans and inanities as before the war. The atmosphere was far less lighthearted, however, for everyone was terrified of being denounced. The feeling of tension and anxiety reminded me somewhat of Germany at the dawn of Nazism.

The Russians were taking full advantage of the defeat and disgrace of Fascism, although their own system was no less lethal. The Nazis had left a tradition of puritanism, xenophobia, governmental encroachment into private life, as well as a police organization, all of which had very much changed the friendly character of Paris. The fantasy, the extravagance, and the "I don't give a damn" attitude that had somehow produced so many men of genius had vanished along with the cafés, the idling painters, the little seamstresses, the bordellos, the boys' brothels, and those easygoing hotels that smelled so pleasantly of opium during the Third Republic.

Paris has never recovered from that inner war and even today, after forty years, some people still lie about their behavior during the occupation. They are afraid of being blackmailed, afraid that someone will find out that they collaborated or failed to resist. They would do better, I think, trying to analyze the reasons for their defeat. The same conditions that led to the downfall of France are now being recreated for the sake of another kind of imperialism.

The highest positions were now occupied by so-called intellectuals, who were more or less consciously prepared to hand over Europe to the Soviets. They, in fact, were the real collaborators, but no one dared to oppose them.

Max d'Ollone had aged a great deal and now seemed a lost and bewildered man. During the war this carefree, absent-minded musician, who understood little of the national tragedy, had accepted the directorship of the Opéra-Comique. When France was liberated, he was publicly insulted and stripped of his pension, his fortune, even his "légion d'honneur." Later he was rehabilitated, but his zest for life had gone forever.

It was very difficult for me to understand the problems, states of mind, and attitudes of the people around me, for I had not been there to witness the dramas that had produced them. I felt, in fact, like a complete stranger in the land of my birth. By my way of thinking, feeling, living, I now belonged to another civilization. Although Europe was in some ways a pleasant and interesting place to live in, it was no longer my homeland, and I did not feel part of it; I was an exile. The little I recognized seemed part of a previous existence, a kind of dream. I could sympathize with the problems of the world around me, but they were not my own. I had become a man without a country, for the changes in India's government and its progressive tendencies now made it impossible for me to live in its ancient, thousands-of-years-old civilization, in that golden age of humanity that I had discovered but was now losing as well.

I felt particularly uncomfortable in France. But I had to grow reaccustomed to Europe—America would probably have been even worse. For a few years, instead of spending the hot season in the Himalayas, I returned to Europe. It was now out of the question for us to take those long sea journeys via the Suez Canal. Flying only took three days. The airplanes always travelled by day, with several stopovers; we would spend the first night in Karachi, the next in Cairo, and the last in Rome, Geneva, or Paris.

I bought a car in Switzerland and began to explore the European continent—Denmark, Holland, Sweden, and Italy.

My visits to Italy made a deep impression on me. It was the only country besides India where I felt I could live. It was during this period of my life that I was forced to move to Madras, then Pondicherry. Southern India was never a home to me. I did not feel that I could live there forever, as I had in the north.

Italy had been totally devastated. The villages were in ruins, the bridges destroyed, the roads rutted and torn up. Here, like everywhere else, people spoke of liberation without knowing precisely what they were being liberated from, though the word, of course, sounded very fine. The Venetians had unanimously voted for "the Republic." When they found out that they had voted for an Italian republic, they were appalled; for them "republic" could only mean the glorious, the powerful, the one and only Republic of Venice which had nothing to do with the kingdom of Italy.

In this country ravaged by war, no one ever seemed to complain. Apart from the politicians—who belong to a special world quite removed from the people they are supposed to represent—no one accused or recriminated against his neighbor. There was too much else to do: making a living, surviving, rebuilding. In Italy, political affiliations did not have the aggressive quality they had in France, nor the ambiguities of the Germans', who were constantly subjected to insults even when their own parents had been exterminated in camps or their children massacred on the battlefield.

During my first visits to Italy, when I was still living in Benares, I rented an apartment in Rome for the summer each year and spent most of my time travelling from one end of the country to the other.

I made several trips to Apulia, where some of the most harmonious baroque monuments in the world can be seen, especially in Lecce and Martina Franca. In spite of its ancient olive groves, Apulia is a region of great poverty, but here the people, though poor, are proud and noble. The families in this area traditionally ate one meal a day, a large plate of pasta at noon, but did not feel degraded by their asceticism. I spent most of my time in Taranto, the ancient capital of Magna Grecia, the Grecian Italy. In certain villages people still speak ancient Greek. The ruins of Metaponte evoke the ancient splendor of the region. Wedged on a narrow strip of land between the sea and the great lagoon (*il mare piccolo*), Taranto has always been a perfect haven for navigators. Today it is a warport that commands the entire Mediterranean. In those days, it was a simple, provincial city with no problems or pretensions. Noblemen and persons of consequence lived in vast, nearly empty houses.

All the people were royalists and even in the humblest homes one always saw the portrait of the exiled king hanging beside an image of the Virgin. The Countess of L., president of the Monarchist party, lived in a patched-up shack lost among the dunes by the seaside. She entertained in princely style in a bare room with sunken old armchairs. A staff of servants was indispensable to her rank, but for reasons of economy was limited to a few graceful little boys of twelve or thirteen who wore short pants and white jackets with golden epaulets decorated with a coat of arms.

One of the party secretaries was called Don Salvatore. He was blind and lived in a small, two-room apartment that he shared with a retired officer who gave him his pension in exchange for two fried eggs and four slices of sausage a day. In order to increase his income, Don Salvatore allowed the sailors of the Italian Navy to change into civilian clothes in his apartment for the modest sum of one hundred lire. Sometimes, while they were changing their clothes, he would avail himself of their charms. A tiny room that served as a kitchen as well as a lavatory was decorated with a portrait of the Queen of England and a political engraving representing the port of Trieste, which was not given back to Italy until a few years later, in 1954. When Don Salvatore entertained distinguished visitors, he invariably served them an *amaretto* of his own confection. When the time came to fill the glasses, he would retire with dignity into the kitchen-lavatory. Since he could not see what he was doing, he would fill his mouth with the liquor and carefully spit out the right amount into each glass, which the forewarned visitors quietly emptied into flower pots.

The poor people of Taranto were cordial and hospitable to anyone they considered a friend. I often visited the ancient city, a small island of clustered houses and tiny streets, connected to the new city by a swing bridge. It was safer, however, not to venture there by oneself. Sometimes a tipsy American sailor was lured into the area by the promise of a beautiful girl, then would emerge a few hours later stripped of all his possessions and without a stitch of clothing on his back. The police hardly dared enter this jungle.

The modern trend towards economic development in southern Italy later led to the creation of a huge metallurgical industry. Gentle Taranto is now a crowded city with ugly modern buildings and luxury shops. Its people, once cheerfully idle, poor but proud, are condemned to live in depressing misery and forced to work in the factories. Taranto has lost its *joie de vivre*. The vast empty beaches that I once knew are now crowded with cabanas and foreign tourists in the summertime.

I visited Amalfi for several years in a row; it was a charming little port, where one rarely saw any foreigners. In those days, this ancient miniature republic was very hard to reach and completely autonomous. There were three hotels. Two of them, the Luna and the Capuccini, were former monasteries; the third, Santa Catharina, had access to the sea, which could be reached by an interminable flight of steps. The residents of these three hotels remained invisible. I made friends with a young fisherman and sometimes accompanied him on his boat trips. He found me a room in an old house overlooking the port.

It was through Roland Bourdariat, a Parisian who had been recommended to me by René Guénon, that I met a very singular man who lived in a beautiful villa by the sea. He was an American and called himself the Baron de Van. He was interested in music and published a luxurious musical review in collaboration with Roland. He and his wife were separated and he lived with his son, a frail boy of ten whom Roland devotedly looked after. The baron was completely under the influence of drugs and had such frequent fits of depression that it was sometimes difficult to approach him. When we were together I often used to play and sing Indian *râgâs*, whose deep and intense emotion he immediately understood. He died the following year of an overdose of drugs, and Roland had to take care of everything—the sale of the villa, the inheritance, and mostly the boy, who had no one but him to turn to and was finally taken back to his mother, an American woman who apparently showed very little interest in her son. A year later, I found Roland dressed up as a seminarian; he had become secretary to a cardinal and now lived in the Vatican. I was spending the summer in a small Roman hotel on the Via Borgognona, where Roger Peyrefitte was also staying to write a book about the Vatican. Roland tried in vain to put the monsignori of the Roman Curia on their guard, but they found Peyrefitte charming and paid no heed to Roland's cautionary advice. He would come to the hotel, looking very prim in his black cassock, and sit inside my car; then the cassock would fly to the winds as we drove off in search of some Roman adventure. At the time of the liberation Roland's father, a very rich antique dealer, had lost everything he owned, and Roland had lived through some difficult years. He later became one of the most respected translators at Unesco.

For several years Rome remained a free and pleasant city.

But little by little, as it grew more prosperous, all the vultures reappeared and the character of the city soon changed. The atmosphere of freedom that one so often finds after wars and revolutions gradually disappeared. Politicians and bourgeois— those rapacious, dishonest, unpleasant puritans who disappear so quickly in periods of crisis—were once more in top positions, setting their police force against the little people and throwing them into prison for stealing three apples, while they, under cover of virtue and righteousness, speculated on rate exchanges and raised the price of living. It was becoming difficult to find an apartment without getting involved in various complications and being unjustly accused of financial illegalities.

During that time I met a very strange character, Roberto, who had once been the friend of a famous couturier and had lived with him in great luxury. Then he had fallen on hard times and became a racketeer and a thief, living on various shady dealings that occasionally landed him in prison. He was a strong, hardy man in his thirties, a kind of small-time Mafia boss, highly feared and respected. For some mysterious reason, he took a liking to me—not unlike those so-called dangerous animals who always seem to approach me so fearlessly. He took me under his wing and never asked me for any money, which did not prevent me from offering him gifts when he needed them. Thanks to him, I was able to explore the strange little world of the Roman suburbs where, though delinquency is the rule, such virtues as solidarity, friendship, and honor also exist.

Roberto once took me to Naples to one of those half-buried dwellings brimming with the strangest specimens of humanity. The *mamma* was a stout matronly figure, good-natured and dictatorial. She had eleven sons and daughters, all thieves and prostitutes. They would sit together, gay, amusing, full of zest for life, around a huge table in a large vaulted dining room. The *mamma* would bring out a large cauldron filled with pasta. Everywhere one looked one could see images of the Virgin or the saints surrounded with artificial flowers; in front of each image was a small, permanently burning oil lamp. Once accepted in this little world, I had no fear of anyone harming me or my car, which was quite luxurious but always seemed mysteriously protected; if some pickpocket happened to take my wallet by mistake, it would reappear an hour later, with nothing removed and a message of apology. When Raymond met Roberto, it was wintertime, and he offered him an old raincoat he no longer wore. Roberto was outraged. One can give a friend a stolen object, but never a hand-me-down. I did not see him for a long time after this; when I did, he told me that had it not been for his own feelings of friendship for me, Raymond would have had cause to regret his insolence. I was not surprised by his attitude and would never have committed such a blunder myself. In this curious environment one can help a friend in need, but only with the greatest of tact. Charity is a form of humiliation and often inspires hate.

This story reminded me of the widow of Francis Picabia who, even when down to her last franc, would invite people to tea, which she elegantly served in chipped, unassorted cups from a lidless teapot. What would she have thought if someone had decided to send her a magnificent new tea set from the five-and-ten?

Through an ambassador friend, I was given the address of a baker's son who had previously lived in Paris and offered me a tiny room in an inn kept by his family, called the Paradiso. I spent several summers with this simple, hospitable, generous, uncomplicated proletarian family. Here I learned to appreciate a nation of courageous, hard-working, open, and independent people whose virtues the modern, exploitative consumer society is trying hard to destroy, though it will never succeed.

The Paradiso

The Paradiso was situated right outside Rome, near a vacant area that ran along the railroad track. It was partially in the country, with shacks strewn here and there and a population always on the verge of delinquency. The owner was a modest, hardworking baker who was always covered with a light dusting of flour. Bread was baked each morning for the entire neighborhood; there was another oven for pizzas. In front of the ancient two-story structure was a huge vine-covered pergola that served as a restaurant in the summertime; a large dining room inside the house was used in winter. The hill beside the inn had been partly scooped out to accommodate a cement platform where, on Saturdays and Sundays, all the young people of the neighborhood danced to the music of a local orchestra. It was the first time I had ever heard modern popular dance music; the Italian and American songs, which were highly expressive at the time, caused me a real emotional shock.

The baker's wife was a worthy Roman matron who cleaned, tidied her house, cooked, did the laundry and ironing, and, most of all, protected and defended her children with unbounded devotion. Whenever she sat down to catch her breath, a tame hen would immediately sit on her lap, and they would cluck affectionately at one another while she gently stroked its feathers.

She had nine children. One of the sons was married and ran the restaurant. Two younger boys helped with the baking and delivered the bread. The eldest son had done very well for himself. His name was Angelo and he had always been the perfect angel in this paradise, being a very pretty boy, pink and fair, lively, intelligent, and amusing. Like all Roman youths, he had gone chasing after a life of adventure and small profit, in the course of which a French diplomat had taken a fancy to him and, for a time, adopted him. For several years Angelo reigned over various embassies, lived in Paris, and even worked as a journalist. Now he had finally returned to the fold.

There were also three daughters. Elsa, the eldest, lived with a tall, hardy female who was as strong as a boxer and never hesitated to exchange punches with men, but otherwise seemed an inoffensive and obliging creature. A younger daughter had left the family for a more or less indeterminate fate. From time to time she would make an appearance, looking very elegant. The youngest girl was still in her teens and remained virtuously beside her mother.

I enjoyed a number of charming and passing affairs with some of the young people who frequented the Paradiso. Whenever the police, who were required to keep an eye on public dancing places, happened to ask indiscreet questions about this stranger who was always hanging about, Elsa would sharply intervene: "How dare you cast a doubt on the honorable character of my fiancé?" "Excuse me, signorina, I was not aware," he would answer, and everything would return to normal.

Elsa even asked me to "try out" her youngest sister's suitors, to make sure they had the proper physical attributes, sufficient ardor, and so forth. I had to give a detailed report.

Raymond felt very bored in Madras and was also having financial troubles. During the war, he had had to declare his sources of income to British officials who then passed on the information to the Indian government. Nehru's policy was to destroy fortunes in the name of certain theories of social justice that usually benefit the state but never the poor. Raymond was suddenly ordered to pay back taxes which he supposedly owed the government for the past fifteen years and represented a large part of his fortune. He decided to leave India. Radha preferred to stay with her father who had become president of the Theosophical Society. She agreed to a divorce in exchange for a life pension.

I was spending a holiday at the Paradiso when Raymond finally arrived alone, lost, and bewildered; even the faithful Kamal had married and gone away. Having spent his childhood on an Algerian farm and gone off with me to Asia at the age of nineteen, Raymond—in spite of his visits to Paris—had never considered living in Europe. He now had to find a new life for himself, a new *raison d'être*. Unlike me, he was not involved in work that could be carried on anywhere. I still had responsibilities in Pondicherry and had to go back. I left Raymond in Angelo's care, and he lived for some time at the Paradiso, which gave him a chance to learn many things. It was a strange experience for this elegant Swiss *grand bourgeois* to suddenly find himself plunged into a little world that seemed straight out of a Pasolini movie.

Raymond took pictures for some articles that Angelo was preparing and patiently taught him the art of photography. Angelo made rapid progress and, with his skill, quick mind, and lively temperament, soon entered the world of fashion and cinema. He became the favorite photographer of all the movie stars, who found his bright chatter highly entertaining. Today he owns a beautiful house in the Roman countryside, filled with objets d'art, with a large swimming pool and a studio where theater and movie stars come from all over the world to be immortalized. Here one might meet Jane Fonda, Ava Gardner, Sophia Loren, Gina Lollobrigida, and Helmut Berger, Alain and Nathalie Delon, Ursula Andress, as well as Fellini and all the great Italian directors. Most famous movie stars are rather uninteresting: they are simple puppets, created entirely by the director, and only play short sequences at a time. Jean Renoir used to say that the ideal actor should never act, never think, and only needed a sufficiently vacant expression to look profound. Those with strong personalities, like Chaplin or Anna Magnani, play only one role throughout their career and are exactly the same in life as they are on film. Theater actors, however, are different, for they create and live their roles.

On Nobility

Roman aristocracy still exists. I have often visited the home of Princess Pallavicini, protectress of Monsignor Lefèvre, the well-known religious conservative who strongly opposes modern trends at the Vatican. She lives in a magnificent palace in the center of Rome. In order to reach the small drawing room where she usually receives her guests, one must pass through great museum-like halls with marvelous frescoed ceilings and enormous paintings by the great Italian masters; the furniture, sumptuous but slightly heavy, is lined up along the walls.

Some of these great families have lost their fortunes: Princess Rospigliosi, a very agreeable woman, lives modestly in a small apartment. Rich or poor, however, they are very dear to the Italian people, who love their princes as much as they love their monuments. One day, while I was out walking with Giovanni Borghese, I was struck by the familiar, though deeply respectful way the neighborhood people would address him in the street: "*Buon giorno, signor Principe!* And how are you today? Ah! It's a sad world we live in now, isn't it?" In Rome one always has the feeling of being at the theater. There is a tacit understanding and a mutual feeling of respect between the aristocracy and the little people, the artisans—the two classes of society with which I feel most comfortable.

Romans are deeply shocked by the behavior of the present pope, who goes around in a white Japanese jeep, shaking hands and mixing with the crowds as though he were a candidate for the United States presidency. His appearances on the balcony of Saint Peter's before busloads of multiracial groups are now an accepted part of local tourism. After the crowds have dispersed, Bernini's noble square is littered with dirty scraps of paper, beer cans, and Coca-Cola bottles. Romans think very little of the pontiff's homilies on abortion, contraception, and the pill, and say that he ought to see a psychiatrist. But the common people, those who cross themselves at every possible opportunity, wear gold crosses on their breasts, touch their sex to ward off evil spirits, and fill their homes with pious images and small altars for the Virgin—whom they invoke before running off to commit a crime or in search of adventure—no longer understand. A religion that has lost all its pomp and splendor and is no longer expressed in the mysterious and sacred language of the Apostles seems just like any other political party. Religion is something magical and has nothing to do with morality or social laws. Rome deserved far better.

ZAGAROLO

Rome is one of the world's great religious centers, but only in the areas surrounding the ancient city does one find those magical places where the forces of heaven and earth seem to meet and one feels the presence of gods. I wanted to live near Rome. I had stayed long enough at the Paradiso and could not enjoy its hospitality and relative comforts forever.

During one of my visits to Rome, Raymond and I began to search for a property in the area. In the course of one of our random explorations, we were shown a beautiful house in the countryside not far from Palestrina.

The village of Zagarolo, which is just below Palestrina, stands on a rocky spur that must once have been the site of a prehistoric colony. Its caverns, hollowed out of the rocks and now hidden by façades, are still inhabited.

The house we were offered was built on a hill called the Labyrinth. We found some fragments of pink marble columns and a few remains of architraves. In ancient times, it was probably the site of a sanctuary.

Yet, even after Raymond moved into the beautiful house, I

still did not like it; I was not comfortable there and could not help feeling that there was something evil about it. Farther up the hill, however, was a peasant's house that seemed far more favorable, and I was able to buy it. I later enlarged it and from then on stayed there for extended periods. The Labyrinth is one of those places where the spirit seems to breathe and peace prevails. The mysterious hand of the gods had led me to a friendly, favorable place where I felt that I could live and work.

People claim that the name of Zagarolo comes from *Caesariolum*, after Caesar, who owned a villa there. For me, however, the word has always evoked Zag, the Cretan name for Zeus.

Only much later—thanks to the research of a historian, Emanuela Kretzulesko-Quaranta, who is married to a Rumanian and lives in the area—did I discover that Zagarolo and its Labyrinth, along with Praeneste (now called Palestrina) had once been the most sacred site of the ancient world. According to legend, Aeneas, after escaping from burning Troy, landed his ship at Circeo, fled through the Labyrinth, and finally found shelter beside the Great Goddess who lived in a cavern on the Praenestan Mountain. Later, Praeneste became the religious center of the Etruscan world, and a temple was built in front of the cavern. The Romans, who came here to worship the Great Goddess in the form of Fortuna Primigenia, enlarged the temple, which became a massive structure. Its interlacing ramps, built directly on the mountain, went down into the valley from sanctuary to sanctuary. It was here that the armies would come to make sacrifices to the gods before leaving on their expeditions. A tall golden statue of the Goddess rose above the temple. It could be seen from the sea through an opening between the Alban Mountains, and the commanders of Roman fleets would invoke it from afar before sailing off into the domain of Poseidon.

Emperor Hadrian, eager to rediscover the wisdom of the ancient people, restored and enlarged the temple and constructed a palace at the foot of the hill from which he could contemplate the sacred mountain; it was not far from the great villa he had built in Tivoli for his pleasure and glory. In Praeneste he brought together many wise men who still knew the secrets of the ancient Egyptian religion. He sent for Greek artisans to pave the great sanctuary and the famous "Cave of Spells" with precious mosaics. These mosaics, considered the most beautiful in the world, have resisted the ravages of time.

The temple was abandoned and sacked, but its imposing structures stood intact until the troops of Pope Eugene IV destroyed them in 1436.

Less than half a century later, in 1484, Francesco Colonna, son of Prospero Colonna and friend of the popes Nicholas V and Pius II, both advocates of humanism, built a palace over the ruins of the sanctuary in order to protect it without changing anything of its basic structure or touching the mysterious passageways that had been hollowed out of the mountain. In his other palace in Zagarolo, Francesco Colonna gathered together the first humanists who were in search of ancient wisdom. Among these were Giovanni Pico della Mirandola, Alessandro Farnese, Nicholas of Cusa, and especially Leone Battista Alberti, architect, philosopher, and probable author of the mysterious symbolic work *The Dream of Poliphilus*, which describes a mystical journey to the sacred sites of Palestrina and Zagarolo. These men were seeking to discover the religious traditions and rites of the ancient world. Zagarolo was a center of development of what was later called the Renaissance, a movement of return to ancient sources that originated in the Accademia Vitruviana in Rome, then the Accademia Romana in Zagarolo. It came to an abrupt end when Pope Paul II, concerned over this return to "pagan" wisdom, arrested the members of the Academy, tore out their tongues, and had them put to death. In the meantime, the movement had spread far enough to influence Lorenzo de' Medici and François Ier, though by then it had become more cultural and had lost much of its original intent, which was essentially religious, philosophic, and ritual. The initial goal was far too openly opposed to the Church, always greedy for power rather than wisdom and truth.

I had gone in search of a pleasant house within a short distance from Rome. Chance—or was it destiny?—led me to a place that had been considered sacred and magical since the most ancient prehistoric times.

CHAPTER FOURTEEN

The Message of India

PUBLICATIONS

In 1960 I left Pondicherry for good and was taken on by the Ecole Française d'Extrême-Orient. I was now officially settled in Paris. I went back to the Hôtel Pont-Royal and lived there for several months. Then, with some difficulty, I managed to retrieve the studio on the Rue Froidevaux and put it back in order. While I was living at the Hôtel Pont-Royal, I worked on a French translation of my book *Hindu Polytheism*, which had already been published in English as part of the Bollingen Series at Princeton.

Louis Renou had told me: "You have learned enough; now you must make use of your knowledge. You have enough work to last you till the end of your life." So I set to work. I undertook, in a series of books, to draw a true picture of the Hindu world on many different levels—philosophic, religious, social, ethical, and artistic. I tried to offer an insight into the profound values of this extraordinary civilization, the only one of all the great civilizations of the ancient world that has survived, whose contribution, were it better known, could revolutionize modern thinking and bring on a new Renaissance. This is probably why people are so afraid of it. The true message of India has nothing to do with the pseudomystical rubbish it is all too often identified with. Little by little I began to study parallel sources in Western antiquity, which led to my book *Shiva and Dionysus*.

A religion is essentially a tradition made up of various heritages, beliefs, superstitions, and rites, but its feeling and atmosphere cannot be expressed in arid theological texts. One cannot form any idea of the day-to-day Christian life of a shepherd from Abruzzi or a Breton peasant girl by reading the works of Saint Augustine or my brother, the cardinal. Similarly, the multiple aspects of Hinduism are not contained in the arid speculations of the relatively modern *Vedanta*, which European Orientalists find so interesting.

My translation work and my attempt to elucidate Hindu conceptions presented many difficulties because no words in any Western language can express the very subtle notions of Hindu metaphysics or cosmology. I had to express one way of thinking through the bric-a-brac of the vocabulary of another. Everything had to be rethought, no word could ever be translated directly by another.

During the years I lived in India, I had been in close contact with the British world. London's Royal India Society had brought out my first book on music, *Introduction to Musical Scales*. In 1949, I published *Yoga, Method of Reintegration*, which was based on Sanskrit texts. In 1964, the Bollingen Foundation brought out a magnificent American edition of *Hindu Polytheism*, which was reissued in 1985 by Inner Traditions International in New York. New Directions had published *The Ankle Bracelet* in 1965; Barrie and Rockliffe, an important work on Indian music, *The Ragas of Northern Indian Music*, in 1968. In France, Robert Voisin of the Editions de l'Arche issued my *Yoga* in 1951, and Edmond Buchet *Le Polythéisme hindou* in 1960, as well as other works I later wrote. My *Quatre Sens de la vie* (1963) was published by the Librairie Académique Perrin, and later reissued by Buchet.

Pierre Bérès was very interested in Raymond's photographs, and published them in 1960 under the title *Visages de l'Inde Médiévale*, one of the most beautiful books ever produced on Indian art; it was reissued in 1985. He had also organized a very large exhibition of Raymond's photographs which were also displayed in 1949 at the Metropolitan Museum in New York. Bérès brought out some of my more difficult works, such as the *Traité de musicologie comparée* and especially *Sémantique musicale*, which challenges the basic principles of all the musical systems; it had been turned down by every other publisher, who considered the book unsellable. Pierre Bérès, a world-renowned expert on ancient books, belongs to that disappearing breed of what one might call "patrons," who choose works simply because they like them. Whether or not they make a fortune from such books is of secondary importance.

My work was something of a problem to publishers because it did not belong to any preestablished category. For those academic quibblers who never pay attention to a text's real content, my work was considered "unscientific" because I translated from Sanskrit exactly as I would have done from English, trying to express the exact meaning of texts but with another vocabulary. They would have preferred for me to translate into a pedantic and incomprehensible jargon, using terms of etymology, weight, and meaning different from those of the Sanskrit works.

But there was a further problem. True Hinduism has very little to do with those mindless ramblings that seem so much more congenial to people in search of a vague form of Orientalism which, like fashionable yoga, does not disturb their habits and is ultimately only a means of escaping reality. My *Histoire de l'Inde*, though honored by the Académie Française, sold relatively few copies. It took a great deal of time—and the passing of some of the luminaries of the academic world—for my work to find its place and its public. The Church, the University, and the false prophets created a barrier of silence that was very difficult to break through. In any case, it did not matter very much to me whether or not my work reached a large audience. Certain things needed to be said and written so that those in search of the truth could find it; that was all that really mattered. I later noticed, however, that many of my "enemies" had adopted my terminology, not only in the field of music but in their translations of Sanskrit terms. My most recent work on Hindu cosmological theory, *While the Gods Play, Man and the Universe according to the Shivaïte Tradition*, has greatly interested many eminent modern physicists, who find Hindu conceptions on the nature of matter and the origin of the world quite illuminating. Two young Americans, Robert and

Deborah Lawlor, who were formerly interested in the work of the Egyptologist de Lubitsch and, after spending some time in India, settled in Tasmania, have recently undertaken an English translation of several of my works. Ehud Sperling, the dynamic director of Inner Traditions International, has arranged to publish them.

RECORDINGS

For many years I studied Indian music and did my best to take notes on its principles and forms. I had to invent a new system of notation to indicate precise intervals, for the existing systems were all quite vague. Only after the war did it become possible to find sound reproduction systems that used other devices besides records and cylinder engravings. I immediately acquired one of the first steel-wire recorders. Later I made a special trip to New York to buy the best of the new magnetic tape recorders, called "Magnecorder," a very bulky machine with two compartments that required a current adapter; the sound, however, was of very high quality. My journey from Europe to America was quite entertaining. I had to spend the first night in Shannon, Ireland, and the next in the middle of a Newfoundland forest, in a hotel built entirely of wood. As soon as I returned to Benares, I began to record some of the best classical musicians, Vedic chants, and traditional popular songs of India. Serge Moreux, artistic director of the French record company Ducretet-Thomson, and his assistant, Roland de Candé, were very much interested in my work. The result was my first *Anthologie de la musique classique de l'Inde*, which included performances by India's greatest musicians—in particular the young Ravi Shankar—none of whom had ever been recorded before or heard in the West. Serge Moreux wrote an introduction so extravagant in its praise that I felt quite embarrassed.

Jack Bornoff, executive secretary of the International Music Council, persuaded Unesco to ask me to create a series of records on the great music of the Orient, then Africa, and hired me as an adviser for his organization. For the first time since its creation, Unesco, which until then had done little more than support the Addis Ababa Philharmonic or the Teheran Opera, became involved in non-Western music. I then undertook a vast recording program in several Asian and African countries: Afghanistan, Cambodia, Laos, Iran, Japan, Tibet, the Middle East, as well as Tunisia and Morocco. Several years later, when the Berlin and Venice Institutes were created, I was able to work with very competent assistants who helped me with the actual recording. Jacques Cloarec, a wonderfully efficient young Breton who became my assistant in Berlin, took over all the technical aspects—selection, editing, texts, photographs, etc.—and made it possible for us to create a very large collection of records.

In the meantime, Serge Moreux had died and no record company seemed interested in non-European music. Only one music publisher, Karl Vötterlee, director of the Bärenreiter company in Kassel, was willing to issue anthologies of Asian and African music. I entrusted the African series to Paul Collaer. It was only much later that Philips, in Holland, decided to publish a history of traditional music on a record called *Les Sources musicales*. After this the Italian company E.M.I., whose director at the time was a very brilliant and imaginative Frenchman, Michel Bonnet, undertook to publish a regional series called *Atlas musical*. In spite of the recent proliferation of exotic records, the quality of these collections has never been equalled. When we left the Berlin Institute, Jacques Cloarec and I had produced one hundred and twenty records.

After the completion of Unesco's vast East-West project, which had cost millions, I learned to my great satisfaction that the general director of this noble organization had declared the record anthologies one of its most important achievements. Unesco, in fact, had made no financial contribution at all.

For Asian and African traditional musicians, the Unesco label, which has very little value in the West, carries a great deal of prestige and represents a kind of international consecration. Once they have been recorded, they become "international-class musicians" and cease to be neglected, scorned, and ignored by their own governments. Radio stations begin to play their music, and their financial situation rapidly improves.

I was far less interested in attracting the attention of Westerners to Oriental music than in helping musicians maintain their traditions. In many cases, my goals were fully realized.

My association with the International Music Council and Unesco was always very pleasant thanks to the remarkable personality of Jack Bornoff, who directed the Council for thirty years and saw that it maintained a relative independence, though it was affiliated with Unesco. As for Unesco, which, in the beginning, was a sort of club for eminent writers, philosophers, and scientists, it has become a political bureaucracy whose various sectors are run by people chosen not for their competence, but for the color of their skin or the politics of their country.

CHAPTER FIFTEEN

Sundry Characters

"Nabokov is the cousin of Lolita's father. He is beyond description." (Letter from Raymond to Pierre, Zagarolo, 29 January 1963)

One year, at an important music conference in Madras, I gave a lecture on traditional music as a measure and expression of a people and its culture, and on the dangers of new developments based not on the culture itself but on foreign conceptions, which are not always compatible. After I finished talking, a Russian-American musician took up certain points of my speech, which he very generously praised. I had met this man many years earlier in Diaghilev's circle. His name was Nicolas Nabokov. After the speeches were over, Nicolas and I remained together for a long time discussing problems of cultural assimilation and the ways in which India's precious heritage might be preserved. This was the beginning of a wonderful friendship and a very fruitful association. A few years later, I helped Nabokov organize a great festival of music and Oriental theatrical arts in Tokyo, which was followed by other festivals and congresses, including one in Berlin on African music.

Nicolas, a cousin of the writer Vladimir, was an exceptionally intelligent man, brilliant, amusing, full of fantasy, and blessed by the gods with all the possible gifts but that of moderation. He was the director of an important organization, subsidized by American foundations, called the Congress for

Cultural Freedom, which helped a great many artists and writers, planned reunions, conferences, and festivals, and published important literary journals such as *Preuves* in France, *Encounter* in England, *Quadernos* in Spain, etc.

These projects, in fact, were probably financed by the American Secret Service. When this was revealed by the American press, all the "liberal intellectuals" who had engaged in the venture left the Congress for Cultural Freedom. I found this attitude very stupid. It is perfectly possible to do good work with bad money provided one can use it as one pleases without compromising one's principles. I had lived long enough in a colonized country to know that cultural subsidies often cover up political interests. But culture is more important than politics and, so long as it is not controlled, there is no reason why it should not be helped. The Medicis, Sforzas, doges, and popes who commissioned artists to build palaces for their honor and glory were certainly tyrants; but what really matters is that they supported Mantegna and Giotto, Carpaccio and Michelangelo, Botticelli and Titian, Bramante and Bernini. Their futile political intrigues and ambitions are of very little import today.

Nabokov was made an adviser to the municipal government of Berlin for cultural affairs and director of the Berlin Festival. He was a personal friend of Willy Brandt's, who was then Mayor of Berlin, and undoubtedly played an important political role, taking part in negotiations for the détente and Brandt's Ost-Politik. He was on friendly terms with the Soviet ambassador in East Berlin.

Nabokov was a talented composer but did not feel very comfortable with dodecaphonism and serialism, for at heart he was a romantic. He composed several ballets for his friend Balanchine. His excellent opera *Raspoutine* was first shown in a rather poor production in Cologne. Scherchen, the great orchestra conductor who had refused to direct the Berlin Orchestra during Hitler's rule (Karajan was chosen in his place), was then living in Italy. He decided to direct *Raspoutine* in the Catania Opera House in Sicily. It was an unforgettable performance.

For the occasion I had invited all my Italian friends, who

descended on Catania in great throngs. I took along Allegra, wife of the famous lawyer Carnelutti, having asked her to dress as elegantly as possible. She appeared at the performance wearing a red gown with a train, great masses of jewels, and surrounded by a group of gentlemen in evening dress. The mayor was dazzled and all of Sicilian society visibly impressed. This was particularly helpful in view of the fact that Nicolas' wife of the time had managed to arrive late, accompanied by a Greek friend of hers who, not to pass unnoticed, wore an enormous cast on his leg, which he had recently broken. Whenever the hotel porter was asked for Mrs. Nabokov's whereabouts, he would answer with great dignity, "Madame has gone out with *her* Greek." None of this was particularly pleasant for a musician whose greatest work was being celebrated that night.

A few years later, Nicolas got divorced and married a fourth wife, called Dominique, a charming, unaffected, amusing, and devoted Frenchwoman who made his last years the happiest of his life. She became very good friends with "le Farfadet", of whom I shall speak later. We were a very close foursome and poked fun at everything, sometimes quite unkindly. Thanks to Nicolas I met, among others, the great actress Anna Magnani, as passionate and spirited in life as she was on film, and many interesting personalities of the musical world, including Leonard Bernstein, Rostropovitch, Balanchine, etc. Nicolas visited me very often in Zagarolo, where he composed some of his last works.

Nabokov's last musical success was *Love's Labour's Lost*, on a Shakespearian theme adapted by the poet W. H. Auden; it was presented in Brussels in 1973. All of Nabokov's friends were there including his four wives, who were not sure quite how to behave towards one another. Willy Brandt, who was then Chancellor of the Reich, had come to Brussels especially for the performance. Mrs. Brandt, who was seated in the main loge, looked very bored and obviously did not enjoy the music. She complained about this to Nicolas, naïvely asking him the name of the composer. It is apparently considered proper for the wives of heads of state to appear at official functions without necessarily knowing what to expect. Mrs. Brandt had obviously not been enlightened by her chief of protocol.

Nicolas came from a noble family that had owned vast territories in the south of Russia and a palace in Saint Petersburg. He claimed to be descended from Genghis Khan. He had all the qualities of a prince and never quite accepted his status as a poor *émigré*. He was officially an American citizen, but felt like an exile. The very word "citizen" was so ill-suited to him that it seemed like an insult. He appeared relaxed everywhere he went but always felt like a foreigner whether he was in France, Germany, or the United States, although he spoke the languages of these countries fluently and without an accent. In the book of memoirs he wrote shortly before his death, he speaks quite humorously of his curious destiny as a man without a country.

Because of his exceptional qualities Nicolas was very useful to various governments, but he was never really supported by anyone. Musicians of far lesser talent were promoted by their own countries as national monuments, but Nabokov belonged nowhere and was acutely aware of the fact.

It was Nicolas who found a way to interest American foundations in the creation of the Berlin Institute. Together we created the Venice Institute and the Association of Festival Directors of which he was the driving force. Whenever we met on our various travels to all the corners of the earth, it was always with great joy. He was the only Westerner I ever knew with whom I could always feel in perfect harmony, with whom it was possible to glide effortlessly and without transition from the most delicate exchanges of wit and pleasantries to the deepest discussions on philosophy and religion. Nicolas possessed a delicacy of soul that only comes with a true understanding of the sacred.

I was deeply fond of Nicolas. He was a wonderful man, sensitive, loyal, and brilliantly intelligent. He played a very important role in my life. His death, in 1978, has left a great void.

Constantin Braïloiu, the famous Rumanian musicologist, had asked me to come to see him in Paris, where he was living in exile. He was preparing a collection of 78 rpm records for Unesco. Braïloiu was a grotesque-looking man, puny and short, with an enormous bald head and a very prominent

brow. When I entered his apartment, which was rather bourgeois but dark and dusty and filled with old furniture, there
seemed to be so many cobwebs I felt as though I were in a
horror movie. In a corner, sunk deep inside an old armchair,
almost invisible, was the monster. Without even a word of
greeting, he asked me in a cavernous voice and an accent that
reminded me of Count Dracula's: "Have you any recordings of
funeral ceremonies? I am a bit of a necrophile." My first
instinct was to run away as fast as I could, but I bravely
resisted the urge, hastily murmuring a magic formula to ward
off the evil eye. In those days I had not yet become acquainted
with the very special world of people who call themselves
ethno-musicologists; most of them are very bizarre and I soon
learned to be wary of them. I gave Braïloiu some very fine
recordings, which, alas! were never used, the collection of
records he was supposed to prepare being quite esoteric, to say
the least. Braïloiu did me a great service, however, for he told
me about a young Pole who lived in Switzerland and had just
invented a portable tape recorder. I immediately went to Lausanne, where I met Stéphane Kudelski, inventor of the first
Nagra, a small-sized high fidelity machine.

Stéphane was what people like to call "a brain." He had left
the highly regarded University of Lausanne after refusing to
take his examinations, claiming that his teachers understood
nothing about electronics. He then moved to a small apartment and began making recording devices that were very
much ahead of their time. Even today, in the enormous factory
he now manages, Stéphane designs machines that will only be
adopted by important companies ten years hence. He also
creates sophisticated instruments that are vital to the leading
industries. He has no competitors. No radio reporter or film
producer can live without a Nagra. I immediately grew very
interested in Stéphane's work and bought one of his first
battery and crank-operated Nagras. Stéphane introduced me
to his parents and I often went to visit this very interesting
family of emigrants.

Stéphane's father was a Polish army officer who had fled to
Switzerland, his mother a distinguished and cultivated woman
from Warsaw's high society. The family had lived through

difficult, poverty-stricken years, and the great Polish lady was somewhat alarmed by the exploits of her son in a world so different from the one she had been born to.

I remained on close terms with Stéphane and followed his meteoric career with a great deal of interest. It was thanks to the Nagras that I was able to produce most of my records for Unesco, sometimes in very difficult conditions. Stéphane agreed to make me an electronic musical instrument based on my theory that certain numerical ratios have an influence on emotional states of mind. This instrument, which was recently completed after ten years of testing, could revolutionize every musical concept known to man.

Stéphane lives in a pretty house above Lausanne with his charming wife Eva and several children, the eldest of whom, André, seems to have inherited his father's gifts.

Menuhin is a warm and sympathetic man. He and his sister Hephzibah, who, alas! died a few years ago, were always ready to defend the oppressed and help unrecognized artists. For a long time Menuhin was the only person besides me who showed any interest in Indian musicians. It was he who launched the career of the great sitarist Ravi Shankar, forcing him on his impresarios and playing concerts with him. He has never hesitated to support my projects and was a board member of the Berlin Institute from the time of its creation. This great musician, however, was always too deeply imbued with his own art to thoroughly understand the spirit of Indian music, which he admires and has done a great deal to promote. His duets with Ravi were a mistake, even though they were very successful with the public. Menuhin also encouraged him to try new musical experiments, which in my opinion was rather unfortunate. But this was not, after all, so terribly important: by abandoning a certain precision of style for the sake of publicity, Ravi opened the door to other musicians who were more respectful of the rules of a great classical art. He has often told me that some day he will retire to India and devote himself entirely to real music and to the forming of new students.

Menuhin's wife Diana has always shown a marked hostility

towards exotic music and sees no reason to hide it. One day, in Geneva, while we were listening to a superb concert of Indian music, she turned towards me, yawning, and asked: "How long is this thing going to last?" Unable to control myself, I replied somewhat sharply: "Like any other concert, Diana, until the intermission." She did not seem very pleased.

In 1955 or thereabouts, when I was still living in Adyar, I met a rather plain American woman in her thirties called Helen who was working for the American consulate. This woman pursued me relentlessly, constantly came to see me in my house or on the beach, tried to make me kiss her, and obviously longed for some kind of intimacy. I found it rather difficult to understand what she really wanted. An English friend of mine soon enlightened me. Helen was a special envoy of Joseph McCarthy, the famous American senator who, in the name of puritanism and anticommunism, was trying to eliminate every person suspected of being a homosexual or a left-winger from American public services; later he went mad. In order to obtain information Helen stole letters, searched wastepaper baskets, and bribed servants. She probably hoped that I would inadvertently betray a few victims.

The effect of McCarthyism was devastating and the entire world is still suffering from its consequences. It is obvious that in a country like India, where most women are inaccessible, homosexuals, because of their wide circles of friends from every milieu and their close relationships with men, are more likely to know things than anyone else. It is also indispensable to maintain contacts with people of varied political beliefs, especially those hostile to one's country. Within a few months, most of the members of the American Intelligence Service were sent away and replaced by decent young married men with families who lived virtuously within the antiseptic confines of the diplomatic world. The United States had completely dismantled its intelligence service and has never succeeded in putting it together again. This has led to appalling political errors, one of the more recent examples being Iran. Espionage and virtue have never gone very well together.

It was around that time, in Paris, that I met Bill. Bill was an artist. He had been part of a team sent by the United States to reorganize the cultural life of Germany, and occupied a very high position. He was a very cultivated, gregarious, and compassionate man, who had made himself very useful and was highly respected by the Germans as well as by members of the international circle. At the height of the McCarthy purge, however, he suddenly found himself relieved of his duties, without any kind of pension or indemnity, without a cent in his pocket to feed himself or pay his rent, abandoned by all. For several months the Germans came to his aid, found him a place to live, and clubbed together to help him out, pay his back rent, telephone bills, etc. Bill did not have a cent to his name.

Bill finally found work. An Englishman, who had performed similar duties for the British government and was occupying a very high post in an international organization, hired him as his assistant. This act of great courage filled me with high regard and admiration for the Englishman; it is always so easy to forget the oppressed. It was at this time that I met Bill.

The Germans, many of whom had lived through the anguish of having to betray their friends to save their own lives and those of their children, had behaved toward Bill with wonderful delicacy. Things were different in France, however. Bill once told me, with tears in his eyes, that I had been one of the first people there to treat him as a friend, without that mixture of reserve and commiseration that makes it so difficult for those who have suffered condemnation to form a new social life. For me he was never "that poor Bill," but simply Bill.

Henry Corbin was a *sufi*. He had found his way through a mystical Persian sect, a secret Dionysian tradition that managed to survive the rigors of militant Islam. This highly learned and spiritual man was now totally integrated in the very closed, esoteric circle of the *sufis*, but was very discreet on the subject and never made a show of it. All the great Persian poets were *sufis* and tried to express divine love through the love of divine creation. They sang of corporal beauty, physical passion, the fairness of flowers and birds, the radiance of nature, a harmonious world in which love, art, and knowledge all merge together in a single quest.

Although Corbin and I rarely met, there was a wonderful

248 · THE WAY TO THE LABYRINTH

understanding between us. We recognized each other without having to say a word, like pilgrims who walk side by side on the road. He belonged to conflicting cultures and seemed to be following different paths; but they led to the same goal, a world where differences and conflicts no longer exist or matter.

This was not the case with Mircea Eliade, the famous prophet of religious history whose superb work always struck me as being based on exterior knowledge rather than actual experience. Although he was always very polite with me, I sensed a certain reticence in this man, as I always did with university-trained Indianists and musicologists.

In the very curious Western world of Indian scholarship, no one, in fact, speaks any Indian languages. All these people's opinions on Indian philosophy are based on English-written texts. Many Sanskrit professors cannot even read the alphabet and need to use transliterations. This was why I was always considered so troublesome. I did not pretend to be a philosopher or a historian, but I knew the subtleties of the language, the meaning of the rites and symbols as well as any Brahman formed in the Hindu tradition. My approach to this extraordinary civilization challenged the ideas of people who did not really understand its spirit. It was as though I were a scholar from Ancient Egypt suddenly and mysteriously transported into the modern age among a herd of Egyptologists. It was perfectly natural that such "men of learning," accustomed to interpreting the vestiges of a "dead" civilization as they pleased, should feel threatened by a survivor who had not only practiced all the rites and sacrifices but understood their psychological and social significance, not only studied them but lived them. For these people I was an intruder who was best ignored; my works were never included in their bibliographies. Like all others, apparently, Eliade feared a reality that might disturb his clever, intelligent, but artificial system of reconstruction.

Corbin invited me to participate in a series of conferences given at a very exclusive club in Ascona, called the Eranos, under the patronage of a disciple of Jung's. I found them boring and pretentious, with psycho-mystical tendencies far removed from human reality. I refused to go back a second time. For me, the search for spiritual values is closely linked with everyday life, a sense of humor, and the pleasure of being alive. My body and soul have never been far apart.

I had met André Malraux at Nehru's house in Delhi during one of his trips to India. When I returned to France, he invited me several times to his house. He was passionately interested in the Asian arts and fully appreciated them. He was a fascinating and brilliantly intelligent man, but terribly egocentric. The only realities he accepted were those he could manipulate as he pleased, so that our conversations were like a dialogue of the deaf. My interpretations of Hindu masterpieces, based on symbolic elements and magic diagrams working together to form a wonderful harmony, clashed with an aesthetic approach whose criteria had nothing to do with the artists who had conceived them. Any theory of art he had not elaborated himself or that differed too much from his was displeasing to him—in fact did not interest him at all. He did not invite me again, preferring the less troublesome views of his usual guru, one of those pretentious Indians who sell Westerners a vague pseudo-Oriental philosophy that flatters their habits.

I did, however, become very good friends with Georges Salles, the great art history expert who helped Malraux prepare some of his books. Georges Salles was a mystic. Underneath his prosperous, distinguished *grand bourgeois* exterior he was a kind of saint. His preoccupations were chiefly of a spiritual nature, and his books—which were published only privately—reveal an astonishingly intense inner life. It mattered very little to him that someone else should get all the credit for his work. I often went to visit him in his large apartment above the Luxembourg Gardens. We quickly established a strong feeling of mutual trust, though we did not always agree on everything.

Georges Salles had a collaborator and companion, an active, disinterested, and wonderfully fine woman called Roberta. Although she came from a very eminent family, she had little use for conventions; but beneath her caustic, humorous exterior and her often blunt way of speaking she was passionately devoted to unselfish ideals. She protected Georges during his last years and brightened his life. When he died in Germany, she brought his body back to Paris. After this, the vultures wasted no time. Shunned by all the family, she stood by while cousins and nephews whom she had never seen tore through the spoils, the clothes, and all the familiar objects she knew so well. She was not even invited to the grandiose funeral. It was I who accompanied her to the church. There, standing discreetly behind a pillar like an anonymous visitor, she witnessed the solemn and hypocritical tribute to the one for whom she had been everything—his companion, his joy, his shining light. A few years later, at her own expense, Roberta published the remarkable *Cahiers* in which Georges Salles had written his reflections on life, art, and death.

Edward Mac Avoy wanted to paint my portrait. The art of portraiture is not like any other. It is based on a subtle form of drawing, evolving into a kind of diagram conceived by a psychologist who delves into the hidden soul of his model. The portraitist then clothes his drawing with colors, creating a kind of aura that situates the character in his own individual world. His work is exactly the opposite of the impressionist's, whose point of departure is appearance.

The sitting sessions were a fascinating experience. The painter talked constantly about all kinds of things, trying to incite reactions on his model's face, making him reveal his true nature through anger, vanity, envy, greed, doubt, or tenderness, of which the sitter became a kind of symbol and incarnation. Mac Avoy's portraits of Picasso, Cocteau, Mauriac, John XXIII, and many other famous people reveal more of their character and the complexities of their personality than any biography. Few portraitists in the history of painting have been able to achieve such a degree of psychological insight.

Not unlike Signorelli, Mac Avoy knows how to express the tragic beauty of the body as well as the anguish on a face. Sometimes, in his large paintings, he hides his cruel and penetrating vision of human beings by surrounding them with flattering details; this has made it possible for him to remain a fashionable painter. A vain woman will willingly believe that the splendor of her jewels, her clothes, and her background represent her more truly than the revealing traits of her face, of which she is totally unaware.

Mac Avoy admits that he has made enemies of several of his subjects who found this revelation and intrusion into their secret being intolerable. The mask, the impression people wish to create of themselves and sometimes come to believe in, disappears beneath the aggressive brushstroke of the painter, who cunningly perceives the reality beneath the appearance.

He pictured me as an odd-looking character eying the Western world with subtle irony. He embellished the portrait with Oriental symbolism that enhanced the expression of secret amusement etched upon my face.

A strong and lasting bond is inevitably created between Mac Avoy and his subjects, almost as though they had lived through a dangerous expedition together. This bond expresses itself either through lasting friendship or enmity, sometimes even unquenchable hatred. Indifference is impossible when one has experienced such a psychoanalysis and probing of the soul. I was fortunate enough to remain his friend. His many subsequent visits to Zagarolo, whose mystery he understood, gave me a chance to appreciate his extraordinary capacity for hard work.

Mac Avoy is also a wonderful storyteller. He has a rare talent for embellishing a story or an anecdote without distorting it. His memories of the people he has painted, together with the paintings themselves, offer a completely new understanding, a ruthless yet affectionate vision of many of the most prominent people of our time.

The hills surrounding the city where Palestrina lived always seem to attract musicians. Petrassi, the great master of Italian music, was born in Zagarolo. Henze, whom I had met in Berlin, came to settle in Marino. I had not seen him since his sojourn in Cuba and his brief dalliance with Castroism.

Once, when I was visiting Henry-Louis de La Grange, I met Sylvano Bussotti, one of the most prominent Italian musicians of the new generation. Soon afterward he came to live not far from my labyrinth, and we became very good friends.

Sylvano is a very engaging man. Beneath a blatant display of paradox and unnecessary drama, which he genuinely seems to enjoy, he conceals a deeply romantic sensibility and great sincerity of character. In the snobbish and fickle world in which he lives, it is the only way he feels he can protect his integrity. What his music reveals is not at all what he wishes for us to see in it; he is like the wise man who pretends to be mad in order to protect himself. His *Racine*, which disconcerted his audience at La Scala in Milan, is a good example of this dichotomy. Sylvano flits through his world of false drama with the airy elusiveness of a will-o'-the-wisp. One must pretend to take his follies seriously in order to gain access to his secret being. As soon as I met him, I immediately sensed and liked the deep and human qualities of this eccentric and whimsical genius. With all due respect to Stockhausen, modern music has irretrievably lost its cosmological dimension and can never again reecho the harmony of the spheres. But in its search for a new vocation, oddly enough, it has reverted to a kind of animism. It explores all the sounds around us—the birdsongs, the murmurings of trees, the buzzings of the crowds, the clamors of the cities, the mysterious spirits that enliven machines. In order to be understood, however, music of this kind needs visual support and representation. The music of today can be quite effective as theater, but does not hold up in the arid, severe medium of a concert hall. With his gift for show and spectacle, Sylvano has been able to find a perfect balance.

By a strange turn of fate, it was in Rome that I rediscovered my old friend Zaher, the King of Afghanistan, who had inspired me to make my first trip to the Orient so many years before. This distinguished and affable man, now living in exile in Rome, leads an obscure and modest existence. His deep devotion to his people was all that ever mattered to him and—unlike so many other rulers—he never tried to use his power to amass a personal fortune. His deep wisdom, his views on politics, and his calm resignation are admirable; but he remains on the alert, suffering the tragic destiny of his people, refusing to intervene, ready to help them should they ever need him.

From time to time he comes to see me, happy to find a friend without political ambitions or interests, with whom he can talk freely and without fear. Most of his family was horribly massacred. Four of his sons were able to escape and now hold obscure positions in various countries. His ailing wife, shattered by her harrowing experiences, makes his everyday life very difficult to bear. For nearly forty years, this wise and moderate ruler, who was adored by his people, was able to maintain neutrality, until the day the Soviets, bent on annexing Afghanistan, organized the four successive revolutions that served as a pretext for them to occupy the country.

Finding Zaher again seemed to close the determining cycle of my life. There was something magical about this return to my point of departure.

CHAPTER SIXTEEN

Berlin

THE BERLIN INSTITUTE

When I returned permanently to Europe, Louis Renou offered me a teaching post at the Ecole des Hautes Etudes. At about the same time, Nicolas Nabokov suggested that I create an institute in Berlin for the study and propagation of non-European musical systems. The Ford Foundation was willing to support the enterprise provided Berlin was chosen as its center; the Americans were in fact quite eager to help finance cultural organizations in this city in cooperation with the Bonn government.

During an earlier visit in 1961, I had been quite impressed with the situation in this captive city. The Wall had just been built. It seemed essential for Berlin's survival and for the defense of the free world that international organizations be established here. I also felt that it was very important for the status of the great musicians of India and other Asian countries to make them known to the Western world.

I therefore decided to accept the Berlin offer, which was a typically idealistic and unreasonable thing for me to do. As usual, I chose adventure over security, easy work, pension, and benefits, which the French university was willing to offer me.

Thus, in 1963, the International Institute for Comparative Music Studies came into existence.

I was to spend about a dozen years in Berlin. I had to create from scratch a completely new type of organization—a project that proved quite discouraging at times and fraught with problems. Raymond, who felt lonely and bored in Zagarolo, soon came to join me and took the administration in hand. We found a lovely old house for the new institute in the suburb of Grünewald—the Neuilly of Berlin—in the middle of a large abandoned garden near a small lake. We had to form a governing board, create statutes, lay down plans of action, and find collaborators. I had no experience whatever of bureaucratic haggling, and German administrations are particularly weighty and repressive. The Institute reissued and developed the journal of the International Music Council, published works on Oriental music, and made it possible to enlarge our record collections. We also organized congresses and concert series.

It seemed logical to create separate divisions for the different cultural regions, but I soon realized that my goals were so far removed from those of the university-trained folklorists and musicologists that no real cooperation was possible. A more capable man would probably have found ways to make use of the musical bureaucrats, but I have always been singularly lacking in managerial qualities. It gives me no pleasure to impose my will, nor do I like to submit to others. When I am faced with the intrigues, ambitions, and bad faith that always seem to prevail in administrations, I feel completely helpless. I can only work effectively with friends whose goals are the same as mine.

One of my first assistants was an Englishman called Peter Crowley, who was interested in Celtic music and had done important work in the field of Tibetan music. Peter was bored to death in Berlin and found solace in whiskey and cheese, which he ordered especially from England. He hardly did any work. A few years later, when the Berlin Senate ordered reductions in our salaries, which the German administration deemed excessive, Peter decided to resign. He then went to America and had no good words for the Institute, which he felt was more interested in musicians than in the science of musicology.

Peter had left an insignificant job on the London radio to

come to Berlin. One day, as I was talking to David Webster, the very amusing director of Covent Garden who was also organized BBC programs, I reproached him for having given Peter so high a recommendation at the time I was hiring him. David laughed: "What kind of manager would you think I was if I hadn't passed him on to you?"

Hans Eckart joined the Institute soon afterward. He was a great expert on Japanese music and an intelligent man. I liked and respected him very much and found him pleasant to work with. He was able to acquire an excellent collection of Japanese books on music that forms an important part of the Institute's library. He spoke fluent Japanese, having lived for many years in Japan, where he had held an important propaganda post during the Hitler years. He also taught at the Free University of Berlin, but the students made violent demonstrations against this "Nazi" and played very cruel tricks on him. In the end he committed suicide.

I was put under a great deal of pressure to hire Kurt Rheinhardt, a specialist in Turkish music and a professor of musicology at the University. He was a very pedantic man who systematically analyzed tape recordings without any thought for the musicians' artistic worth: the more false notes they played, the more interesting he found them. From his analyses he drew conclusions that were scientific but, in my opinion, absurd. I had a great deal of trouble rewriting and abridging his book on Turkish music; but despite reservations we published it nonetheless. In the end the Institute's budgetary restrictions gave us an excuse to relieve him of his post.

There was also an Indian group—Vivek Datta, his wife Marie-Thérèse, who was Belgian, and a Bengali friend of theirs, Mukund Lath. They were supposed to continue my work on Sanskrit texts, but nothing came of it. We also invited Pandit M.D. Pant, one of the Indian scholars who had taught me Sanskrit in Almora. He did not remain with us for long, but did excellent work preparing texts for publication. It took us some time to make him understand that in Berlin it was not at all proper to throw banana peels and other kinds of rubbish out of the window.

Jacques Brunet spent two years at the Institute. He had just returned from Cambodia, where he had been an adviser to Sihanouk. He was a very nervous man and in rather poor health. He did not like Berlin. I steered him towards Indonesian music and he did extremely well. Now he teaches in Paris.

I soon found that parcelling out work into separate research divisions was a mistake. It was far easier and much less expensive to ask outside specialists to prepare the books and articles we needed. We did not offer courses, therefore had no need for a permanent scientific staff. It did not take me long to realize that our most valuable colleagues were the musicians and not the ethnologists and musicologists from the university. Musicians are instantly sensitive to the quality of music, its artistic worth, and the personality of the artist, even when the system is foreign to them. It was Simha Arom, an Israeli musician commissioned by his government to create an orchestra in Africa, who discovered the wonderful music of the Pygmies, of which we made records. He also prepared some of our best tapes on African music.

Christian Poche, who spent a short time at the Institute, offered us precious contacts with the Arab world. Born in Aleppo, he spoke Arabic and was on close terms with all the musical circles in the Middle East.

After him, Habib Touma became a permanent member of our staff. This Christian Arab, born in Israel, only felt comfortable away from politics, in neutral territory. It was through him that we met Munir Bashir, the great musician from Baghdad.

In order to improve our public relations Raymond hired Prince Rudolf of Lippe, a pleasant and polite young man. He gave several receptions in his bare and beautiful old apartment, but did not prove to be very useful. In Berlin there is hardly anyone left from the old royal court. Under Willy Brandt, the governmental bureaucracy tended towards socialism and was not at all interested in such people. It was obviously a mistake to hire a prince.

It was through Rudolf that I met a very interesting Russian *émigré*, a writer and philosopher called Vladimir Tchelitcheff. He lived in the suburbs in one of those little houses with a tiny garden, where working-class people like to grow a few vegetables. From the outside, his one-story wooden house looked like a rustic cabin. But the inside, however, with its cluster of tiny rooms, looked like an Oriental covered bazaar, strewn with rugs, bursting with art objects, paintings, and precious wall hangings—a perfect setting for Scheherazade. Here I spent many pleasant afternoons sitting around a samovar and talking to a man of rare intelligence and wisdom who spoke without a trace of bitterness of a world gone forever.

John Evarts left the International Music Council to join us in Berlin. His excellent relations with the international musical world and his gregarious personality were very valuable assets to the Institute.

Once in a while, venerable personalities, who had probably spent most of their lives in exile, would reappear on the scene. The famous music critic Hans Heinz Stuckenschmidt, who had recently returned from America, became an excellent friend of ours and got actively involved in the work of the Institute. Helmut Becker, director of the Planck Institute, and Antoinette—his very nice wife who came from Alsace—introduced me to Berlin society. This gave me an opportunity to meet Willy Brandt, who was then reigning over Berlin.

One of the most interesting of these long lost figures was the architect Ernst Charoun, who was building the new Concert Hall not far from the Brandenburg Gate, in a bleak, desolate part of the city that had been totally destroyed during the war. Like Le Corbusier, Charoun was a brilliant product of the Bauhaus, the unconventional arts and crafts institute that played such an important role in the artistic world of Germany before the war and was closed down by Hitler.

Charoun and I had a number of fascinating discussions, for he believed in the value of pentagonal forms in architecture. The Concert Hall was entirely made of pentagons. I found this very interesting because the pentagon and the golden section that derives from it play a fundamental role in the architecture of Hindu temples. Five is the number of life and provides structures with a kind of soul. The properties of the pentagon were also used by cathedral builders. I have written about this in my book *Le Temple hindou*. Charoun had rediscovered this essential principle and, in the last years of his life, put it into practice in the important monuments he built in Berlin.

For the acoustics of the Concert Hall, Charoun called on a well-known specialist, Fritz Winckel, who had experimented with pistol shots in the most famous auditoriums in the world and recorded the resonances. The results were rather surprising: the acoustics were perfect for pistol shots but, unfortunately, not ideal for music. They had to make changes and hang floating panels from the ceiling. Karajan was named conductor of the new orchestra, and the people of Berlin, who are always ready to make a joke, called this bizarre-looking structure "Karajan's Circus." I attended the inaugural concert which took place during the very tense period following the building of the Wall. People were not allowed to applaud. In an atmosphere of religious silence, the orchestra, which later became one of the most famous in the world, played Beethoven's Ninth Symphony. It was as though the people of this fallen city were paying homage to their millions of dead.

Egon Seehfelhner, a Viennese I had known for many years, was then artistic director of the Opera. The Opera House was huge and very plain, having been built in great haste when the former theater, located in the Communist zone, suddenly became inaccessible. The seats were fairly inexpensive and one met all classes of people there. The opera productions were outrageously modern, but one often heard excellent singers from France, America, and Italy. I once met a young Frenchman with a superb bass voice who claimed to be a member of the Paris Opera. When I told him that I had never seen his name on a program, he replied: "That's quite true. I *am* part of the company, but I'm considered too young for a role." In France even the performing arts were controlled by bureaucracy. I doubt very much that anything has changed since.

We had to find a chairman for our board of trustees. Nabokov suggested an eminent Englishman, who was also very elegant. When I went to fetch him at the airport, he seemed rather taken aback. I was wearing one of those very expensive plaid ties with a small design that are considered so chic in England; his was identical. He hastily retreated to his hotel room and changed his tie.

It was a bad beginning. I soon realized that he thought of his chairmanship as a strictly honorary title and was not the least bit interested in our projects or goals. We did not appoint him.

At a congress in Rome I had met a Swiss woman whom I liked very much, called Marguerite de Reding. She was president of the Jeunesses Musicales and a member of the finance committee of the International Music Council. I spoke to her about our problems finding a proper chairman for the Institute. She said: "Why not ask my husband? He is far more clever than he appears." For many years, Baron de Reding had been director of the Radio Helvétique and an active member of several humanitarian organizations. He was indeed a fine man, and also very kind. We named him chairman of the board of the Institute and found his dedication, his knowledge of legal matters, and his ability to solve difficult problems with tact and diplomacy quite invaluable.

He got on very well with Raymond, whose intelligence, dedication, and competence he greatly appreciated. The baron helped Raymond relieve me of all my administrative problems. Nicolas Nabokov, who was a member of the board, was quite exasperated by the meticulous way this skinny little man would analyze problems and deliberately make speeches so long and so boring that his weary opponents, in the end, would do anything he wanted. Nicolas always called him "le baron de Crac," a comic character in French children's books.

The baron met a tragic end. Active and adventurous for his age and a great lover of hunting, he had gone on one of those surprise trips that are sometimes organized by tourist agencies. The journey ended on the island of Comodo, near Bali. This island is known for its giant prehistoric lizards, which can still be seen today. After the customary visit to the hill from which one can safely watch the monsters, the baron, who was a very independent man, refused to return by the same path as the rest of the group, claiming that he had found another. He was never seen again. There was nothing on this abandoned island—neither hotels nor restaurants—so, after waiting for him for several hours, the group finally got back on the boat, leaving the poor man's suitcase on the beach with a note: "Good luck, Mr. de Reding!" A search party was sent especially from Switzerland, but never found a trace of his body. Marguerite had a very difficult time having him pronounced legally dead.

Egon Kraus, an eminent member of the National Committee of Music in Germany, agreed to replace Rudolf as chairman of the board. Like his predecessor, this kindly, cultivated, and efficient man proved to be immensely valuable.

EMSERSTRASSE

When we first came to Berlin, Raymond and I spent several months at the Savoy, a very old hotel with small apartments where Herbert von Karajan often used to stay with his loyal secretary André von Mattoni, whom I had known in earlier days in Vienna when he was a young actor. I was eager to live in an old house, but there were very few left in Berlin. I was finally sent to a man who handled the properties of long-gone Jewish families and refused to rent them out to Germans. Mr. Kirchenbaum was a distinguished and courteous old patriarch and very much interested in music. When I went to see him, however, he told me that nothing was available. He politely asked me to leave him my address and spent a few moments deep in thought. Then he got up, went to the next room, and brought back a Hebrew newspaper he had just received. I had recently given a lecture in Jerusalem, and my photograph was on the front page. After this, of course, Mr. Kirchenbaum offered me a dozen different apartments. I chose one on the Emserstrasse, very near the Kurfürstendamm, West Berlin's great commercial avenue. It was a large third-floor corner apartment with windows that looked out onto an empty lot and a church with a garden. The building was part of a large complex that had been partly demolished; it was riddled with machine gun fire and in very bad condition. We had to redo the bathroom and kitchen, which were in ruins, repair the floors, put new plaster on the walls, install electricity, etc. The rent, however, was moderate. The staircase and landing were rather sordid, but the apartment, once we had fixed it, sunny and pleasant. Raymond lived there with me for some time, then found himself a huge, crooked apartment in another half-ruined building not far from mine. My housework and cooking were done by a series of very pleasant students who used to come for a few hours each day, which made it possible for me to give small receptions.

Young Germans, like Americans, do not consider it demeaning to take on humble jobs in order to earn their bread while pursuing their studies. Dietmar, who was studying painting, became a well-known fashion artist and now lives in Paris. Hacky, his successor, was an astonishingly beautiful young artisan who had come to my apartment to install carpeting. Nicolas Nabokov, who happened to be there when he came, was quite impressed and told him that he had all the qualities of a dancer. When Hacky turned eighteen, he came to ask me how he should go about following Nabokov's advice. That very day I had an appointment with Lindenberg to meet the assistant of Tatjana Gsovsky, the ballet mistress of the Berlin Opera. I took Hacky along and everything was settled: the next day, he started taking lessons. I also hired him as a cook, which made it possible for him to live. Hacky had never seen a ballet nor heard about Nureyev or Stravinsky. He made rapid progress but gave up dancing a few years later and went into the theater. Since then, he has become a movie cameraman.

Manual labor is an excellent thing for the young. Modest and temporary jobs allow them to remain independent and to keep an open mind about their future. The idea of work as strictly salaried, taxed, controlled employment with pensions and benefits implies making an early choice, which frequently leads to disaster. It creates false social categories, prejudice against manual labor, encourages idleness in adolescents— who remain under the control of their families—and encourages unemployment. It deprives individuals and small businesses of useful extra help. A law allowing the young to work part-time without having to pay taxes would seriously reduce unemployment, perhaps even delinquency.

Across the hall from my apartment lived a war widow whose fear of bombings had nearly driven her mad. She was convinced that ghosts came through the walls of her apartment to persecute her. From time to time, wearing the scantiest of costumes, she would ring my doorbell in the middle of the night and ask me to chase away the evil spirits. She even proposed marriage. This way, she said, we could break down the wall and share a magnificent apartment. I found her attitude typically German: for them, practical things always come first. Sometimes she would tie a sheet to her window at night, climb down completely naked to the apartment below, and lock herself in the kitchen. The tenants had to call the police.

One day, while I was entertaining guests for lunch—Nabokov and Shepard Stone, a very important representative of American foundations in Europe—the doorbell rang: "Police inspector! Homicide." Intrusions of this sort are always quite embarrassing. The police asked me if I knew my neighbor's brother; I answered that I had never seen him. When my guests went to the door, a dead body was spread across the landing. No one was allowed to leave. The madwoman had poisoned her brother and kept him tied to a chair for several days. The wretched creature was taken away in one ambulance and the body in another. I never saw her again. There are many war widows in Berlin, women who were traumatized by the loss of their husbands and children, the massacres, the terrible bombings and, in the end, the occupation by Russian soldiers who ceaselessly raped the women of the city, even the little girls.

When I left the apartment on the Emserstrasse, the amiable Mr. Kirchenbaum brought an action against me, which I lost. It seemed that, according to our agreement, the apartment had been in perfect condition when I moved in; now it had to be entirely redone. I was rather surprised and wondered if this lack of honesty and fair play was really necessary. "What else could you expect?" was the disagreeable reaction of most of my German colleagues.

A Ghost Town

West Berlin, like a shop window of the Western world, lives face to face with the desolation, poverty, and gloom that reign over East Germany and other so-called Socialist countries. I witnessed the reconstruction of the city and its growing prosperity; I saw how this capital, once the freest and most modern in Europe, then crushed by Nazism and devastated by war, gradually recaptured its spirit and gaiety and regained its marvelous orchestras and theaters, its night life, and, most of all, its sexual freedom, which is the true measure of genuine freedom, always and everywhere.

The transformation of Berlin in the space of just a few years was quite astounding—materially, culturally, and spiritually. This city, one of the liveliest centers of Western culture at the beginning of the century, was gradually reborn from its ashes and rebuilt amid the ruins in the most difficult possible conditions.

And yet, like a solitary ship on a dangerous sea, floating in the middle of a hostile and unpredictable Communist ocean, Berlin generates a feeling of insecurity. At any moment this world could become submerged, paralyzed. The air is dense with that anxiety which, to a lesser extent, pervades the Free World, a feeling of vague fear and apprehension, as though it were about to be invaded by an army of Huns.

Berlin is a ghost town. In spite of its luxuriousness, its apparent prosperity, its theaters, concerts, and pleasure spots, it is a city without a real population. Most of the people who live here were originally attracted, as I was, by its artificial facilities and have come only to accomplish a specific goal. Artists are offered large grants, businessmen pay lower taxes, students are exempted from military service, but in fact everyone lives in Berlin temporarily and has a home elsewhere. Nothing is ever truly created here. The city lacks a real people; it has no artisans, no solid intellectual atmosphere. As long as Germany remains divided, Berlin will continue to float on a dangerous sea towards an unknown destiny.

In Berlin one is constantly aware of tragedies that are never mentioned, of that dangerous and unpredictable zone where humiliating and frightening searches are systematically conducted, but which must be passed if one wishes to leave the city. I once spent several hours answering questions about all the people whose names I had marked in my address book. In recent years the situation has somewhat improved, but though searches are less frequent one never knows when they will begin anew.

Sometimes one could sense a human drama behind these

abominable police searches. Once, when I was transporting an Indian musical instrument, a customs officer spent hours poking around my car, asking me questions about the instrument: did it belong to me? could I play it? I found it hard to understand what he really wanted. Finally, when we were out of earshot, he suddenly turned to me and whispered very softly: "You are a musician. So was I, *before*—I was a violinist." Then he let me go.

There are many people in Berlin whose parents or children have remained on the other side. They simply wait, hoping that someday they will be reunited. One of the boys who worked for me at the Institute had suddenly found himself completely abandoned and penniless at the age of fourteen, along with his twelve-year-old sister. Their mother had gone to visit relatives in East Berlin and was put in prison. A student who worked as a guard for the Institute once tried to cross the Communist zone on the expressway and returned . . . two years later. He too had been imprisoned. Now, since the détente, East Berliners over sixty-five are granted permission to visit the Western zone but cannot stay longer than twenty-four hours; if they do, they lose their homes, their pensions, and all social benefits.

Peter, a young refugee whom Raymond had helped, waited ten years before he could see his mother, who lived wretchedly on the "other side." He gave her a dress and a pair of shoes, which were brutally snatched from her by a customs officer. The poor woman went home in tears, with patches on her clothes and holes in her shoes.

In Berlin there are also many refugees from neighboring countries—Russian Poles, Hungarians, Czechoslovakians—whose families have been scattered or annihilated. They choose to live in this sanctuary because it is close to home, and wait hopelessly for news that will never come.

Some Jews like to come to Berlin for a nostalgic visit to the cherished places they remember from childhood. We once accompanied a woman, a well-known musician who now lives in London, on a search for the site of her childhood home. Even the street was gone. Her life had been particularly tragic. After fleeing Germany she had become an Egyptian citizen and played an important role in the musical world of Egypt. Then came Nasser and another exodus.

Thanks to the grants offered by American foundations, many foreign artists live in Berlin, but most of them find it difficult to adapt to Berlin life. Gombrowicz, the famous Polish-born South American writer, spent two gloomy years in this city dragging out his incurable melancholy. He longed to recreate a café life but always found himself alone at the Café Zuntz, his friends having abandoned him at the last moment. The English poet W.H. Auden drowned his boredom in alcohol. Gilbert Amy only appeared occasionally. Xenakis lived in a very pretty, nearly empty house not far from the Institute, and we saw each other from time to time. He was always talking about the architecture and mathematics of music. Sensing my reticence, his wife, who was a very lively and amusing woman and a talented writer as well, once told me: "In spite of all his theories, Iannis is a real musician." I entirely agreed with her.

The Berlin Institute gained a reputation that far exceeded its importance, not for its achievements—which were really quite modest—but for its defense and support of musicians from non-European cultures. It played a very important role in Asian and African countries, encouraging traditional music and urging government and radio to support their own musical heritages without any feelings of inferiority.

This was a recognized fact in Asian countries. Indira Gandhi once wrote me: "You have done so much for making India's music known in Europe."

Zoltan Kodaly, the famous Hungarian musicologist who was Bartok's friend and successor, came secretly to see us so that he could learn our methods. This created a minor incident, for the Berlin authorities were furious not to have been warned of the arrival of this eminent personality.

Arthur Greenberg, director of a New York research group on medieval and Renaissance music, came to the Institute to study certain elements of Persian music which he felt he needed to understand in order to reconstruct the style, rhythms, and ornaments of ancient Western music. Unfortunately he died before completing his project.

LE FARADET

Raymond had come to Berlin to help me. He was an excellent, conscientious, and efficient administrator; but he had grown gloomy and irascible and sometimes caused me problems. I often regretted having allowed myself to be dragged into this venture, which was far more difficult than I had imagined and absorbed all my energies in matters of little importance. I went through periods of deep depression.

The gods chose this time to send me a member of their cohort, one of those mysterious beings Hindus call *ganas*, fantastical and mischievous youths who like to play tricks on gods and men. This *gana* looked like a *korrigan*, the sprite-like race of children that fairies in Britanny sometimes leave in cradles instead of human babies. Cocteau used to say that such beings were light of blood. This *korrigan* became my guardian angel. I called him "le Farfadet" [the Sprite]. He loved to dance, sing, and tear about in a red English sportscar. But there was nothing that he could not do; he could organize and put anything in order without even seeming to touch it.

He did not have any of the ambitions of the men of this world, whom he mocked. He lived in an entirely different realm.

He could manipulate people, charm them, and make them do anything he pleased. Any project he got involved in seemed like a game, but he would accomplish it, as though by magic, with wonderful precision and efficiency. Le Farfadet poked his little nose into everything, put everything right, averted intrigues. It was thanks to this celestial aide that the Berlin Institute became such a huge success. The gods, once again, were helping me fulfill a destiny I did not feel quite capable of handling on my own.

In spite of our interesting projects, le Farfadet suffered from his exile in Berlin. The German mentality did not agree with him: he felt like an ambassador who has been sent far away to a forlorn African republic. But he bravely accomplished his mission and, once the Institute's goals had been achieved, helped me to disengage myself and leap into new adventures. Ten years of efforts had completely transformed the status of

Asian musicians, who were now entirely incorporated into the world of international music, recognized, accepted, and invited to play concerts. This was an important first step; now I had to attack the more serious problem of making known the other aspects of Indian culture—its philosophy, religion, and social structures—a project to which I thereafter devoted my time in my labyrinthian retreat, under the skillful and light-handed protection of le Farfadet.

In Venice I had met a highly respected young Italian composer of Hungarian origin called Ivan Vandor, who had lived for long periods in Tibetan monasteries and published several excellent works on Tibetan music. He had also worked at U.C.L.A.'s Institute of Oriental Music, an organization run by Mantle Hood. I asked him to become my assistant and, in 1976, left the Berlin Institute in his care.

I had found my freedom at last.

The hill of the Labyrinth was covered with vines, some of which I continued to maintain. Le Farfadet grew quite interested in the rites of preparation of Bacchus' sacred brew. We studied various methods and learned to recognize the days most favorable for winemaking according to the movements of stars, a system still used by peasants. There are many subtle differences between real wine and the industrialized product that goes by that name. Philippe de Rothschild kindly invited us to Mouton so that le Farfadet could learn some of the traditional techniques which he, unlike most wine producers, still observes.

Our visit to Mouton was wonderful. Philippe has the style and the manners of an English noble lord of old; in fact, he has done very beautiful translations of Elizabethan poetry. His American wife Pauline who, alas! is no longer with us, was one of the most remarkable women I had ever met. Never in all my life have I seen such refinement in the art of living as I found in their home.

The Bordelais countryside is both hideous and fascinating. The vast plains with their endless rows of low vines and rocky and grayish soil are quite sinister. From the outside, the house, though very large, does not pretend to look like a castle; but the beautifully decorated interior, the quality of the objects and furniture, the refinement of the service were a perpetual enchantment to me. Each meal was served in a different place. A strange, fairy-like creature was hired especially to make new flower arrangements each day; Pauline would open a special album and choose the table linen, the precious chinaware and crystal that matched the flowers. We celebrated the new year with Stephen Spender and two famous American scientists, and drank wines that were exactly one hundred years old.

Monsieur Raoul, master of the wine storage cellars, initiated le Farfadet into the secrets of the trade. The wine was fermented in oak vats and never touched a metal object. It was stored in new barrels that were always kept filled, drop by drop, so that the precious brew never came in contact with air. The temperature of the vast cellars was strictly controlled.

The result of this investigation vastly improved the wine of the Labyrinth, though it made no claims to greatness.

I saw Pauline again many times in Paris. She was passionately interested in ideas and also quite fond of me, though she felt some reticence about my polytheism. One night we had dinner together in a very common working-class *bistrot* where I often came to eat and whose prices were the only ones I could afford at the time. It was run by a very beautiful woman called Madame Giselle, who reigned with absolute authority over the bar adjoining the restaurant, which she kept in perfect order, though it was frequented by all the neighborhood riff-raff. Pauline had often admired the character of Carmen on the stage, but meeting this character in the flesh was quite another matter. The contrast between these two women, both very beautiful, both in total control of their own special domain, made me wonder what would have happened if Louis XIV had suddenly found himself face to face with the Emperor of Ghana. These women belonged to two totally different worlds but each enjoyed unquestionable prestige over her own territory. One reigned over the Mafia and its violent, courageous, daring men who possess their own special brand of chivalry; the other, over the most sophisticated society, with a graciousness and freedom of spirit that only come with the near absolute power conferred by great fortunes.

These two women eyed each other with curiosity and obvious interest. Pauline, who would never have dared enter such a place alone, was delighted with the experience. Madame Giselle was dazzled by her furs, whose value she had assessed from the very first instant.

When I returned to Mouton a few years later, I was happy to rediscover its pleasant, cultivated, and open-minded atmosphere and Philippe's warm hospitality. Nothing had changed and yet everything was different. The furniture and objets d'art seemed to have grown rigid and had a museum-like funereal quality. All life was suspended, like the clocks that people used to stop at the instant of death, and the survivors seemed like ghosts. Pauline was dead and, like a flower that has lost its perfume, the house had lost its soul. I was filled with a strange anguish and a deep feeling of sadness.

The Death of Raymond

While Raymond was reacquainting himself with Europe in the Paradiso's proletarian atmosphere, he had met a good-looking, almost illiterate young Italian called Franco. Later the two men moved into a charming apartment on the Via Nomentana. When Raymond bought the property in Zagarolo, he made Franco his factotum.

Franco was a shrewd and obsequious youth who dreamed of being adopted by Raymond. He feared me because I was always putting Raymond on his guard, which, alas! proved to be of no use at all.

While he was living in Berlin, Raymond met a young East German refugee called Peter, who had spent several years in shelters that sounded all too much like children's penal colonies. Peter was a gentle, maladjusted boy, completely oblivious of material things and unable to fend for himself. He became as passionately attached to Raymond as a baby chick to its mother.

Raymond was happy with Peter but, with the typical perversity of a right-minded Protestant, the fonder he grew of Peter, the more he felt he owed Franco, and the more he indulged and favored him.

He always insisted on throwing the two boys together; as a result, the atmosphere around him tended to be highly charged.

Raymond had accompanied me to New York for an important conference. His two favorites were with him and, being part of the congress, were invited to the White House and presented to the First Lady. Raymond went directly back to Zagarolo, and I to Berlin. A few days later, while I was entertaining Nabokov and Balanchine, who had come to listen to tape recordings I had just brought back from Soviet Georgia, I received a telephone call announcing Raymond's death. He was only fifty-six.

I arrived in Rome the same night. They had placed Raymond on his bed, and his beautiful white face was like a statue's. A whole lifetime of affection, companionship, and shared ventures had suddenly come to an end; my friend had deserted me. Franco bustled about making all the funeral arrangements, in total control. Peter was completely shattered, desperate, pitiful; I spent most of my time trying to calm him down. The faithful Pierre Arnal, Raymond's oldest friend, was there also, a last witness to his first love.

I was filled with a strange feeling of anger. I was furious with Raymond for having died. I sensed somehow that it was his fault, without quite knowing why. The Italian doctor, taking no chances, had asked the local forensic expert to prepare the death certificate: heart attack. A few days later, however, Raymond's uncle, "the Buffalo," who practiced medicine in Switzerland, expressed some doubts about the cause of his nephew's death. The young German physician who had looked after him in Berlin was categorical. The violence and the symptoms of the attack that had killed Raymond an hour after he had been gaily drinking coffee on the terrace left no doubt whatsoever in his mind: he insisted on an autopsy. Raymond, in fact, was already suffering from heart problems, and knew that he was in danger. A month earlier, on August 31, 1968, he had written to Pierre Arnal: "At our age, the future may not be so very long."

I found myself facing a difficult dilemma. A judicial inquiry risked poisoning the lives of all those present for months, even years; then there was Raymond's family, a possible scandal. The risks were too great. No one could help Raymond now. I decided to do nothing. I consulted with old Dr. Burnier and Raymond's brother, who both agreed with me. The German doctor never forgave me.

According to Raymond's instructions, Franco alone was responsible for the funeral arrangements. Raymond had expressed the desire to be cremated and mentioned it in writing many times. As early as 1945, he had written Pierre Arnal: "Do you find life amusing? I do, I do most awfully—not only amusing but perfect. But if I am to leave it—when I do leave it—I don't want to wallow under six feet of cheap earth. No indeed! I shall burn like the good Hindu I am. Har Sharan will be set ablaze one last time, once and for all." (Benares, 7 March 1945). Har Sharan (He who is protected by the Liberator) was the Hindu name Raymond had been given at the time of our initiation.

But Franco had other plans. Raymond was not a Catholic, so there could be no rites. A small group of eight people accompanied Raymond through woods all pink with flowering wild cyclamen, to a modest tomb in the cemetery of Zagarolo. Franco, who led the procession, had invited one of his prostitute friends to walk with him—a girl he had probably picked up on the street—thinking he would look finer that way. I was far too upset to intervene.

Franco inherited the property in Zagarolo and most of Raymond's fortune. Raymond had told Peter that a large sum of money was deposited in his name but had done nothing about it. I managed to remedy this, though it was not easy for me.

I was never able to recover the books and objects I had left in Raymond's house. Franco even resorted to blackmail concerning the right of way to my house. While we were discussing matters in the lawyer's office, we were asked if it was necessary to put in writing our informal arrangement about road maintenance. Franco, whose bad faith had been evident throughout the interview, exclaimed: "But that's not necessary since Alain says he'll do it!" It was a typically Italian attitude. We belonged to different worlds, but he knew that in my scheme of things a word had the same value as a signature.

Franco fired the entire staff without even giving them notice. I took on the gardener and the cook, Mario. Mario died four years later of a heart attack, and Franco two years after that in an auto crash. The gods have kept their secret.

Franco's brothers divided the property between them, and the fortune was soon dissipated. The magnificent grounds became a kind of suburban shantytown filled with rabbit hutches and corrugated-iron shacks, separated by barbed-wire fences and littered with rubbish. Fortunately, my house and domain remained separate.

CHAPTER SEVENTEEN

Musical Landscapes

CAMBODIA AND LAOS

In 1956, when I was affiliated with the Ecole Française d'Extrême-Orient, I made a long visit to Cambodia and Laos in order to study and record their music.

Cambodia was an exquisite country, peaceful and harmonious. Under the very humane government of Prince Sihanouk, everything seemed bright, peaceful, and unclouded. The famous Cambodian Royal Ballet was suffering from attempts at modernization, but the orchestra was still excellent. The Khmer culture, inherited from ancient Champa, is one of the great original traditions of the world, not linked in any way with India or China, as can be judged by the music. During certain periods of history, this culture had spread throughout Burma, Thailand, even Java and Bali, but was at its most authentic in Cambodia. I also taped various kinds of religious and popular music, dance orchestras, and public festivals.

The custodian of Angkor was a very old architect called Marchal, who seemed almost an archaeological monument himself. Though eighty years old, he was still quite lively and went on incredible expeditions on the Mekong River or in ruin-scattered forests. In the village of Siem Reap, near the temples, he owned two houses right across from each other, separated by the main thoroughfare of the town. His French wife lived in one house, his Cambodian wife in the other. He would sleep or take his meals in whichever one happened to suit his mood; this, no doubt, allowed him some diversity in his diet. He judiciously smoked a few opium pipes a day "to ensure his longevity."

André Malraux was considered the national enemy and was still wanted by the law for stealing sculptures from temples. This, I may add, saved them from being later destroyed when the barbaric warriors of Pol Pot used the temples as fortresses.

The architecture of the temples was very impressive, but I found the sculptures rather monotonous and far less interesting than those of India.

Not far from Angkor I recorded magicians' orchestras, whose strange music originates from Jinn-worshipping mountain tribes that are quite different from the Khmers. The people from these very primitive tribes later formed Pol Pot's ferocious army. The complete destruction of the Cambodian civilization by the Khmer Rouge, who in fact are not real Khmers at all, was a frightening genocide. People sometimes wonder how the Olmecs and Mayas were annihilated. Yet in our own time, under our very eyes, we have witnessed the total eradication of a people and its civilization.

Laos was very different from Cambodia, a rough and closed country mostly populated by mountain tribes. People used to say that until 1940 the French tea planters who wanted to force the peasants to work for them would burn their crops; the men, who had families to feed, then had no choice but to work on the plantations. Once they were taken on and surrounded by guards, those who had gathered the smallest crop during the day were sweetly tortured each night with the electric current from a telephone dynamo. This form of Stakhanovism was apparently quite effective. The memory of this gentle treatment may perhaps explain why, when they later had the chance, the Laotian mountain men proved to be so ferocious.

Vientiane was an ugly, modern little city. There was only one hotel, a kind of barracks made of reinforced concrete, where Sikh soldiers sent by the United Nations had destroyed all the *bidets*, which they considered obscene.

The only way to go from Vientiane to the royal capital of Luang Prabhang was by a small four-seat airplane that transported great heaps of vegetable crates and live chickens, as well as an occasional passenger. It flew extremely low, threading its way through narrow mountain passes. When I expressed my surprise to the pilot, he admitted: "This plane cannot fly any higher. But I am well paid—these are the wages of fear."

Luang Prabhang was nothing but a small village, consisting of a single street lined with fine trees and a few scattered houses. The temple and the palace were the only important monuments.

The palace, all made of carved wood, was very beautiful and surrounded by a vast enclosure. The Royal Orchestra was an imitation of the Cambodians', but quite good. The popular music was entirely different, however. Laos is the kingdom of the *khène*, a mouth organ from which is derived the Chinese *sheng*. The *khène* is a nostalgic-sounding instrument that echoes through all the Laotian villages. Here one also finds sets of sacred gongs, which are considered the soul of the village, the voice of the guardian Jinn. If the gongs are stolen or destroyed, the village disintegrates and its people go elsewhere to find a more favorable Jinn. In spite of wars and political oppression, Laos seems to have suffered less than Cambodia. The music of the *khène*, a true folk art, is apparently still played in the villages, which consist of huts perched on top of wooden posts, as though on the edge of a lake.

Return to Kabul

In 1959, I went back to Afghanistan, this time to record music. I was invited by Christian Belle, who was ambassador at the time and had once been deeply involved in Parisian artistic and cultural life. People called him "little Christian," as opposed to the "great Christian" Dior. The embassy was a charming old house. Christian had converted a former hammam, with a vaulted ceiling and blue ceramic tiles on the floor, into a series of rooms. The garden was surrounded by walls and filled with four-leaf clover. The queen of the embassy was a Siamese cat who sat majestically on a pink velvet stool and nobly acknowledged those who came to pay her homage. It was strictly forbidden for anyone else to sit on that stool.

This time my visit to Afghanistan went very smoothly. A

number of musicians from various regions had been invited to Kabul so that I could record their music. Ahmed Ali was now curator of the museum and was still very proud of his glorious expedition to Kafiristan.

Kabul could now be reached by air from Delhi. It was no longer the end of the world, but there were no modern hotels as there are now, and the country had not yet been invaded by hordes of tourists. The tribes still led a rugged pastoral life under the peaceful and popular reign of Zaher Shah.

I had been asked to try to make contact with a young Italian girl who had married an Afghan "prince" on the Côte d'Azur. This proved to be quite difficult. The Italian embassy knew nothing about her. Moslem harems are a closed and secret world. I appealed to the palace for help and, as a special favor, was finally granted permission to see her.

I was taken to a large farm surrounded by high cob walls, at the end of a long, rutted, and muddy road. Inside the enclosure was a vast courtyard crowded with animals, chickens, and filthy old women, with several primitive-looking mud and brick structures built along the sides. In one of the corners was a tiny little room, which the young woman had decorated with hideous modern furniture covered with a blue silk-velvet fabric that shimmered in the light. Here was her oasis, her pathetic tribute to Italian vulgarity, absurdly incongruous within the context of the farm. On the walls were artificial silk hangings representing Mecca, the kind one finds in the bazaars of Port Said, which the girl obviously preferred to the elegantly sober rugs of Afghanistan. I was the first European she had been allowed to meet. She cried, spoke of running away, but I could do nothing for her; there was no hope. The heavy wooden door that led out of the courtyard was a boundary that she would never cross again.

IRAN

In 1957, I went on a trip to Iran for my record collection project. I have gone back many times since. At first I found very little encouragement for my work. All the Iranian officials told me that "the ancient music of Iran no longer exists and interests no one." Iranians were busy building a new Opera, creating a new symphony orchestra. Everyone spoke of Mozart and Verdi.

It was through Imbert de Laurens Castellet, the chargé d'affaires in Teheran, that I met Ernest Perron, who was to provide me with the key to the real Iran.

Ernest had had a very remarkable career. As a boy, the Shah had been sent to a Swiss school where Ernest's father worked as a gardener. A deep and passionate friendship had gradually developed between the shy, sensitive, and frightened son of Reza Shah Pahlevi and the fair, vigorous, honest, radiant Swiss youth. When the Shah ascended the throne, he was terrified by the responsibilities and intrigues of the palace. He sent for his friend Ernest who became a kind of *éminence grise* and reigned over Iran for over twenty years. It was he who encouraged the Shah to create the liberal regime that distinguished the first part of his reign from the harsh and bloody dictatorship of his father Reza Shah, a former officer of the Czar's army who had seized power by overthrowing the ancient dynasty of the Kajars. It was to Ernest that Iran owed its agricultural reforms, hospitals, roads, schools, social benefits, food distribution programs, not to speak of the liberation of its women.

Ernest was made official Chamberlain of the Palace and given the title "Excellency." He became the protector of the minorities—Armenians, Kurds, and Jews. Though deeply religious and a fervent Catholic, he never tried to proselytize and felt a genuine affinity for Iranian mysticism.

Two events altered the course of his career. He was struck down by polio, which changed him from a tall, handsome man to a misshapen Quasimodo. Then the Shah was obliged to marry. His first wife, the sister of King Farouk, was not important; but the second, Soraya, was a vain, domineering, and ambitious creature who dragged the weak-willed Shah into the international jet-set life of luxury hotels, winter sports, yachts, and casinos, which made a deplorable impression on the religious, sometimes even fanatical Iranian people. Then, feeling seriously threatened by the assassination attempts of Soviet-inspired revolutionaries, the Shah gave free rein to his secret police to ensure his protection. Ernest was appalled, but the Shah no longer listened to him. Soraya did everything she could to humiliate him and drive him away from the monarch. Though Ernest was still the official palace chamberlain, he withdrew into the home of Princess Shams, the Shah's youngest sister, who was married to the Minister of Culture Pahlbodh. She felt the highest respect for Ernest and never abandoned him.

Soraya was hated by the people. Farah Diba, who succeeded her, was a far more modest woman but not strong enough to control the wild extravagances of the coronation ceremonies, whose inordinate splendor gave the Shah's enemies an un-hoped-for weapon and deeply disturbed the lower classes. Furthermore, the Shah was gravely ill. The nervousness and authoritarianism that characterized his last years of his reign were partly due to his illness.

On the whole, however, Iranians had no reason to be un-happy with the Shah. Under his reign the country's prosperity had grown by leaps and bounds. The only victims of ruthless persecution were dissidents, most of whom were financed by foreign countries; students who had been sent at the govern-ment's expense to study in Europe and America, only to be recruited by left-wing extremists; and political troublemakers who were considered heroes by Western "intellectuals." Ad-mittedly there were flaws and a good deal of corruption in the government, but on the whole non-politicized citizens had nothing to fear. No one interfered with their private lives. Adulterous women and homosexuals were not massacred. Teheran had become an enormous and extraordinarily pros-perous city. The destiny of a people rarely hinges upon reali-ties, but on slogans. The numbers of victims of the Shah come nowhere near the great masses of unfortunate people who were massacred by Khomeini. The real problem was that mod-ern Iran had been patterned after the Western mode, which caused deep resentment among the dispossessed religious hierarchy as well as the Moslem Shiites, a small but tradition-ally violent group of fanatics.

Through Ernest and his friends, I was able to meet several great artists, above all Nur Ali Boruman, a blind musician who played the Iranian lute or *tar*, but lived far removed from public life, for his family was descended from the ancient Kajar dynasty. Golpayegani, his young student, was a wonderful singer. I also became friends with Teherani, the great Persian drum virtuoso who played the *dumbak* (or *zarb*), and Hussein Malek, master of the *santur*. My most moving encounter was with an extraordinary flutist who lived alone, destitute and abandoned by all, in a miserable little shack near Isfahan. A loyal disciple who bought him food each day was the only person who ever came to see him.

Modern Iran was not interested in such people. Here, as in Nehru's India, the process of Westernization seemed irreversible.

I spent a great deal of time making tapes of these musicians and published two records of Iranian music under the Unesco label. I was able to arrange a few concerts in Europe which met with a great deal of success. The results were spectacular. One day, the wife of the French Ambassador asked the Empress Farah: "Where can I hear those marvelous musicians Daniélou recorded?" "What musicians?" replied the puzzled Empress. Finally they were invited to play at the palace, then on the radio. The International Music Council organized a congress on traditional music in Ispahan. A school was founded under the direction of Nur Ali Boruman, with the help of Dariouche Safvate, who had recently taught at the small center of Oriental music that was created in Paris within the Institut de Musicologie by Nelly Caron, Tran Van Khé, and myself. The music of Iran had been brought back to life. The local press wrote several articles about me. I was offered a professorial post at the University of Teheran.

Ernest was delighted with these developments for which he was partly responsible thanks to his many loyal friends in the ministries, radio, and press. He grew quite fond of me and we remained in close correspondence thereafter. Ernest's letters were very beautiful, full of simplicity, faith, and humility; they were the letters of a saint. His last message to me was written a few days before he died as a result of falling off a horse, for in spite of his infirmity he had never stopped riding.

If the Shah had not drifted away from Ernest, the fate of Iran would undoubtedly have been quite different; but historians of the period have been curiously reticent about the role played by this exceptional man.

Nur Ali recently died. The music school has been more or less closed down by Khomeini, and all the radio recordings were erased by the mullahs. The marvelous music of Iran may not survive this mad fanatic who is trying to destroy the cultural tradition of his country in the name of a simplistic religion—though true Shiism, in fact, is a deeply tolerant and mystical faith, altogether different from what now goes by that name. What will happen to the magnificent musical tradition of Iran, no one can say. It is more than likely that it will eventually be replaced by Russian-style pseudo-folk music and disco beats with an Oriental flavor.

Not long ago, I received a visit from a young musicologist who had spent several years in Iran studying music and had actively participated in the revolutionary movement. He complained now of having been chased out of the country and wanted me to help him find work. He was clearly very eager to take advantage of the comforts of the Free World before going off elsewhere to sow the seeds of revolution and death. He wanted my support, but he had come to the wrong address.

Thirty miles from Teheran, at Galand Bagh, the home of the former Iranian Ambassador to Rome, Nizam Sultan Khajenouri, I witnessed the ecstatic ceremonies of the *sufis*. Like many Iranians who otherwise appear quite modern, Nizam was a *sufi* and deeply involved in the poetic and mystical tradition which all the greatest Persian poets have belonged to.

The ceremony took place in an isolated building in the garden. Ernest and I were served tea in a comfortable little room furnished with rugs and cushions. Then we slipped through a narrow door into a large adjoining room filled with men sitting on the floor. It was very dark. We sat discreetly in a corner, against a wall. The silence was awesome, overwhelming.

Little by little, almost imperceptibly, a low murmur of prayers seemed to rise from this motionless crowd of bodies. Then someone began to intone a low chant, which the others, still murmuring, took up in unison. The chant grew gradually louder and louder, and more and more rhythmical, until it became almost deafening. A man stood up and began to dance, making a strange animal-like droning sound and head movements which the Greeks used to compare to those of bulls. Then others joined him. The dance became more and more frenetic, the chants gradually changed to shouts. The clamor was fantastic, overwhelming. Drums began to play, giving a tempo to the dance. I felt completely dazed, almost hypnotized. Time and space seemed no longer to exist. The movement and the noise formed a kind of cone that rose to the sky and seemed to communicate with an unknown world. The dancers acted as though they were intoxicated. They went into a trance, shouting and calling out strange incomprehensible words. The droning went faster and faster and became more and more spasmodic, mingled with invocations to Allah.

This frenzy lasted over an hour. Then the exhausted participants began to fall on the floor, one after another, in a sort of cataleptic fit. The clamor slowly died down, then suddenly ceased altogether. The room looked like a battleground covered with prostrate, motionless heaps of bodies. A blessed silence, like a mysterious presence, descended upon the room, enveloping these victims of faith. Ernest and I slipped quietly out the door, still completely deafened, still under the spell of our strange experience, the magical act of communication with the unknown we had witnessed: we felt transformed, like different men. We remained for a long time in the quiet and peaceful little room without saying a word to each other, then walked through a lovely rose garden back to the main house.

I have never dared to record the *zekhr* ceremonies. The religious nature of this kind of experience is far too intense for me to even consider introducing so profane an element as curiosity. Two of my assistants, who were less personally involved, succeeded in doing this: one in Syria, the other in Yugoslavia, among Moslems of Albanian origin. I was able to produce two superb recordings of these ceremonies. Jochen Wenzel, a skillful young technician who accompanied the researchers, was strongly marked by the violence of the experience.

While visiting a noble Iranian, I was persuaded to take part in an opium session. A few friends and I gathered in a small dark room whose walls were decorated with blue ceramic tiles, the kind that can only be found in Iran. There were several layers of precious rugs on the floor, with large cushions to lean against. Two or three young men wearing Persian costumes, who seemed to step out of ancient miniatures, served us tea. Then one of them brought in a brazier and pipes that looked like bamboo flutes. He melted down and lit tiny balls of black resin, then placed them in the small silver bowls at the end of each pipe. He brought one to each of us with slow, graceful, protective gestures, as though he were offering a soothing drink to an ailing child. We had to inhale the acrid and aromatic smoke very slowly and deeply, then the attentive youth would remove the pipe. No one said a word. The stillness in the room was like the silence of a mysterious ritual.

The graceful acolyte glided noiselessly from one reclining body to another, like an angel of death skillfully dispensing small doses of dreams to his victims.

Apart from its poetry the experience was not particularly pleasant for me. I love the reality of the world far too well to willingly let myself go to any form of intoxication. The next day I was deathly pale, ill, nauseous, ready to faint. I never repeated the experience.

AFRICA

The International Music Council had decided to hold its annual meeting in Yaoundé, in Cameroon. The Chamber of Deputies was placed at our disposal, and we lived in the Hôtel des Députés, a kind of primitive barracks kept by a white adventurer of undetermined nationality who ran a quite good restaurant, a vestige of the French presence in the country. The congress mostly included representatives of various African countries who wore ties, spoke elegant French or English, and seemed, for the most part, not only very vain but totally ignorant of African traditions. Africa, the last continent to be subjected to European rule and fragmented into innumerable ethnic groups to begin with, was deeply affected by colonization. Part of the population had been converted to Islam. African society and its way of life were profoundly disorganized by low-church Christian missions. There is practically nothing left of the great empires and royal courts, which were once important centers of artistic culture.

Like everywhere else, the "natives" who took over the country from its colonizers were formed by European standards
and taught to scorn their more backward brothers, who clung
to the beliefs and customs of their ancestors. Many of them
are married to white women or have mixed blood. They no
longer belong to any culture and have become very much like
the former colonizers, whose prejudices and methods they
have adopted; they also make a show of a brand of nationalism
that mainly consists in destroying their cultural heritage. It is
a complete waste of time to ask them about local traditions. All
the records of African music that I published were made by
foreigners.

Europeans, who are in control of most of the country's
affairs, live among themselves in small provincial groups.
They treat the new leaders with shrewdness and the poor
with contempt. Most of them are mediocre people who put on
airs of insolent superiority which they have no right to in their
own countries.

Nature in tropical Africa is beautiful but hostile. In Douala,
Cameroon's commercial port, the climate is torrid. The Ivory
Coast is richer but even more alarming than Cameroon. The
development of the country depends on a deeply hostile collaboration between races who cannot understand each other on
any possible level. Senegal is an arid country that gives one a
foretaste of Maghreb. Although it has a few resources, it is
very cleverly organized for the tourist industry. The climate is
pleasant and there are vast beaches and luxurious hotels,
where only the lower orders of servants are black. It is impossible to make contact with the people. The influence of Islam
has added an element of hostile aggressiveness and haughti-
ness to the behavior of mediocre, second-rate people, making
Africa, with its tyrannical leaders, its indolent population, and
its fancy white slaves, an extremely unappealing place; and
because all participate in the running of commerce and industry on a non-autonomous basis, the moment their collaboration breaks down, the country disintegrates into civil war,
extreme poverty, and famine. Westerners are so convinced of
the superiority of their social and economic theories and the
benefits of their industrial civilization that they feel it a moral

duty to export and impose them on other nations for their own good. Exporting democracy or socialism is a method of colonization just like Christianity or Islam. Since Africa has always been organized on a tribal basis, this leads to the extermination of the least fit in artificial nations that cannot function without outside help.

Nowadays, people often speak of African civilization and culture; such terms, in the circumstances, seem something of a joke. In a context favorable to their own customs, their beauty, and their poetry, black Africans have a great deal to offer, and though their values, knowledge, art of living, and vision of the world may seem archaic to us, there is much that we could learn from them. Very little is left of the real, the authentic Africa, however. Nearly everywhere one goes, missionaries and colonizers have destroyed the harmony of black institutions and hidden the sculptural beauty of the human form under sordid rags or European-style suits. Moslems, on the other hand, have imported their long tunics, their turbans, and their puritanism.

Only a few isolated groups—the Pygmies, the most ancient inhabitants of Africa who now lead wretched lives in the forests where they have sought shelter—have been able to preserve their culture, their philosophy, their religions, and their music, vestiges of a nearly forgotten golden age. Africa is a sad continent.

In the bastardized society in which we live, people refuse to accept the notion of "pure races" and all that is implied by the term: physical harmony, nobility of character, and other virtues. And yet, whatever their social rank may be nowadays, these types are instinctively recognized for what they are.

In one of the oldest and most beautiful *hôtels particuliers* on the Rue de Varenne in Paris where she was living at the time, the Baronne de La Grange once gave a reception for a select group of people in honor of her son Henry Louis, the famous biographer of Gustav Mahler on whom an award was being conferred. Some of the most illustrious titles of French nobility were present. Suddenly, with just the right amount of delay, a very tall, very elegant African entered the room. With the most perfect simplicity and courtesy of manner, in which one could detect just the slightest trace of condescension, he paid his respects to the baroness and shook hands with some of the guests. A slight shiver of excitement went through the room. What royal personage might this be who was willing to honor the occasion by his presence? After exchanging a few words with people whom he seemed to know, this remarkable-looking man, to everyone's astonishment, took his post behind the buffet. It was Hassan, the African cook Henry Louis had brought back from the Ivory Coast.

The USSR

My continuing search for surviving elements of traditional Asian music and my participation in Unesco conferences and gatherings at the Institute put me in frequent contact with Soviet "specialists." The Soviets are an extraordinarily conservative people. All their beliefs—social, religious, literary or musical—were defined at the end of the nineteenth century, during the era of their prophet; they have remained unchanged ever since. The Soviets' ideology belongs to bourgeois dissidents of a bygone age, and they struggle against problems that have little more reality today than Don Quixote's windmills. If they had not also retained the repressive methods of the czarist era and a contemptuous attitude towards peasants, this might be considered laughable. They believe in the absolute superiority of the European bourgeois civilization; such progress, however, ends in 1883, the year of Marx's death. The heights of musical art, according to them, were reached by Tchaikovsky, whom they would probably send to a gulag for immoral practices were he alive today. Contemporary music seems a dangerous threat to the established order. All other musical cultures, whether they are local or exotic, are considered primitive, archaic, and picturesque relics whose only possible function is to add a bit of local color to Western compositions such as Balakirev's or Borodin's. All this makes the Soviet Union a fundamentally colonialistic nation, working for the good of a backward populace. They do all they can to improve, orchestrate, and russianize the so-called popular traditions. Anything that differs from the most conventional type of Western music belongs to the category of "folklore," a term that is not only condescending but falsely complimentary; for as Xavier Grall once remarked: "Folklore is the culture of slaves." Acceptance of any form of local art is an encouragement towards nationalism.

My absolute refusal to record the orchestral arrangements of the "folklore" of the Eastern Republics of the Soviet Union led to constant clashes that sometimes took on the character of a political conflict. Although I never made any attempt to hide my convictions and refused to travel to Russia except at the Soviet government's expense, I was nonetheless invited there several times. My objections to the "orchestral improvements" of folk music were termed colonialistic, even fascist, with that remarkable talent Marxists have for inverting realities. And yet, after some of the conferences in Moscow or Alma Ata where I had proved myself most stubbornly unyielding, those same musicians who had stigmatized me in public would chase me into lonely corners or elevators and beg me to continue my crusade.

In Azerbaidzhan, while listening to a folkloric orchestra that was playing for me alone, I very rudely interrupted the concert and insisted on hearing some of the soloists. I was particularly interested in one of them, a superb player of the *tar* (a kind of lute), and arranged to go to his home so that I could listen to him play. When I asked him why, with all his wonderful talent, he had ever agreed to play for this abominable orchestra, he answered: "What else can I do? It's all because of Western imperialism." I soon realized that this ambiguous expression really meant "Moscow." When I invited him to play some concerts in Western Europe, he said: "It would give me great joy to be able to accept. Unfortunately I should probably break my leg a week before leaving."

In the Republic of Georgia Jacques Cloarec and I recorded superb improvisations of polyphonic songs, which are typical examples of Caucasian music. I found myself having to duplicate all the tapes. We spent an entire night working with the technicians on the Tiflis radio, who had told me: "You must take the tapes with you, otherwise you will never get them."

"Unimproved" traditional music is apparently considered anti-Marxist.

The unfortunate young woman who accompanied us from Moscow as a spy-interpreter was in a state of great anxiety during our trip to the Eastern Republics. The only foreign language she knew was French—a rather special kind of French, for she had been trained to escort Algerian Arabs. She shamelessly addressed me by the familiar "tu" and spoke with a very picturesque, well-imitated accent. Unfortunately for her, we met several German-speaking musicians and musicologists during our trip, and she was unable to report our conversations. I felt very sorry for her. Her reports were incomplete and, whatever the reason may be, lapses of this kind are no laughing matter in Moscow.

Thanks to Stalin, who was Georgian, the Republic of Georgia has a fairly autonomous government. In the Tiflis hotel where we stayed, busts of Stalin were carefully hidden in closets along with ancient icons. Georgians live in relative freedom and are far less terrorized than other Soviets—they are a cheerful, alcoholic people with rather loose morals. Georgia is a kind of Italy of the Soviet Union. In the hotel restaurant, people at the other tables were already tipsy at breakfast and would insist on offering us bottles of wine and glasses of local brandy. Our young but austere Moscow interpreter lived in terror of the vigorous, strapping young men who would constantly try to corner her in staircases in the hope of pinching her bottom. It was a far cry from the sinister hush of Moscow hotels where each floor is guarded by an imposing female martinet who observes any unusual movements and meets all visitors' questions with a formidable silence.

One of the pleasantest things about the Soviet Union is its respect for privileges, inherited from the Czars. The amenities and advantages accorded to the *Nomenklatura* are exactly the same as those defined by Peter the Great for the aristocracy. When a visitor is an official guest, all traces of official quibbling seem to mysteriously disappear. While normal travelers leaving the airplane are subjected to interminable inspections—passports, customs, money, subversive literature—one is greeted by a charming young woman holding a red card. The somber officials blushingly apologize for having dared to ask a question, and one walks freely past all the controls with an acute feeling of superiority towards that contemptible mass of plebeian tourists, who line up in endless queues.

I felt slightly ill after my trip to Georgia. When I returned to Moscow, I was graciously escorted by car directly to the airplane that was taking me back to East Berlin, thus avoiding all the airport controls.

On the East Berlin airfield I was greeted by a young Russian officer with a car who drove me straight to my home in West Berlin. We crossed the Wall through a special gate, and I was never subjected to any kind of inspection—not even for my passport. Life is very beautiful in the USSR if one happens to be "official"; when I returned there as an ordinary guest, things were far less agreeable.

The Soviet Union is the only country in the world today that still maintains an aristocratic tradition. A select oligarchy enjoys unlimited privileges, leads a life of astonishing luxury, and shows the deepest contempt for the rest of the population, which lives in wretched conditions similar to those of the English working class of the nineteeth century. The Communist leaders of so-called capitalist countries apparently see nothing else besides the sumptuous *dachas* outside Moscow and the luxurious resorts on the Black seacoast that are forbidden to the public.

Greece and Mount Athos

In Greece I did a certain amount of research on Byzantine music. This country and its magical islands are deeply imbued with history and still maintain a great variety of traditions. Some of them seem derived from antiquity, while others show hints of Turkish influences as well as very ancient Macedonian, Albanian, and Balkan musical traditions. Religious music termed Byzantine is most probably derived from the Romans. Like everywhere else, these traditions are threatened both by folklorists who would like to adapt them to so-called public tastes, and purists who try to reduce them to the level of a written document. The musicians, who are the true heirs to the tradition, are not asked for their opinion. These simple village people are raw material and apparently exist for no other purpose than to be exploited. I was horrified to see the famous musicologist Simon Karas high-handedly explaining to a group of musicians I was about to tape how they should sing and correcting them as though he were a schoolmaster directing a children's choir.

Dora Stratou, a very pleasant woman who has been organizing folk concerts in Athens for many years, introduced me to many island musicians. I asked them: "It seems to me that this music must have been quite different in the past. Wasn't there a drone?" "Of course there was! But it's now considered out of fashion." Then, to their great joy, I recorded some of their wonderful ancient songs. Dora was bewildered: "You've been doing concerts for me for ten years," she told the musicians. "Why haven't I ever heard these songs before?" "You never asked us," was the naïve reply.

Through José Garza, a Mexican director of Unesco's radio services, I had met a former minister of the King of Greece, Lambros Eutaxias, a man of vast culture and a great lover of music. He owned a superb property in Eleusis, which I visited several times. I wanted very much to visit Mount Athos, and he offered to accompany us. So we all set off—Lambros, one of his loyal servants, Jacques, and I—to make tape recordings of the Orthodox Easter ceremonies in the monasteries. The presence of an important man like Lambros made it very easy for us to obtain the required authorizations. Athos is a magical place. It has been cut off from the rest of the world since the beginning of time, and the luxuriance and unbridled fantasy of nature are quite astonishing. There are hundreds of varieties of plants that exist nowhere else. At the end of this long peninsula looms the high mountain that Poseidon brought over from Asia: it was the first Olympus. Solitary monks live in cells scooped out of the rock that were once occupied by Dionysian hermits. One of these monks secretly led me to a stone altar not far from the Grand Lavra monastery, where bulls were sacrificed in pre-Christian times.

The Holy Week ceremonies were very impressive with their superb chants and sumptuous ecclesiastical vestments. Jacques spent every night taping the music while I unheroically went to bed. He had some problems, however—tangling up his microphone wires in the dark sanctuaries, and damaging his equipment. We also had to walk long distances between monasteries during the day.

It was a real pilgrimage, stimulating to the mind but exhausting for the body. The monks graciously invited us to share their meals, which, it still being Lent, consisted of bean gruel—a curious reminder of the conflict between Christianity and the ancient world, which did not allow beans to be eaten at ritual meals. Fortunately, Lambros's servant had prudently brought a secret cache of food and even a few heartening flasks of sacrilegious whiskey.

But alas! the monastic population of Mount Athos is slowly dwindling. A few dozen aging monks manage with great difficulty those vast monasteries where thousands used to live. Russians, Bulgarians, and Rumanians are no longer allowed to come to this peaceful haven, and young Greeks are little inclined towards the contemplative life. One reason for this decline in the population of monks may be the puritanism of modern life. It has become difficult for them to share their austere cells with charming little monklets, as was once the custom, which makes for a very arid life in this sacred place where no females are allowed to enter. The Blessed Virgin who took the place of Rhea, goddess of the Mountain, is very exclusive: no other woman may enter her enchanted domain.

On a promontory high above a tiny harbor, where small boats circling around the peninsula sometimes like to stop, we feasted Easter Sunday with two obliging customs officers who, breaking the endless monotony of their uneventful lives, roasted an entire lamb on an improvised spit in the courtyard of their fort. Nothing had changed since the day that ancient ship carrying Ulysses and his companions was borne here by the winds.

MEXICO AND SO-CALLED LATIN AMERICA

José Garza, who had recently left Unesco, invited me to visit him in Cuernavaca, a millionaire's town with an "ideal climate," neither hot nor cold, with no spring or autumn, which, in fact, makes life amazingly dull. The atmosphere of this small town, with its aging men and women who have nothing to do but await death, reminded me of Whispering Glades, Hollywood's luxurious cemetery.

I was happy to accept the invitation, which also gave Jacques and me a chance to explore this magnificent country. Garza was a collector of pre-Columbian art and bought choice objects from clandestine tomb diggings at very low prices. His house was like a museum, with the finest examples of Olmec art I have ever seen: life-size heads made of crystal and jade, gold masks, and hundreds of statues of gods.

My search for vestiges of musical traditions was fruitless. We travelled nearly everywhere in the country. It would probably require much time and patience to discover any signs of such traditions, which have been kept very secret, for Mexico, like all the other countries in so-called Latin America, is entrenched in a Hispano-devotional mishmash of missionary Christianity—one of the worst forms of religiosity, with no value whatsoever on any level.

I once told José that he had the eagle-like profile of an Aztec warrior. He was quite insulted. "Every single drop of blood in my body is pure Castilian!" exclaimed this great lover of pre-Columbian civilizations whose admiration obviously did not include the descendants of that great people, totally reviled and scorned today.

In Venezuela, a country of skyscrapers and shantytowns, the Institute of Ethno-musicology has spent the past several years gathering specimens of traditional South American popular music. I vainly searched for material to record. The so-called native music of these countries consists of byproducts of Spanish music or Basque-style songs saturated with guitar harmonies. The steamroller of colonialism has completely crushed the Indian soul and obliterated even the memory of its past. It survives only in a few isolated groups lost in the Amazon jungles or in inaccessible regions of the Andes, among people who have been reduced to such a level of poverty and fear that one can no longer use the word "culture" to describe the vague memories they have preserved of their glorious past.

I encountered the same problem in Jamaica and Cuba, not to mention the French West Indies. This caused me some serious problems with Unesco, for those countries complained of not being represented in my record collections. I had created these collections for the sole purpose of defending cultures threatened by Western influences. I was certainly not about to give equal standing to triumphant colonialism.

Morocco and Tunisia

I returned to North Africa in the hope of finding traces of its brilliant civilizations and some remnants of the remarkable Islamic-influenced Spanish culture that once found refuge in this part of the world. Algeria, now infatuated with Marxism, has become hostile to all its traditional arts. I had hoped that in Morocco, which is still considered very conservative, I would find enough material to make a few records. Jacques and my secretary André Laprade drove down with all our recording material while I flew over to Marrakech, where we were supposed to meet. As it happened, I was forced to go all the way to Tangiers, where they were being held by customs officers, and pay their way out. Tangiers, once a center of trafficking, contraband, and pleasure, is now completely dead. After a short stay in the gloomy city of Rabat, we established our general headquarters at a friend's house in Marrakech. Although it was May, the weather was so cold and gray that I had to escape, shivering, into one of the large hotels. Unfortunately for us, the king was in residence at his palace and, as a result, the city was fiercely guarded by the police and by members of the Secret Service. Each night we had to drive our cook back to her home, otherwise the poor woman would probably have found herself in prison.

Our search yielded very few concrete results. The music schools here are afflicted with modernism of a very low order. So-called Andalusian music has lost all its style and refinement. The only place where we were able to hear beautiful mystical chants was in a monastery. In Fez we recorded a very fine soloist who played the lute.

Surrounded by walls like a medieval Italian town, Fez is the only city in Morocco that seems to have kept its character. Its narrow streets are filled with artisans who skillfully work copper and leather, weave fabrics, rugs, and wall hangings.

But alas! Unesco has made plans to build a low-income housing development around the city, presumably to improve living conditions.

Though Marrakech is much acclaimed by tourists, I found it detestable. This ancient market town, where mountain tribes used to come down for supplies, has no architectural or cultural value whatever. Foreigners, who live in luxury hotels or insipid and antiseptic villas completely cut off from the rest of the city, come here for the vaguely exotic local color or the cheap pederastic encounters that are readily available in impoverished countries. I used to see ridiculous characters coming out of the Club Méditerrannée, right on the main square, dressed up in their sky blue or cyclamen pink *gandurahs*.

Because of the many years I spent as an Indian "native," I am instantly sensitive to the hate and contempt lurking beneath an appearance of friendly curiosity towards the insolent rich, who find such a picturesque charm in poverty. At the slightest hint of an Islamic revolution, all those charming young Moroccans would be only too happy to slide a dagger into the bellies of the not so very generous foreigners who court them. All monotheistic religions—Islam more than any other—are intolerant by nature. Their followers consider themselves a chosen people to whom truth has been personally revealed by "God" through their prophet. This leads to an acute feeling of superiority in the name of which all crimes, genocides, and acts of vengeance are considered heroic deeds in a holy war.

In spite of Bourguiba's strict regime, Tunisia has been far more successful than Morocco in adapting modernization to its culture and has managed to preserve the charm of its villages and landscapes. Salah-el-Mahdi, director of the Tunis Conservatory and all the country's musical organizations, arranged two visits for me, which allowed me to meet traditional musicians as well as popular groups. I was able to make some very interesting recordings. Here, however, like everywhere else in North Africa, the great musical traditions are disappearing. Soon there will be nothing left but the dull, mediocre, adulterated music which radio stations blare out from morning till night in all the Arab countries.

CHAPTER EIGHTEEN

Venice

VENETIAN EPISODE

The American foundations that had supported our venture in Berlin were pleased by the achievements of the Institute and the prestige it had so quickly gained on an international level. In spite of my violent diatribes against the destructive methods used by "Socialists" in the countries they rule, and their opposition by principle to my way of thinking, even they had to acknowledge the importance of the Berlin Institute and all it represented.

Contrary to its usual practice, the Ford Foundation renewed the support that had helped create the Institute, but was forced to stop after the sixth year. According to their statutes, they can help set up an organization but are not allowed to support it indefinitely. The Institute's financing was then taken up by the Berlin government. From that time on, I had to face constant interference on the part of a pernickety municipal bureaucracy that paralyzed all our initiatives and seemed unable to understand the special problems of an international organization. The situation in Berlin, moreover, made my contacts with Soviet-influenced Asian countries quite difficult. In order to continue promoting Oriental musicians, I had to create a second, completely independent institute in Venice. The directors of the Ford Foundation understood my problem very well and generously contributed to the new organization. The Cini Foundation agreed to let us install our offices in the wonderful monastery of San Giorgio. I decided to donate my collection of books on the East to the Oriental division of the San Giorgio library. My collection included hundreds of Sanskrit manuscripts on music as well as card indexes and outlines for textual editions. These books and manuscripts were beautifully arranged and classified and have become available to researchers.

Pierre Arnal agreed to help me and took charge of the administrative department. His wife Solange made herself very useful running the secretarial and accounting offices. She and Pierre were valuable collaborators and contributed greatly to the development of the Venice Institute. In the somewhat hostile atmosphere of this strange city, we lived together like a family. It was a period of intense work and wonderful harmony, but Pierre, who was not in very good health, suffered a great deal from the Venetian climate. After three years of living and working together with us, he and Solange were forced to leave and settled in a beautiful old house in Aix-en-Provence. Jacques then took charge of the administrative and accounting departments.

It was necessary to spend part of the year in Venice. After staying a few months at the elegant but sinister Bauer Hotel, I decided to look for an apartment. The hotel porter introduced me to a very old marquise who wanted to rent out her charming house in the arcades of the ancient cloister of San Zaccaria. The marquise was a very interesting character. It was rumored that she had once been d'Annuzio's mistress; in any case, she had never changed since the time of her famous affair and remained strictly *modern style*. She was a very frail old lady who always wore floating red tunics, with long white hair falling loosely down her shoulders and back. She admitted to being eighty—out of vanity, people said—but was probably somewhat older. She lived on the top floor of a palazzo on the Grand Canal, in an enormous apartment draped with heavy red curtains, which made it look like some kind of theater. Everything around her had crystallized during her period of glory. She was a charming and amusing woman and seemed to have stepped out of another age. She never left Venice and spoke with horror of Rome's monumental traffic jams—in the days of horse-drawn carriages. She was actively involved in spiritism and table-turning, thanks to the help of a priest from San Giorgio who had invented a very subtle device for the recording of spirits and ghosts!

D'Annunzio had lived in the small house of San Zaccaria at the time of his affair with the beautiful marquise, but its history of illustrious tenants went back much further. Another famous lover had lived there a century earlier, when nuns from a neighboring convent were persuaded by Casanova himself to climb up through the window to this charming love nest.

The house was not very comfortable but had a great deal of charm, and I was unable to resist the temptation. I had to redo the beautiful ruined floors, restore the baroque stuccowork, install a bathroom and a kitchen, as well as central heating. I wanted to make a garden on the terrace, but in Venice nothing is ever simple. We bought enormous earthenware pots, but finding the soil to fill them with was a real gangsters' operation. We had to send gondoliers armed with large bags to steal soil from the islands, then transport it from the Canal to the house. Bringing in small trees and plants we had bought on the mainland was another complicated operation. The result was quite beautiful, but drew complaints from the Fine Arts Administration; by planting trees on the roof we had altered the layout of the square, listed as a historical monument. In the end, of course, everything worked out very well.

Then we had to furnish the house. In Venice one can still find remarkable craftsmen who specialize in painted furniture, chandeliers, and mirrors. I became friends with some of these artisans, who made me some wonderful replicas of ancient models. It was as expensive as buying antique furniture, but I have always found it more interesting to encourage fine craftsmen than to fill the pockets of antique dealers. Our small house in Venice became a real jewel. For several years I spent part of my time there and even bought a large motorboat with a cabin. Jacques planted a Breton flag on the stern, which drew criticism from the French consul. The boat went very fast. We hired a very pleasant Venetian called Mirco, who spun it elegantly around the Canal and made it prance about the waves like a thoroughbred mare.

Venice is delightfully theatrical when a pale sun shining

through the haze infuses it with a golden light. It is a wonderful place to visit, but not at all pleasant to live in. The population is hostile. Venetians loathe all those foreigners who want to save their city and create all kinds of organizations to bring it back to so-called life. The powerful Venetian Republic is as dead as the Roman Empire; consciously or not, its survivors wish only to scuttle their ship and sink down with it into the Adriatic Sea. Thanks to their deleterious fumes, the powerful Marghera industries are working very actively towards eroding the marble façades of the city. I was fascinated by the vast industrial zone of Marghera, with its architecture of smoke stacks, pipes, cranes, and reservoirs; it looks like a kind of science-fiction fairyland engulfed in a cloud of multicolored fumes, spitting out sparks that reflect on the pallid waters on a film of shimmering oil. I took many pictures of it. It would take another Guardi to paint the frightening and magnificent new Venice of the twentieth century. The air of the city is sometimes so unbreathable that people faint on the streets. It did not take me long to realize that my boat was completely useless, for the gondoliers' unions refused to let anyone else berth along the quays. The enormous funds that were collected to "save Venice" have always mysteriously disappeared without leaving a trace. A number of romantic millionaires who wanted to settle along the Grand Canal in its beautiful palazzos were, if not openly expelled, at least driven away by all manner of harassments. When Bestegui tried to restore the Palazzo Labia, his extravagances were greeted by various manifestations of hostility. Xenophobia has become a permanent attitude among Venetians, a great fallen people who wish only to die in peace. When people talked about Count Cini, who has done more than anyone else to restore the monuments and create a new cultural life in the city, they would scornfully murmur: "But he comes from Ferrara!" In this closed and intensely alcoholic world, puritanism has reached the heights of absurdity. I was unable to find an apartment for my Roman cook, the owner having stipulated that no one outside his family should be allowed to visit him. Though the Institute's secretary came from an aristocratic Venetian family, she never succeeded in finding an apartment, the reason being that she was single; she was forced to marry in order to find a place to live. After my house was broken into twice—though it was right across the street from the police barracks—I gave up trying to live in Venice otherwise than as a typical foreigner, spending a few pleasant days a year in one of its sumptuous hotels. I reduced the Institute's work program and conducted its remaining activities from a distance.

Venetian society, whose rival *salons* were so well described by Baron Corvo in the nineteenth century, now gravitated only toward three poles linked to the great industrial fortunes of Marghera. On opposite banks of the Grand Canal reigned the two enemy branches of the Volpi clan: the "Frenchwoman," widow of Count Volpi, and the Countess Cigogna, his daughter by a first marriage—a very nice and active woman who was deeply involved in Italia Nostra, a group of defenders of the country's cultural heritage.

The sultan of Venice was unquestionably Count Cini, whose palazzo was filled with extraordinary paintings and various art objects—a large Botticelli and a gallery filled with Guardis. He was a gracious host and, with the help of his very charming wife, entertained all the interesting personalities who visited Venice. A remarkably clever businessman, he readily admitted to having made only one mistake in his life, that of growing old. Two minor centers of attraction were the permanently unfinished residence where Peggy Guggenheim kept vast collections of paintings and dragged out her unbelievable longevity, and the Polignac Palazzo where the Duc de Caze came to live from time to time. Both of them have since died.

The Countess Cini was a passionate traveller. Each year she went on an expedition to a different Oriental country. I helped her prepare the itineraries and choose interesting places to go to, off the beaten track. She was a very good photographer and always came back with excellent films. I told her about relatively unknown cities of the Rajasthan, from which she brought back some very fine pictures. We became good friends. She gave sumptuous lunches, with a waiter in livery standing behind each chair, and always insisted on placing me at her right, which was sometimes embarrassing. I met Ezra Pound several times at her house. The great American poet, once a friend of Mussolini's, had never recovered from his cruel period of imprisonment after the war. He seemed to have made a vow of silence, listened passively to conversations, and never answered questions. He was looked after by a kind of housekeeper-companion, a pleasant, cultivated, wonderfully devoted woman called Olga Rudge. Years later I was quite surprised when she told me that Ezra Pound had been in the habit of taking notes on the various things I said in his presence. It was difficult to imagine this impassive old man recording people's conversations.

I was visiting the Cinis the day Henri Cartier-Bresson came to their palazzo to photograph Ezra Pound. It was very interesting to see how the great photographer managed to capture the fleeting expressions on the silent poet's face.

I had met Stravinsky several times during my life. Once, after lunching together in Paris, he told Nabokov that he wished he had known me better, but added: "I am too old now to make new friends." While visiting New York I was invited several times by his wife Vera. Nabokov, being the Stravinskys' most devoted friend, was actively involved in organizing the great musician's funeral; for, though Stravinsky died in New York, he had expressed the wish to lie beside his friend Diaghilev in the old Orthodox cemetery in Venice.

Nabokov came with Vera and Stravinsky's assistant Bob Craft. The "other" family consisted of the musician's sons, whom people ironically called "les truffes du Père Igor," a dreadful play on words that sounded like "Périgord truffles" in French but really meant "the ninnies of father Igor." They had not been in contact with their father and did not help organize the funeral. The two groups never exchanged a word.

Jacques and I found ourselves involved in the details of the funeral as though we were members of the family. Jacques photographed the funeral rites, which were celebrated with great pomp in the enormous church of San Giovanni e Paolo. The young Greek Orthodox priest who officiated was a magnificent cantor and looked very elegant in his black silk robe. It is normally forbidden to celebrate Orthodox rites in a Catholic church, but if one is willing to pay the price, it is always possible to find loopholes in the rules, even in the largest church in Venice.

The rites of interment, which took place in the dilapidated old Orthodox cemetery in the shade of its ancient cypresses, seemed touchingly simple and quiet after the magnificent pomp of the church ceremony. The grave, placed right alongside Diaghilev's, was covered with a perfectly plain gray stone slab without any ornament; but it was signed Manzu, therefore worth its weight in gold.

A small incident took place a year later, during the commemorative ceremony. After the solemn mass in the Greek church, everyone went to the cemetery and waited vainly for the Orthodox priest to arrive. No one had remembered to hire a boat for him. Jacques had to dash off in my boat to fetch him. After the priest arrived, there was a new delay. He had grown mistrustful and refused to complete the ceremony until he had received his check. Vera and the priest walked away for a few moments to settle this detail with the help of Adriana Panni, the robust director of Rome's Accademia Filarmonica and a loyal friend of Stravinsky's.

PIERO

Piero was a very good-looking, fair-haired Venetian youth of eighteen who was the product of a broken marriage and had run away from home. One day my Roman cook Guerrino discovered this little urchin at the railroad station, sleeping on a train. Piero was looking for work, so I hired him to help around the house. In the atmosphere of calm, quietness, and understanding he found in my home, he quickly blossomed; he felt very proud in his elegant livery with its golden epaulets. I became a kind of second father to him, a protector he could trust and who gave him new confidence in life.

Then came the blow. Piero had been with us one year when we discovered that he was a drug addict. He entertained friends in his room, and they smoked drugs together; we found all kinds of pipes and syringes hidden in the drawers. I found myself in a serious dilemma. Italian law is terribly severe about drug possession, even in very small quantities. All my circle of friends, colleagues, and servants felt endangered. A father might have taken the risk; but a group mostly made up of homosexuals is automatically considered a corrupting influence by the police, the judges, and society in general, and an ideal subject for a scandalous news item. In the end I was forced to send Piero away. He was sad to leave but behaved very sweetly, without asking for anything. There was no fuss, no complaint.

From time to time he would come back to see me for a bit of comfort and quiet affection. Finally he disappeared altogether.

His mother, I was told, had placed him in one of those institutions where sadistic doctors claim to cure drug addicts with tranquilizers, shock therapy, painful withdrawal, isolation, and various other tortures. I never found out what happened to him. Perhaps he is locked up in prison somewhere—perhaps he has died by his own hand. If he were living a normal life, he would surely have come back to me. Piero's story has left me with the most incurable remorse. Even after all these years, I still think of it nearly every day. I betrayed a delicate and sensitive human being who had turned to me for help. Whatever the risks may be, it is always wrong to abandon those who have come to one for shelter, even though they may be criminals.

Using drugs is not a crime. It is a remedy against the anguish and melancholy of adolescents struggling in a world that refuses to recognize the most pressing needs of youth, their right to pleasure and love. With patience, understanding, and affection I might have helped relieve Piero of his anguish, his need, his addiction to drugs, which was only a substitute for happiness. I did not have the courage to take this risk, which was not mine alone. I have never forgiven myself for having abandoned Piero, for not finding a way to defend and protect him.

Finally I left Venice. My sojourn in this city was one of those episodes which, like a beautiful trip or movie, leave one's mind filled with images, but with no real enrichment.

THE FESTIVALS

When I undertook to promote Asian musicians and consolidate their position in their own countries, my work involved something more than making records and doing technical research. I had to find ways to bring these artists to the forefront of the international music scene. As recently as fifteen or twenty years ago, no festival or theatrical agent would even have considered placing what they called "folklore" on the same footing as the great music of the West.

In 1960 or thereabouts, I helped Nicolas Nabokov organize the first large Oriental music festival, in Tokyo; it was a beginning step towards integrating the great traditions of Asia into the international music world. This festival included the finest artists from India, the Middle East, Korea, and, of course, Japan. It gave many young westernized Japanese musicians a chance to discover the Nô and Bunraku traditions, which they had never seen before. The festival was extraordinarily successful. For the first time, the Indian Kathakali troupe, which had never before left its village—not even to go to Delhi—was shown before an international audience. This festival marked the first step, in Japan and elsewhere, towards a rediscovery of ancient musical cultures that had not been influenced by modern trends. At last they were being viewed as important art forms rather than as vestiges of outmoded traditions.

Nicolas then organized an African festival in Berlin. His ventures, however, tended to look rather like colonial exhibitions. What I wanted for "my" artists was the same kind of concert hall background that one would have chosen for Menuhin or Karajan, rather than Oriental museums or folkloric organizations. But artists' tours are always very complicated; in order to cover expenses one must take considerable financial risks. The Berlin Senate, which supported the Institute, refused to do this.

Nicolas and I felt that it would be a good idea to create an association for the directors of the large festivals, but it had to be located elsewhere than in Berlin. This was the main reason I decided to create the Venice Institute.

The festival directors were not very enthusiastic about the project itself, but liked the idea of meeting in a relaxed, pleasant atmosphere. Thanks to the Cini Foundation, we not only enjoyed a prestigious setting but were able to entertain the participants elegantly, meet them at the airport with launches or my own personal boat, send them to good hotels, and organize dinners in the private dining rooms of Harry's Bar.

It took us quite a long time to achieve any concrete results. Festival directors are usually more interested in exclusive rights over artists than in cooperative efforts. In any case, it was very interesting for me to meet those slightly mysterious characters who control all of Europe's musical world. From time to time musicians and critics would participate in our meetings, people such as Stockhausen, Jerzy Grotowski, Maurice Fleuret, Claude Samuel, Jean Robin, Mrs. Karlweiss, etc.

Ninon Karlweiss was a remarkable person. This tiny, very active woman of modest appearance, who claimed to come from Auvergne, was one of the best theatrical agents in the world and spent all her time flying between New York and London, Paris and Tokyo, Rio and Oslo. Her judgment was absolutely infallible. She was constantly discovering new artists and knew from the first moment she heard them how much success they were likely to have. The greatest theatrical producers could take on any of the artists she recommended with their eyes closed. With her astute, instinctive sense of quality, this apparently hard-nosed businesswoman made herself tremendously useful to a large number of deserving musicians; with mediocrities, however, she was quite merciless. On the whole she was a nice woman and I liked her very much. Once, after a trip to Brazil, she brought back a group of Voodoo dancers from Bahia. I saw one of their first performances, which was staggering. But after being forbidden by various towns to cut a rooster's throat on the stage, then soak in its blood—and other essential details—the participants lost their inspiration and the performances were far less intense.

Ninon Karlweiss died quite suddenly, while fully active, like an airplane that mysteriously disappears into the night.

The first person who took the risk of organizing a large European tour for the Kathakali dancers was Thomas Erdos, the concert manager and producer of the Baalbek Festival in Lebanon. It was an enormous success, but Thomas had so much trouble lodging, feeding, and transporting these amiable Indians that he swore he would never do it again. Many of the people who accompanied the musicians had nervous breakdowns.

One night, while I was in Berlin, a hotel manager telephoned me at midnight: "I will not keep your artists for another moment in my hotel!" In a fit of anger, the sister of the Indian dancer Yamini Krishnamurthy had viciously bitten his arm.

We organized a tour for an important group of gamelan players and Javanese dancers. The first performance took place in Venice. Everything had been prepared by Surya Brata, a famous Dutch musicologist who specialized in Indonesian music and had adopted Javanese citizenship. He arrived with a very mediocre group, quite different from the one we expected. The performance was dreadful. I was so mortified I hardly dared show my face. The tour threatened to be a financial disaster, for most of the concerts were cancelled. Brata was a mass of nerves and gave himself injections— right in front of everyone. He just stood there, blissfully unaware of the calamity.

We often had trouble with turbaned ladies with "a passion for India and all that kind of thing." During concerts, they would climb on the stage to burn incense and offer garlands to the artists. They swooned with admiration before the master's spirituality. I was sometimes rather brutal: "If you really want him to be inspired, why not give him a bottle of whiskey?" In Berlin those orientalized ladies, who practiced yoga and transcendental meditation, convinced the Dagar brothers (the great Indian singers) that electricity was not spiritual and that they should insist on a candlelit stage. The concert was to take place in the Charlottenburg Palace, and the artists' insistence on candlelight caused the security service a great many problems. All during the rest of the tour, the musicians remained convinced that candles were the height of elegance and that vulgar projectors only showed lack of consideration for their art.

The inauguration of the Shiraz Festival was an unforgettable event. The hotels, which had been built for the occasion in the middle of the desert, were barely finished and still surrounded with barbed wire fences. We travelled from one building to another in old carriages. The hotel staff spoke nothing but Persian, which was very inconvenient for the foreign guests: when Cathy Berberian ordered coffee, she was given fried eggs. In spite of the beauty of the surroundings, the creation of a festival in Shiraz was strictly a millionaire's idea:

artists and audiences had to be transported from Teheran by military airplane. The unexpected sounds of the music of Schönberg, Ligeti, and Boulez must have made Darius turn in his grave, which for thousands of years, in the great silence of the desert, had been left untroubled.

For the inaugural concert, which took place in the ruins of Persepolis, an orchestra in formal dress was scheduled to play a Tchaikovsky symphony at dusk. But the ghosts that haunt this magical place were apparently disturbed by the music. A mischievous Jinn, taking the form of one of those small tornados that suck in all the sand in the desert, blew away all the scores in the middle of the symphony, which suddenly ended on a false note. Other concerts,—such as the one given by the Indian oboist Bismillah Khan in the tomb of the Persian poet Hafiz, were intensely poetic and never to be forgotten.

It was in Shiraz that I met Maurice Fleuret, the brilliant music critic who for many years was principal adviser to this remarkable festival with its unique blend of Asian and European pageantry. Maurice is an interesting man with a peculiar turn of mind and a passion for modern European as well as Asian and African music. Although we disagreed about everything, we became very good friends. Our conversations have always been very interesting and useful to me, for they made me realize that a work of art can be judged and appreciated from totally opposite points of view and according to different value systems. I always know in advance that any interpretation Maurice admires will strike me as a travesty and that whatever he finds interesting in Indian music has nothing to do with what it means to me and to those who play it. And yet whatever it is he is searching for exists also.

In spite of all these problems and misadventures, my efforts to promote the great musicians of Asia in the West were completely successful. It is no longer difficult to organize tours for musicians from different cultures. The problem is preventing theatrical producers from making the wrong choices. In Berlin, where we were able to organize concerts regularly, there now exists a large public of enlightened music lovers who know how to recognize and appreciate the talent of the best artists of India, Japan, Korea, and Indonesia.

CHAPTER NINETEEN

A Hindu's View
of the Western World

A WORLD ADRIFT

During my childhood I learned to distrust anything that had to do with the ideas and beliefs of the world in which I had been born, and established a vigorous system of defense. I refused to become interested in what people called culture or in any of the serious topics of conversation that were discussed in my family circle: religion, literature, philosophy, politics. Science was apparently not considered a part of culture, which made it easier for me to study mathematics and physics without anyone making remarks.

When I returned to Europe after twenty years of study in the most sophisticated circles of traditional Indian culture, my thinking was based not on Western philosophy, of which I knew nothing, but on the Hindu cosmological theory according to which theology, metaphysics, ethics, and human and social sciences are seen as various applications of common principles of a universal nature, rather than as separate entities. These principles can be represented as kinds of proto-types, geometrical or mathematical formulae whose properties can be traced in all aspects of creation, from the composition of atoms and galaxies to animal and human societies, but also in the structures of musical and spoken languages and, finally, in the mechanisms of the mind.

From then on, all forms of organized thinking, the study of any subject filtered more or less consciously through my mind according to six methods whose conclusions, though often contradictory, make it possible to view problems in a well-balanced manner. These methods, which Hindus call "points of view" (*darshana*) include cosmology, more specifically the "measurable" (*sâmkhya*), which places any problem within the context of universal structures or macrocosm; *yoga*, which considers it in relation to man's inner universe or microcosm; "rites" (*mîmânsa*), which allow one to experience the relationship between the human and the supernatural; and metaphysics (*vedanta*), which relate to the invisible, suprasensible world. The *vaisheshika*, on the other hand, is the experimental or scientific approach, and has to do with the world as it is perceived through our senses, while logic (*nyaya*) allows the mind to establish connections. To these various methods one may also add the study of the nature of language (*vyâkarana*), considered an imperfect instrument for the formulation and communication of all we experience through the senses, which allows us to define the contours of our thought but whose limitations must be recognized so that we do not confuse words with ideas.

For many years I had grown accustomed to the extreme intellectual discipline of Hindu scholars. With them it was possible to discuss any problem without ideological interference or limited preconceived notions; one could think and try to go to the heart of things according to different value systems, without the prejudices or limitations that are created by set beliefs. Vijayanand never found it difficult to discuss ways of life or opinions about the world and the divine that were different from his own; he would analyze them logically without ever allowing himself to make judgments or trying to reconcile them with his own value system or the life he had chosen or been fated to adopt by birth. The *darshana* doctrine is a solid basis for well-balanced thinking. What may be true on one level is not necessarily true on another. Any hasty and superficial generalization not only leads to absurdities but is morally, socially, and intellectually dangerous. All systems are defined and limited by their data, and become false when they try to go beyond their postulates. As a result, many different relative truths can coexist without negating one another. The important thing in any kind of research is to determine at the outset the limitations of its given data. This is why science, for Hindus, is necessarily atheistic, for the study of the material world does not lead to the notion of God. Yoga, on the other hand, is theistic for it leads to mystical experience, while in cosmology the "first causes" of the universe must be impersonal. A realistic approach towards any problem must necessarily take these contrasts into account; a doctor who allows his religious beliefs to interfere with the exercise of his profession not only betrays science but religion as well.

Armed with this baggage I began to renew my contacts with Europe, which appeared to be suffering from a deadly disease, a kind of cancer with some cells developing in an incontrollable manner and contaminating the others little by little. There is a limit to this kind of development, however. The countryside and wooded areas of our lands are slowly being devoured by giant urban anthills, with less and less vital space to breathe in. Certain aspects of life have grown disproportionately in relation to others, creating a serious disequilibrium. The desire for prosperity has stifled the quest for wisdom and the joy of being alive. I often used to wonder why modern Westerners were so agitated and so seldom happy. The truth is that Aryans, from whom all the dominating forces of Europe have descended—Achaeans, Dorians, Celts, Romans, Teutons, and Russians—are a predatory people. Having recently invaded a large part of the planet, populated the American and Australian continents, imposed their languages on Africa and sometimes even Asia, they have finally reached a limit, and their forces of expansion are beginning to turn against them. It seems unlikely that they will ever be able to control themselves. This is one of the great problems of history: when a natural equilibrium is destroyed, certain animal species tend to multiply to the point of self-destruction.

I was quite amazed by the incoherence of ideas, the naïveté of beliefs, and the low level of reasoning that I found in Europe. Armed with their very dubious theories, so-called intellectuals seek unrelentingly to change the world without studying its logic or trying to understand its cause or purpose. They claim to "reform" society on the basis of unrealistic postulates that do not take into account the nature or role of the human animal within the framework of Creation.

Each person puts forth his bible, his taboos, his beliefs, and seems only to have a choice between various erroneous systems whose individual merits are discussed with a great deal of bad faith. Discussions always seem to focus on critical interpretations of "prophetic" texts rather than on an effort to understand reality. Only a few "scientists" working in very limited fields seem able to escape dogmatism, but the moment they move away from these specialized areas they become as incoherent as everyone else.

No one seems capable of recognizing the point where the valid elements of a theory become absurd. A so-called ideology can very quickly turn into blind faith. People choose their arguments, their proofs, and deny any evidence that contradicts them. This kind of artificial game can only result in a distorted value system imposed by various forms of tyranny; for when one reaches the extreme limit of a lie, there is no other choice but to destroy the evidence of one's opponent and physically annihilate those who maintain and defend it. History has only too often proved this.

On this level, the French seemed particularly flighty and irresponsible. I had grown accustomed to philosophic joustings between Indian scholars, where the loser was forced to recognize and accept the point of view of the victor: Buddhism, as a result, disappeared from India as soon as its philosophic bases were seriously challenged. The French love to engage in discussion but are always afraid to draw conclusions. Each person defends his position with tendentious arguments, tries to prevent his opponent from talking, and makes no effort whatever to understand what he is trying to say. French television debates never do anything to clarify issues; most of the time they are ridiculous skirmishes between people of very obvious bad faith.

Korzybsky, the famous American linguist, has attributed many of the problems of the Western world to the verb "to be" taken in the sense of identification (the "is" of identity). One can "be" nothing else besides oneself. One "belongs" to a group, and "believes" in a doctrine; one cannot "be" a Marxist or a Christian. Because there is no formal criticism of language, Western thinking is often vague, confusing, even dangerous. Words are used that no one can understand; they serve as sacred formulas and cannot be challenged without risk. People equate words with ideas and seem quite surprised and disappointed when the results of their efforts turn out to be the exact opposite of their original goals.

Cocteau used to tell a funny story in pantomime about his meeting with Charlie Chaplin. He deeply admired the great actor and was thrilled at the idea of meeting him. But, during a short trip they took together, they were completely unable to establish contact, and their exchange of ideas was limited to such comments as: "How do you do? What a lovely day!" etc. Neither of these two brilliant men seemed able to sustain the conversation.

I have often encountered the same problem. No matter how interesting they may be to me, or how much I respect them, there are people with whom I cannot establish any kind of contact. When Julien Green and I met over a glass of port, we found it impossible to rise above the most banal and superficial level of conversation. I experienced the same thing with Lenny Bernstein, the orchestra conductor, and many other famous people.

Yet I am sociable by nature, and interested in people of all kinds. I often used to wonder why I so quickly and instinctively became reticent on meeting certain kinds of notable figures, but found it so easy to communicate with others. I have finally come to the conclusion that I cannot relate to people who are fired by any kind of belief, whether it be religious, political, or artistic. I have grown far too accustomed to an open and inquiring attitude towards all things—myths, morality, society, or science—and only feel comfortable with people who, at least in their thinking, are completely without ready-made ideas or taboos.

One of the reasons I got on so well with Raymond was because of his iconoclastic sense of humor, which always seemed to find the weak point in the noblest assertions and the comic element in the most sacred taboos. This did not mean that he had no values, but showed on the contrary how much more real they were to him when stripped of all emphasis and embellishment.

Tagore, like Max Jacob, was always ready to laugh at his fine pronouncements a moment after he had spoken them. Another man I would call a "free spirit" was Nicolas Nabokov. But whenever people, instead of simply being themselves, wish to be labeled as Christians, Moslems, Communists, Democrats, Fascists, or Socialists, I feel as though their minds were dead and see no point in trying to establish contact.

In a world based on systems of belief, free spirits tend to lead marginal lives. A typical example is François Michel, whom I met when he was preparing the *Encyclopédie de la Musique*, published by Fasquelle, and liked from the first moment I saw him. Though a marvelous pianist, he never made a career in music. It is impossible to belong to a clique and still maintain one's integrity. As a result François Michel has continued to lead a nomadic existence, and I sometimes see him in completely unexpected places, which he visits for brief periods of time.

One of the personalities who most strongly impressed me was Jean Genet, a kind of ascetic saint and a totally disinterested man who, in spite of his fame, managed to remain marginal. He spent his time and money supporting thieves, those miserable sinners society imprisons and mistreats because of their unorthodox attempts to redistribute worldly goods—something that everyone agrees should be done but seems unwilling to carry through. Among Hindus there is a moral code for thieves as well as for prostitutes. They are considered special kinds of castes that can be found in all societies, with as much right to spiritual growth as anyone else. There is no reason why a thief or a prostitute should not also be a saint: their ways of life are unacceptable only from the standpoint of social conventions, which have nothing to do with the inner life. One might even say that the true thieves are those who accumulate property and wealth. This is why Brahmans are not allowed to possess more than the barest necessities; why Hindu monks, instead of forming monasteries, must lead a nomadic existence. For warriors and princes, commercial activities are strictly forbidden.

Whether under the rule of capitalism or socialism, Western countries are completely dominated by the bourgeois mentality—in Hindu terms the spirit that motivates the third, or mercantile, caste. This is true not only because of the power associated with money but because of the importance of material concerns and, above all, snobbery. This word which, according to some, comes from the Italian *snobile* (without nobility), characterizes a caste whose interest in intellectual matters is nothing more than a desire for social advancement, power, or profit. In the political world people easily speak of the proletariat and the ruling class, but seem to forget the most powerful group of all, the merchants and the businessmen—useful, but unproductive and parasitical—who control everything connected with money but have long since overstepped the bounds that should exist in a well-balanced society.

Whether one is dealing with literature or the arts, philosophy, politics, or science, it is impossible for an idea or a principle to achieve recognition or success unless it conforms to certain fashionable and ready-made standards that are geared towards commercial interests or ambitions of power in the name of which all other values are sacrificed. In the artificial and pretentious world we live in today, independent spirits who try to find their own truth and live according to their personal ideas and tastes are viewed with suspicion. Snobs go about extolling the artistic fashions of the day as though their merits were absolute. In all artistic domains snobs seem to lead the way, not even realizing that by calling graffiti "sublime," cacophonic jumbles "musical masterpieces," and banal literary forms "works of art" they are only yielding to vulgar commercialism. They have lost all sense of reality, which generates ludicrous, even perverse attitudes in their politics as well as in their personal lives. Their judgment has been so totally conditioned that they cannot think seriously or adopt rational attitudes regarding the world and its problems. It seems as though the links between cosmology and science, art and the sacred no longer existed. Ideologies—even certain diseases—become "the latest thing," when in fact the problems are deeply vital. Fashionable Communism goes hand in hand with faddish and short-lived musical crazes or feigned enthusiasm for painting styles that are totally devoid of talent, aesthetic interest, or even technique. I was quite astonished by the difference in atmosphere between the avant-garde circles of my youth, when artists flirted with the absurd without taking themselves seriously, and the postwar intellectuals who pondered over it with pedantic solemnity.

Snobs are vain and naïve people who are easily used and manipulated by powerful plutocracies and other types of imperialisms. Intellectuals, unfortunately, are often part of the flock.

In the Hindu world, "knowledge" is considered above all a heritage. It is one's duty to pass it on and, if possible, add a few elements that will serve to develop and keep it up to date. As a result, those who have been deemed worthy of carrying this burden have a heavy moral responsibility, especially in the choice of their disciples. Knowledge is like a calling. Some forms of knowledge must never be transmitted to ambitious or irresponsible people. The greatest problem of a scholar is to find a disciple, a receptacle (*pâtra*) who will be worthy of this sacred trust.

One of the most astonishing aspects of the evolution of Western society is its total irresponsibility and anonymity regarding the transmission of knowledge. Knowledge has become collective. A learned man or scientist is nothing more than an easily replaceable cogwheel in the machine of "progress." Nowadays, in the excitement of new discoveries and their applications, the legacy of the past is completely left aside. The keenest minds are taken up by specialized branches of science, their findings immediately thrown into the communal melting pot of all these sorcerers' apprentices, without a thought for the use that will be made of them. There is no longer any such thing as a responsible individual, only a vast community of brains. This community apparently has no guide, no presiding force, and seems to drift along aimlessly at the mercy of chance. But is it really a question of chance? Might we not be victims of an evil force goading us along with the promise of a few so-called material advantages, but leading us in fact to the total destruction of our own species? This process is obvious on all levels of society.

Only occasionally does a scientist, like Oppenheimer, have sufficient courage and insight, at the end of a long career, to recognize the great dangers of the world he has helped to build and the irresponsibility of collective science in its blind pursuit of an unknown and frightening destiny—a destiny everyone is aware of and no one really wants.

Many of the principles that have revolutionized Western science were not really unknown to other civilizations; but the choice of disciples and the applications of these ideas were strictly kept under control.

Certain elementary notions such as the relativity of space, time, dimension, the energy potential of matter, and the mathematical archetypes that are common to matter, life, sensation, and thought—all of which I studied in Hindu cosmology—are considered great new discoveries in the Western world. But no attempts are ever made to apply this knowledge to a better understanding of the nature of the world or to the dynamics of creation; instead it is used in experimental physics for its most destructive qualities.

The mastering of those forces that have given birth to matter, the universe, and life can only serve to destroy them. This is why all of us secretly await the final and inevitable catastrophe, for there is no other solution. The futility of the Western world dancing on top of the atomic volcano is, at any rate, an astonishing sight to behold.

The vital music of our time is jazz, rock, disco, the popular song. What people call modern music, most often abstract compositions completely devoid of acoustical or psychological meaning, only interests a small group of conditioned music lovers. I, for one, find it deadly boring. Nowadays even the masterpieces of romantic music are too often played coldly, precisely, with no thought for anything but technique. Gone are the days when simple folk would go about humming Verdi arias or Neapolitan songs to themselves, when children learned *die Forelle* or *Ständchen* without ever having heard of Schubert. A gloomy, disquieting silence has fallen upon a modern society that is saturated with the blare of radio music and the images of television advertisements.

Sometimes I sit down at the piano and play a Schubert

impromptu, a short piece by Grieg, a Mozart fantasia, or a melody by Fauré only to remind myself that music still exists. Other times I turn to my *vînâ* and suddenly feel myself enveloped in a world of beautifully precise and meaningful sounds, full of poetry and emotion.

What the fate of contemporary music may be, I cannot say. I do not believe that it can be leading to anything. People seem to have forgotten that music is a language—the language of the soul, the language of the gods.

SOCIETY

Young animals that live in the forests soon learn to make as little noise as possible for fear of attracting the lurking tiger. The children of poor peasants work along with their parents and know that the food on their table comes from the seeds they have sown, and from nothing else. Indian children share the lives of adults. By prolonging childhood to absurd lengths, the Western bourgeois system of education produces a society of shallow minds that have spent too many years living outside reality and are accustomed to functioning in a vacuum, constructing systems not based on experience.

Revolutions, murderous wars, and genocides are created not by artisans or peasants, who from infancy are always in touch with the problems of everyday reality, but by the idle classes who have no idea what it means to be hungry. Most of the problems of the modern West have been caused by maladjusted members of the *petite bourgeoisie* who spend their lives daydreaming instead of trying to learn. Whether one is speaking of Rousseau, Marx, Lenin, Sartre, Aragon, or Adorno, all revolutionary theorists are idealistic bourgeois who drag the popular masses into ill-conceived ventures of which the people, not the initiators, are always the victims.

Jean-Paul Sartre used to inspire me with the same feeling of discomfort and revulsion as Gandhi—another product of a rich bourgeois family—whose sentimental theories, humble façade, and unrealistic ideals of nonviolence led to the division of India and to one of the greatest massacres in history, a massacre not only of human beings but of an ancient civilization.

When belief in a doctrine or ideology becomes a substitute for a serious and responsible study of facts and possibilities, it inevitably leads to the opposite of what is expected. The striking example of Soviet concentration camps has not impressed people conditioned by Marxism, any more than the genocide of the Albigensians or Incas has kept Christians from preaching charity and love of their neighbor; nor has the tragic example of Nazism prevented dictatorships from multiplying.

Marxism, which seeks to replace Christianity, has adopted its system of absolute conformism, enforced by laic "bishops" who demand blind obedience. People who consider themselves rational have grown so accustomed to accepting questionable dogma and obvious lies that they cannot react, or are afraid to do so. They seem to have lost the ability to recognize independent or well-balanced forms of thinking, which they systematically reject.

The list of populations victimized by ideologies grows longer and longer. Slogans and propaganda, which no one dares or feels able to oppose, preclude all other forms of social action or a more realistic style of politics.

In the traditional Hindu education, the *anâdhikari vedanta,* or "philosophy of fools," offered a series of cautionary examples against generalizations that overstepped the boundaries of their premises. One of the simplest of these was: "All living beings are equal before God. Therefore my wife, my mother, and my daughter are equal. Therefore I may sleep with all three of them." Western social theories are all too often reduced to this level of reasoning.

No true social justice can exist unless it is based on an awareness of the profound inequality between individuals and the diversity of their roles and aptitudes. Social justice consists in putting each individual in his proper place according to his needs and nature. The same thing is true of the different races. Each one has its own reason for being, its own qualities, capacities, and beauty. There is no such thing as an inferior or a superior race. A hunting dog is different from a sheep dog, a Percheron is not a race horse, azaleas do not need the same soil as asparagus. As Ananda Coomaraswany used to say, a rose *per se* is no more beautiful than a cabbage; they belong to separate categories, and no conclusions can be drawn unless the different levels of evaluation are strictly defined. A wolf is no better than a lamb, but when kept within the same enclosure, they are certainly not equal. Political systems built on oversimplistic premises can only lead to the elimination of all those who stand in the way, all those who are not sufficiently "equal" to allow this ideology to triumph, whether they are above or below the chosen norm.

This is when egalitarianism leads to bloodshed. All people are supposed to be equal but only according to the model of the average, pseudo-Christian European. No one thinks of being equal to the Pygmies, the Santals of India, or the Amazonian tribes. According to the Hindu tradition, there are four basic human breeds, four distinct races that appeared one after the other, each playing an essential role in the harmony of the world.

The appearance of any autonomous community within a group provokes an immediate reaction: rejection. In order to avoid such a reaction, it is necessary to find a recognized place for this community and a means of coexistence within the group. It is not enough to deny it or to ignore the differences. When a single term is used to describe totally unrelated elements, it is obvious that no solution can ever be found.

The term "racism" is used to describe an irrational hostility towards minority groups. This often has nothing to do with race. According to popular superstitions, which are always seeking magical explanations for everything, Protestants, Jews, and homosexuals are threatened by the same kind of ostracism. People even speak of "anti-youth," "anti-aristocrat," and "anti-working class" brands of racism. This vague and indefinite attitude serves as a cover for so-called colonialistic anti-racism. "Minorities" may differ from the predominant group by their language, religion, race, the color of their skin, their customs, and their territory. The problems are different in each case; but they will never be solved without a facing of reality, a clarification of the terminology, and a definition of the rights and duties of each group.

Instead of allowing these different races to coexist, people prefer to encourage a mass bastardization of all human species, although such a solution contradicts the basic notion of equality. Here again, instead of contemplating, admiring, and trying to understand divine creation in all its glorious multiplicity, they do all they can to destroy it. All the living things of this world—plants, animals, human beings—have their own *raison d'être* and their right to exist. Upholding this right is the only true form of justice. In the West, communities that refuse to allow themselves to be assimilated are constantly threatened by absurd and irrational racism. The fact that their distinctness and autonomy are denied, that they have no official or legal status or any definite role, causes the popular imagination to view them as kinds of secret societies or Mafias.

The Hindu social system was conceived to preserve the integrity of all human species, to find a secure place for each human, religious, ethnic, and racial entity. India has always been a sanctuary for native or foreign minorities. It is the only system that has ever been able to establish a tolerant, multiracial, multireligious, multicultural society, which Moslems and Christians have vainly sought to destroy. The Indian system, like any other, has its faults, but it deserves to be examined in depth instead of being portrayed as an abomination by people who have never been in contact with its happy victims. This attitude is typical of the Western mentality which loves to twist problems around and indulge in vague notions.

Because I lived so long in a world that was striving to defend itself against Westernization, I am acutely aware of the subtle arrogance of assimilative antiracism, the hypocrisy of missionary efforts, and that particular form of blackmail which refuses any kind of dialogue except with collaborators who betray their people and their cultural values. Soviets and their minions like to call me a racist because of my firm stand against the russianization of Afghan "barbarians," the "improvements" of Asian musical cultures, and the conversion to Christianity or Marxism of nations threatened by the dominance of colonialist powers.

The "benefits" of the industrial civilization are imposed "for their own good" upon people who are already quite satisfied with their way of life, the result of long experience. They soon find themselves enslaved by gloomy factory work, deprived of their gods, their pride, and their moral code. The weakest are soon eliminated altogether.

In my childhood, intolerance and the rejection of human principles in the name of so-called ideals were represented by "right-wing" parties. France was still shaken by the Dreyfus Affair, and such men as Léon Daudet stubbornly maintained the same stupid, narrow-minded attitude. After the Second World War and the trauma of Nazi persecution, the "leftists" took advantage of the situation; it was now their turn to collaborate with a form of tyranny that supposedly benefited the nation. In neither case was serious thought ever given to the promotion of freedom, justice, and human happiness unless it conformed to an obligatory moral and social ideal—in other words, tyranny.

In traditional India, marriage is neither the result of a chance encounter nor of love's illusions. Children are married off by their parents when they are ten or twelve, according to a very strict system based on racial selection, the choice of profession, and the compatibility of horoscopes. Financial matters do not come into play; a shepherdess can marry a prince. The female members of a young boy's family include not only his mother and sisters, but a little girl who is his wife. There is no need for him to seek out a female companion. At first the games they play together are fairly simple, which does not prevent him from having other experiences. At an age when Western couples are only beginning to consider the essential duties of marriage, the Indian wife already has several children and lives with other women in the gynaeceum. Although she occasionally meets her husband, they do not live as a couple.

In India there is a society of women as well as a society of men, whose preoccupations, interests, and distractions are different but complementary. The Western "couple," more and more isolated in the world of today, has become an anomaly and creates a kind of prison whose principal victims are the children.

In southern India one also finds matriarchal societies. I have always felt great admiration for those hard, responsible, authoritarian women who so competently manage vast establishments, with large tracts of land, herds of animals, servants, a family, and those flowerlike, dainty, elegant, impeccably groomed men who devote their time to games, sports, theater, music, literature, and war. The result is a charming and culti-vated society in which the role distribution seems far more reasonable than in the West. In these matriarchal societies the level of literacy and culture is higher than anywhere else.

Man is like the male fig tree: he bestows his seed. He can produce thousands of children. Procreation is little more than an incident along his sexual journey. Of all the millions and millions of genes he can transmit through the sexual act, only a few serve towards reproduction; the rest are wasted accord-ing to the vicissitudes of life and pleasure. Havelock Ellis scandalized his time by declaring: "Man is polygamous by nature." In answer to his critics, he added: "I never met a man who had not enjoyed sexual relations with several women. I mention this only as an experimental fact." It would have been more accurate for him to say: "Man is polyvalent by nature." In traditional India, a six-year-old schoolboy has already studied texts of the Kama-sutra which explain all the secrets of loveplay and its variations. These diversions are very impor-tant, for they possess a mystical value linked to practices of tantric yoga, which forbid relations with the wife except in preliminary exercises. The aggressive puritanism of contem-porary Indians is a result of the British influence. Raymond, who had been driven by jealousy into marrying Radha, was nonetheless aware of the magical value of other types of sexual acts. He wrote: "I have always felt suspicious of acts that correspond too closely to the animal nature of things." (Benares, 3 November 1948)

According to the Hindu system, the preservation of the species is an essential duty, which is why interracial marriages are strictly forbidden. Whether or not one believes in religion or rituals, the responsibility toward an unborn child is a basic moral duty. Hindus believe that children born of interracial marriages have ambiguous personalities and lose the heredi-tary qualities of both races, thereby causing the corruption and ruin of any society. Individual freedom is only restricted if it is harmful to a third party. This is true of procreation since it involves the unborn child and the future of the species. If one does not wish to have children, the sacramental aspect of marriage is meaningless.

The solemnization of a marriage which is nothing more than a legalization of sex is the prostitution of a holy rite. It seems to me that many of the family problems of our time are the result of a conception of marriage as a simple channel for erotic energy in a puritanical society perverted by moralistic Christian nonsense. The quality of the product, the child, does not seem to be taken into account, except perhaps among the Jews, with undeniable success.

Every once in a while truly exceptional men and women are born who are superior by their intelligence, their tastes, and their talents. They can belong to any race or social circle. They are mutations who modulate the evolution of the species. A society can be judged by its willingness to accord them the status they deserve as well as their freedom of action. When it refuses to do so, these mutants, on whose shoulders hangs the progress of mankind, are likely to end on the cross or in concentration camps.

A small number of men have a special role to play in society and seem to have been marked from birth for a destiny other than procreation. In all ancient civilizations, the *shaman* was always androgynous. He was a priest, a poet, a magician, and a healer. He dressed like a woman and took a "husband." He was treated with the highest regard. The supposed celibacy of priests is a legacy of this tradition. The same is true of certain women—priestesses, musicians, poetesses, sacred dancers— who used to live by the hundreds in temples and played a very important role in Indian culture.

The fear of homosexuality is one of the strangest maladies of the Christian world. Every evolved being is, to a certain extent, bisexual. One does not become a homosexual. During certain periods of our lives, such relationships may be preferable to others. All adolescents go through a homosexual phase during which they feel the need for passionate attachments, the friendship and advice of an older man, and sexual experiences that are neither solitary nor procreative. In the West, an adolescent cannot confide his sexual problems to his family, which makes a point of ignoring and condemning them. This is the dangerous period when his ties to his parents and brothers suddenly break down. He needs an older friend to guide him, counsel him, teach him the art of love, and help turn him into a happy, relaxed, well-balanced man ready to face the world instead of rebelling. Frustration of this deep and basic need is one of the principal sources of violence and delinquency as well as many of the psychological problems of adult men. Experiences of this sort do not stand in the way of a young man's parallel or subsequent desire for marriage once he is ready to face the responsibilities of fatherhood. Egalitarian societies that try to fit everyone into the same mold and refuse to acknowledge the essential and beneficial role of homosexuals pay dearly for the consequences.

I am what people call a virile man. I am daring and adventurous. My long years of training in sports, dance, and yoga have given me far more strength and serenity than my brother, the cardinal, ever had—for to the end of his life he remained a nervous, frail, and agitated man. I can leap into adventures without even thinking of the risks involved, and have never known fear. I enjoy the company of men who possess these same qualities and feel somewhat repelled by effeminate boys and those weak, fainthearted, prissy men who can be found among woman-chasers as well as among homosexuals.

Once, when I was in Venice, I invited the parents of one of my associates for lunch. I obviously did not fit the mental image the average Frenchman forms of the "typical" homosexual, whom he usually designates by a number of pejorative terms. The moment I left the room, my associate's mother admiringly exclaimed: "But he's a regular he-man!" When I founded the Berlin Institute, a few kindly souls felt bound to inform the president of the Ford Foundation of my proclivities, to which he curtly answered: "It is certainly not obvious. Do you know anyone better qualified for the job?" The incident went no further.

I became integrated into the Hindu world without any trouble, without making any sacrifices. Through a series of erotic adventures I became aware of the subtleties, the mild taboos, and all the nuances of behavior and feeling that distinguish particular civilizations. For a married man, such a degree of integration would be unthinkable. A European wife could never adapt to the traditional role that is expected of Indian women, nor would interracial marriage be the answer, since it violates the most basic taboos of Hindu society.

I have always had the feeling that my destiny, which in a way seemed to have an existence of its own, could only be accomplished if I remained unattached and without social responsibilities. I could not have a family or children. This is why the gods granted me the privilege of a nature that would keep me free from the inevitable social ties that go with having a family, while also allowing me the high level of eroticism that is essential for mental equilibrium.

Once, during a dinner party given by Enrico Fulchignoni, the Italian philosopher, I was asked various questions about polytheism and explained how every aspect of the world is a particular projection of God's mind; so that for a tree, God is a tree, for a bull, he is a bull, for a man, he is man, for a woman, woman, and for a Negro, he is black. All this seemed fairly acceptable. But when I added that for a homosexual God was androgynous, I noticed that several women were shocked. I found this reaction very interesting. If I had said that God was inevitably Christian for a Christian, or Moslem for a Moslem—or even that a Marxist, though his choice is strictly ideological, thought more or less consciously of God as a Marxist—my statement would have struck my listeners as just another paradox. They seemed totally unable to accept the idea that homosexuality was a fact of nature, therefore part of the divine order of things.

In India I learned that the first duty of man is to understand his own nature and the basic elements of his being, which he must fulfill to the best of his ability. His second duty is to respect the reality of other people. This is why he cannot conduct his life on the basis of general moral principles, at least not according to social conventions that are worthless from the point of view of human or spiritual fulfillment. No man should ever try to appear different from what he is by birth and natural aptitude, or reject the special role that has been given him as an individual or as a member of a species;

nor should he attempt to impose upon others a code of behavior that might prevent them from fulfilling their true destiny.

I have never found it difficult to accept myself as I am. In this sense I have been very fortunate.

RELIGION

The main purpose of religion is to provide men with a sense of the supernatural and an awareness of the divine nature of the world. The word "religion" is probably a translation of *yoga* (that which connects), and refers to the fundamental link between the Creator and the created, man and the divine. The social groupings that go under the name "religion" are altogether different, however, and form a further category to be added to such human entities as race, language, tribe, and country. Religion is the most effective instrument of conquest and domination. A defeated people that is forced to adopt the religion of its conquerors loses its individuality, its rituals, its beliefs, and the magical protection of its gods. As a result it becomes vulnerable, therefore submissive and easily assimilated.

Mystics adapt more or less successfully to the dominant religion of their culture; they remain marginal and are generally mistrusted by society. For others, religion is a means of conquest, a pseudo-divine pretext for domination, corruption, and genocide. The total lack of judgment and critical sense of many Westerners which causes them to form fanatical and irrational sects in nearly every domain—social, moral, religious, as well as artistic—is mostly a result of the age-long tyranny of Christianity. They have grown so accustomed to expressing themselves through scriptural exegesis, distorting the meaning of texts more or less ingeniously, that their faculty for logical thinking has become paralyzed. This was true of my brother, the cardinal, whenever he was led into topics of conversation that challenged the foundations of the doctrine which he *had* to believe in. I learned long ago that believing was the opposite of knowing. People do not need to believe when they truly know; they only believe in things that they do not know. Belief is always a very poor counselor.

There is nothing original about Christianity such as it appears today. It is part of a system of religious and moral thought that originated with Mahavira and ancient Indian Jainism, which influenced Ikhnaton, Moses, and shortly before Jesus, the Master of Justice and the Essenes. With its worship of the Trinity, the Virgin, and the Saints, Christianity—like *Mahayana* Buddhism—reincorporated certain elements of polytheism. In the Christian religion there is no connection between theory and practice. It probably runs counter to all of the teachings of Jesus, who was essentially a liberal dissident. What we know of his doctrine was written, modified, and expurgated long after his death and in a spirit totally different from his.

The gnostics of the early Christian era, who attempted to place the teachings of Jesus within the context of his time and man's ancestral religious experience, were viciously eliminated by a Church obsessed with power. After years of internal conflicts and mutual accusations of hereticism, Christians were finally able to establish a system of politico-religious authority so stringent and so terrifying that any sign of independent thinking or attempt to return to the original teachings of Jesus was immediately suppressed. Dissidents were put to death and all their works destroyed or burned, including certain parts of the Gospels that were considered apocryphal. During the Renaissance a new attempt was made to link Christian teachings to ancient forms of wisdom, but this too was quickly put down.

From the time it set itself up as a political and missionary system, Christianity has done all it could to conceal its sources, disregarding all the other ancient traditions, claiming to have invented everything. This is why, even today, Westerners are still so ignorant of the sources of their culture or the meaning of their rites and customs. All attempts to link cosmological and theological thinking, science and religion, have been rejected. In the higher spheres of the Church, the only topics worthy of attention seem to be moral and social behavior, to which one might add a violent antisexual fanaticism, a kind of reverse *Kama-sutra*, which can only be of interest to psychiatrists.

Protestantism made it possible for certain Christians to es-

cape the massacre of "heretics" at the hand of an all-powerful
Church. Scientific research, freed from the bonds of dogmatism that had paralyzed it for centuries, was finally allowed to
develop. But this reformed Christian church has evolved
within a framework of theological and moral concepts without
a solid cosmological foundation. This is why, instead of leading
to serious considerations on the nature of man, the world, and
the divine, it has concentrated on scientific discoveries and
their applications. The Protestants' traditional reliance on the
Bible—a mixed bag of protohistoric anecdotes—as the obligatory source of all knowledge has severely restricted their freedom of thought. Until I returned to Europe, the British world
was my main contact with Western culture. As a result of
political events, these relatively liberal-minded Protestants
had some smatterings of knowledge—incomplete and distorted, to be sure—of Indian ideas. France seemed far more
closed and remote.

I had lived in a culture whose religious conceptions were
very close to those of the pre-Christian era. After my return
to Europe, I was surprised by the great numbers of feasts,
rites, customs, and superstitions that greeted me everywhere I
went; but although they were very familiar to me, no one
seemed to know what they actually meant. Then I remembered hearing an old Brahman explaining the myth of the
nativity of Christ to a group of ignorant, bewildered missionaries. Why was the God-child—like Ganesha or Hephaestus,
son of Hera—born of a virgin, symbol of the first feminine
principle? Why was he born in a cave, in the belly of the
goddess Earth—the traditional site for mysteries and initia-
tions—surrounded by an ass and a bull, the impure and the
sacred beast? What was that star that guided the Wise Men,
who came from three different continents and held secret
doctrines representing the three different modes of initiation?
Why was Jesus riding on an ass, like Shiva, when he entered
Jerusalem? Why did he have twelve companions, like the Sun
among the signs of the zodiac? Why did he befriend a prostitute, symbol of sacred love? Why, like Dionysus, did he turn
water into wine and walk across the waters? And what was
the Cross, the symbol of universality and life, of the union

between fire (the masculine principle) and water (the feminine principle), besides a simple instrument of torture? How and why did Christians come to forget the real meaning of all these myths and symbols, which are common to all the gods? The same is true of rites, sacred formulas, texts, the architecture of temples and their magic orientation. All the feasts, whose universal meaning has disappeared, are linked to the passage of the stars and seasons, as are thousands of other customs. All the sacred Christians sites are inherited from antiquity; saints have simply taken the place of gods and retained their magic qualities. Vatican ceremonies are in no way different from those of ancient "pagan" rites. It was in trying to understand the obvious similarities between the surviving rituals and symbols of the West and the rites of ancient civilizations, which are very close to some still existing in India, that I became interested in the Dionysian cult. Here, I found a conception of the world, of the divine, of happiness, that is very similar to ancient Shivaism and still survives, without anyone being really aware of it, in the mysteries of Christianity. Seen from this angle, the West became far less alien to me, and seemed only a world adrift that needed to find its moorings, its sources, and its origins.

The Christianity of mystics and humble people has very little to do with Church dogma, which they must accept for want of anything better. Many Christians still feel the need to commune with divine mystery in all its multiplicity, whatever names they choose to give it. Many of the people I have met in recent years are struggling hopelessly in the miasma of arbitrary and contradictory beliefs that seems to characterize the modern world. Sometimes they are attracted to so-called initiatory sects or recruited by pseudomystical adventurers, especially by certain types of Indians who preach a very simplified form of Vedanta and exploit their credulousness.

Westerners often speak of Oriental "wisdom" without realizing that this so-called wisdom is simply an attitude of realism in the pursuit of knowledge, whether the field be science, philosophy, religion, or social organization. The little that I could explain of Indian philosophy and cosmology seemed to them an important new discovery; in fact I was only describing certain very rudimentary aspects of Hinduism that have been taught in the traditional world for thousands of years and have somehow been forgotten and lost in the West. Most of the problems of today are a result of monotheistic ideologies taught by prophets who believe themselves to be inspired and claim to know the truth. This is obviously absurd, for there can be no single, absolute truth. The reality of the world is multiple and elusive. Only those who succeed in freeing themselves from various forms of monotheism, dogmatism, blind faith, Christianity, Islam, and Marxism can ever hope to approach the multiple aspects of the divine, understand the proper place of man within the scheme of Creation, and discover the true path of tolerance and love as well as the good will of beasts, men, and gods.

People have often asked me whether I could suggest a line of conduct, a method, and a "religion" that might bring the Western world out of its predicament or at least help some people to fulfill themselves. But I am neither a master nor a prophet. In a world that is hastening towards its own destruction, man's only hope, according to the theory of cycles, lies in individual salvation. Hindus believe that we are approaching the last stages of the kali yuga, the age of conflicts, which must inevitably end in a cataclysm. Only when the greater part of humanity has been destroyed by an underwater explosion will Kalki, the last "messiah," appear on his white horse and grant a few individuals a reprieve in this wondrous adventure man has known on Earth.

CHAPTER TWENTY

Balance Sheet

Who Am I?

"He is here. No! He is lost in Chinese civilization or in dance, painting, music, life. All the rest is for me." (Raymond to Pierre, Paris, 10 January 1932)

"We also have to go on all kinds of boring errands, and Alain is coming with me because I don't know the way. He finds this very tiresome, he has no time to paint and hardly ever dances, and when he can't do *his work* he feels terribly sad, and I am very sad too. I feel as though I were committing a crime. It's true! It's almost as though I were keeping a bird from breathing. And Alain is a bird—when he dances, he flies . . ." (Ibid., Montsouricière, 5 March 1933)

I have always been a hard worker. I cannot bear to be idle. The positions that I have held never tied me down for very long, which left me a great deal of time to study and learn. My greatest fault is that once I have mastered a subject or a technique, I feel no desire to exploit it or turn it to my advantage, and immediately want to go on to something new. I once estimated that I was qualified to practice thirty-two different trades and professions. It is very difficult, therefore, to place me in a category. For some people, I am a Sanskritist, for others a musicologist. I am also a historian, perhaps even a philosopher. In my youth I was quite a good pianist, a dancer, a singer; I also played the Indian *vînâ*. Painting is another of my accomplishments, and I am no amateur. I write equally well in French, English and Hindi, speak Italian in my day-to-day life, and am a good translator. I am a competent photographer, with expert knowledge of darkroom and laboratory techniques, film developing and touching up. I am also something of an architect; I drew the plans and took all the measurements of many of the houses I have lived in. I know a great deal about recording methods and the editing of magnetic tapes. A good jack-of-all-trades, I can do electrical and carpentry work, and am an expert at repairing broken china and glassware. Whenever a pitcher or a valuable plate is broken, everyone in my house is delighted; the pieces are brought to me, and I spend a few happy hours putting the object together again. Those who come to my house expecting to find some kind of guru, with a long flowing beard and Oriental robes, are often quite disappointed to learn that I can drive a car; worse still, that I will happily drive a Porsche at speeds exceeding a hundred and twenty-five miles an hour. How does one classify such a character? Is it any wonder that I turned to Hindu cosmology, which seeks fundamental principles common to all forms of life, techniques, and arts, as a guiding philosophy? I have always searched for secret links between all the different aspects of the world, principles common to music, language, architecture, but also to the physical harmony of the living being—plants, beasts, and men. That was how I discovered Dionysus.

Many people think of philosophers, sages, even "intellectuals" as untidy and unathletic people who cannot deal with practical, everyday things. This is a very dangerous notion. The body and the spirit are more closely linked than we realize. How is it possible for someone who cannot take a car engine apart to understand anything of that infinitely more complex machine, the universe, or that astonishing computer that controls our body, the brain? The various techniques of yoga allow us to achieve unity between our bodily and mental faculties, our physical harmony and spiritual fulfillment. A man who cannot use his hands is mentally deficient; his mind is not in touch with the real world, therefore he can only do harm. "Intellectuals" who are unable to repair an electric plug, yet claim to guide other men, will never lead them to wisdom or happiness.

I have always felt a strong feeling of kinship with artisans, a wise and happy people who are constantly in touch with the form and the substance of the world. But those who sell themselves to the highest bidder—the factory workers and the employees—are a joyless and soulless breed who drag on their dull lives wearily awaiting retirement and death.

When we speak of a journey, we can do little more than describe its exterior and anecdotal side—the incidents, the places where we have stopped, the people we have met. The same is true of the journey of life. The continuity of our experience, the invisible, indefinable thread which, like Ariadne's clew, guides our destiny through a maze of objects, places, and forms, is too subtle to be described. The deep feelings that urge us on, the subtle forces that guide us, seem to have nothing to do with the events of our lives or the people whose images are fixed in our memories; yet those are the exterior elements, the highlights that mark the different stages of our destiny.

A memoir is not unlike a travel guide describing, in reverse, the itinerary that we have followed. It cannot trace the evolution of our inner being, the feelings of joy and wonder that our journey has evoked, or the hidden motives of destiny as it guides us through the pitfalls of life.

As I write these memoirs, I feel that I have said nothing of what was most important in my life, my real *raison d'être*. Perhaps, behind these various anecdotes and reflections, a sensitive and knowing reader will have caught a glimmering of that other journey, the journey of the inner man, which unfolds far beyond the range of human adventures, meetings, and passions, in a reality that cannot be expressed by words.

I have never gone back to India. I know that the world I lived in will always exist but has simply retreated into its shell, waiting for the storms of the modern age to clear away. In order to find it again I should have to go through the new europeanized India that is so alien to me. It would take me a long while to readjust to its customs and rites, to that way of life, eating, and dressing, without which there is no possible access to the traditional world. There would be nothing new for me to find, nothing I did not already know in the former existence I was granted by the gods in that kingdom beyond time and space—the wondrous and eternal land of India.

On Death

When life comes to an end, all the elements that form a living being revert to raw material from which new life is made. The cells of the physical body combine with the soil that will feed plants, animals, other men. The elements of noncorporeal matter dissolve into the cosmic intellect, or universal consciousness, in order to serve again. What is divine in man melts into divinity, for there is no real barrier, and "when the urn is broken, the space contained within it melts into the infinity of space."

It is clear that all living things—bacteria, plants, and animals—survive not as individual beings but as organic, noncorporeal matter. At what stage of their evolution could hominids have acquired everlasting individuality? It seems, according to studies on Australian aborigines, that even in the Paleolithic Age living beings were believed to have two souls; one returning to the soul of the universe; the other, individual, disintegrating after death, though sometimes it could survive for a short time as a ghost. Hindus call "transmigrant body" the different vital essences that are liberated after death and, like corporeal elements, reassemble to form other living things. Sometimes, especially when death is sudden, this process does not take place right away, which explains the important role of funeral rites.

It is easy to understand how the simple-minded of the world, basing their beliefs on these premises, came to speak of union with God or transmigration, forgetting that the link between the different elements that form the individual "self" could then no longer exist. All that remains of the single, separate, individual man once his brief life is over is his creation: his offspring and his work.

Man only survives through the perpetuation of "his" species—which is why preserving racial purity is so important to Hindus—or through his work, the objects he has made, his writings, and his teachings.

Promoters of Heaven and Hell have carefully fostered man's

illusory belief in personal survival, which is manifestly absurd, for none of the inner faculties—memory, thought, intelligence, the concept of "self"—can live on once the physical body is gone. All that survives is our genetic memory, which passes onto other beings; but we cannot sense it or feel it.

This terrifying idea of eternal survival in an ill-defined beyond—as though anything with a beginning could possibly not come to an end—is the reason behind the tremendous fear of death so often found among Christians. It is this fear of the beyond that makes them cling to life. But death is such a simple thing, a final slumber in which all the elements of our being dissolve, become inanimate matter, and return to the workshop of the gods who fashioned us, like a broken vase that reverts to potter's clay.

Death then appears to be the end of a wonderful journey; and when it is finished we can sleep without fear, dissolving into other beings who will continue the voyage. Those who leave their organs to posterity subconsciously understand this.

There comes a time in our lives when we begin to count backwards. Like a soldier who is about to be discharged, we count the days that are left. We try to organize our time in the hope of finishing our work. We no longer wish to undertake, only to complete. It is one of the most beautiful periods of our lives: the most peaceful, as we await our well-deserved rest after so many strains and struggles. Now we can give all we have; not only the physical objects that stand in our way, but all the experience, wisdom, and tenderness we have acquired, forming that precious soil on which new lives, new experiences will develop and flower.

Life has brought me so much joy, so much sweetness, pleasure, friendship, happiness, and knowledge that the only fear I have is that I shall not have given all there was for me to give before I sleep.

The grapes have just been harvested. Le Farfadet is transformed into Bacchus. The wind is blowing through the trees. A gentle rain is perking up the garden. Our dog in the greenhouse is suckling her young.

All the naked heroes, Orestes, Homer, Achilles, Hercules,

have come back to life; I can hear them carousing in the swimming pool among the angels and saints of the village. Their shouts and swearing fill the air, mingling with birdsong and the rustling of leaves. In the distance lies the Eternal City, bathed in a red glow of late afternoon sun; I am too far to hear its sound and clamor.

The large, open room where I love to work looks out in all directions, revealing every landscape. I can see the Alban Mountains, dotted with tiny villages, and the terraces of the ancient temple resting on the Praenestan Hills.

Faces from the past, captured in a moment of perfect harmony, gratefully come to life in the paintings on my walls. Between my piano and my books I have just completed the seventy-ninth turn of the spiral of my life.

Here, in the heart of the Labyrinth, I have done my best to bring together these memories.

October 1986

BY THE SAME AUTHOR

IN ENGLISH

Hindu Polytheism. Bollingen Series. Princeton: Princeton University Press, 1964. Reissued under the title *The Gods of India*. New York: Inner Traditions International, 1985.

Introduction to the Study of Musical Scales. London: India Society, 1943; New Delhi: Munshiram Manoharlal, 1979.

The Ragas of Northern Indian Music. London: Barrie and Rockliffe, 1968; New Delhi: Munshiram Manoharlal, 1980.

"The Secret of the Tantras." In *The Congress of the World*. Texts by Jorge Luis Borges and Alain Daniélou. Milan: Franco Maria Ricci Editore, 1981.

Shilappadikaram (The Ankle Bracelet), translated from the Tamil. New York: New Directions, 1965.

Shiva and Dionysus. London: East-West Publications, 1982. New York: Inner Traditions International, 1984.

The Situation of Music and Musicians in Countries of the Orient. Florence: Leo S. Olschki Editore, 1971.

While the Gods Play, Man and the Universe according to the Shivaïte Tradition. New York: Inner Traditions International, 1986.

Yoga, Method of Reintegration. London: Johnson Publications, 1949.

SCHEDULED FOR PUBLICATION:

Hierarchy and Social Order. Hindu Traditional Society. New York: Inner Traditions International, 1987.

Musical Semantics. New York: Inner Traditions International, 1987.

IN PREPARATION:
Manimekhalai (The Saintly Courtesan), sequel to *The Ankle Bracelet*.

IN FRENCH

Le Chemin du labyrinthe. Souvenirs d'Orient et d'Occident. Paris: Laffont, 1981.
La Fantaisie des dieux et l'aventure humaine. Monaco-Paris: Le Rocher, 1985.
Histoire de l'Inde. Paris: Fayard, 1971–1985.
Shiva et Dionysos, Mythes et rites d'une religion préaryenne. Paris: Fayard, 1979–1985.
Le Polythéisme hindou. Paris: Buchet-Chastel, 1960–1982.
Les Quatre Sens de la vie, la structure sociale de l'Inde traditionnelle. Paris: Buchet-Chastel, 1963–1984.
La Sculpture érotique hindoue. Paris: Buchet-Chastel, 1973.
Le Temple hindou (avec illustrations). Paris: Buchet-Chastel, 1977.
Inde du Nord, traditions musicales. Paris: Buchet-Chastel, 1966–1985.
Sémantique musicale. Paris: Hermann, 1967–1978.
Le Bétail des dieux et autres contes gangétiques. Paris: Buchet-Chastel, 1983. (Second edition)
Shilappadikaram (Le Roman de l'anneau), traduit du tamoul. Paris: Gallimard, 1961–1981.
Le Shiva svarodaya, ancien traité de présages et prémonitions, traduit du sanskrit. Milan: Arché, 1982.
Yoga, méthode de réintégration. Paris: L'Arche, 1951–1983.
Théâtre de Harsha, trois pièces traduites du tamoul. Paris: Buchet-Chastel, 1977.
Traité de musicologie comparée. Paris: Hermann, 1959.
Visages de l'Inde médiévale. Photographies de Raymond Burnier. Paris: Hermann, 1949–1985.
Dhrupad. Poèmes. Thèmes d'improvisation des principaux ragas. (traduit du hindi). Paris: Editions Nulle Part, 1986.

In German

Die Indische Musik und ihre Traditionen. Leipzig: Deutscher Verlag
    für Musik, 1978.
Die Musik Asiens swischen Missachtung und West-Schatzung. Wilhem-
    shaven: Heinrichshoffen, 1973.
Einführung in die Indische Musik. Wilhelmshaven: Heinrich-
    shoffen, 1975–1979.
Musikgeschichte in Bildern-Sudasien. Leipzig: Deutscher Verlag für
    Musik, 1978.

In Italian

Le Città dell'amore. Milano: Ricci, 1976.
Siva e Dionisio. Roma: Astrolabio, 1980.
Storia dell'India. Roma: Astrolabio, 1984.
Yoga Metodo di Reintegrazione. Roma: Astrolabio, 1974.

In Spanish

El Congreso del Mundo, El Secreto de los Tantras. Texto de Jorge Luis
    Borges y Alain Daniélou. Milano: Franco Maria Ricci Edi-
    tore, 1982.